AGP System Architecture

MINDSHARE, INC.

Dave Dzatko

Edited by Tom Shanley

ADDISON-WESLEY

An Imprint of Addison Wesley Longman, Inc.

Reading, Massachusetts • Menlo Park, California • New York
Don Mills, Ontario • Harlow, England • Amsterdam
Bonn • Sydney • Singapore • Tokyo • Madrid • San Juan
Paris • Seoul • Milan • Mexico City • Taipei

For more information, please contact:
Corporate, Government and Special Sales Group
Addison Wesley Longman, Inc.
One Jacob Way
Reading, Massachusetts 01867
(781) 944-3700

Library of Congress Cataloging-in-Publication Data
Dzatko, Dave.
    AGP system architecture / MindShare, Inc. ; Dave Dzatko ;
edited by Tom Shanley.
    p. cm.
  Includes bibliographical references and index.
  ISBN 0-201-37964-3
  1. Computer graphics. 2. Computer architecture. I. Shanley, Tom.
II. MindShare, Inc. III. Title.
  T385.D988 1998
  006.6--dc21

                                                            98-43463
                                                                 CIP
ISBN: 0-201-37964-3

Sponsoring Editor: Karen Gettman
Production Coordinator: Jacquelyn Young
Set in 10 point Palatino by MindShare, Inc.

1 2 3 4 5 6 7 8 9-MA-0201009998
First Printing, December 1998

PC System Architecture Series

MindShare, Inc.

Please see our web site (http://www.awl.com/cseng/series/mindshare) for more information on these titles.

80486 System Architecture: Third Edition
0-201-40994-1

AGP System Architecture
0-201-37964-3

CardBus System Architecture
0-201-40997-6

EISA System Architecture: Second Edition
0-201-40995-X

FireWire® System Architecture: Second Edition
0-201-48535-4

ISA System Architecture: Third Edition
0-201-40996-8

PCI System Architecture: Third Edition
0-201-40993-3

PCMCIA System Architecture: Second Edition
0-201-40991-7

Pentium® Pro and Pentium® II System Architecture: Second Edition
0-201-30973-4

Pentium® Processor System Architecture: Second Edition
0-201-40992-5

Plug and Play System Architecture
0-201-41013-3

Power PC System Architecture
0-201-40990-9

Protected Mode Software Architecture
0-201-55447-X

Universal Serial Bus System Architecture
0-201-46137-4

For Kim, Cassidy, and Logan

Contents

About This Book

Chapter 1: The Need for AGP

Chapter 2: The AGP Solution

Contents

Contents

Chapter 4: The Signal Groups

Contents

Contents

Chapter 6: AGP Commands and Ordering Rules

Chapter 7: AGP Request Transactions

Contents

Chapter 8: AGP versus PCI Transactions

Chapter 9: 1X, 2X, and 4X Data Transactions

Chapter 10: Fast Write Transactions

Chapter 11: The Physical Environment

Contents

Chapter 12: AGP Configuration

Figures

Figures

Tables

Acknowledgments

Thanks to the Intel engineers who attended MindShare's AGP pilot courses. Their suggestions and insights were invaluable.

Thanks also to Tom Shanley and Don Anderson of MindShare for their patience and support during the long writing process.

About This Book

The MindShare Architecture Series

The MindShare Architecture book series includes: *ISA System Architecture, EISA System Architecture, 80486 System Architecture, PCI System Architecture, Pentium System Architecture, PCMCIA System Architecture, PowerPC System Architecture, Plug-and-Play System Architecture, CardBus System Architecture, Protected Mode Software Architecture, Pentium Pro and Pentium II System Architecture, USB System Architecture, FireWire System Architecture and AGP System Architecture.* The book series is published by Addison-Wesley.

Rather than duplicating common information in each book, the series uses the building-block approach. *ISA System Architecture* is the core book upon which the others build. The figure below illustrates the relationship of the books to each other.

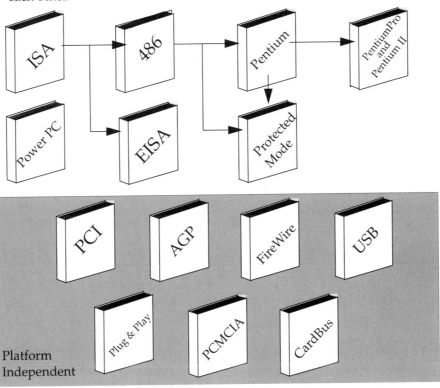

Cautionary Note

The reader should keep in mind that MindShare's book series often deals with rapidly-evolving technologies. This being the case, it should be recognized that the book is a "snapshot" of the state of the targeted technology at the time that the book was completed. We attempt to update each book on a timely basis to reflect changes in the targeted technology, but, due to various factors (waiting for the next version of the spec to be "frozen," the time necessary to make the changes, and the time to produce the books and get them out to the distribution channels), there will always be a delay.

Organization of This Book

The book is organized as follows:

Chapter 1: describes some of the motivating factors for the creation of the Accelerated Graphics Port (AGP). Some of the limitations of PCI graphics are discussed in the context of rendering a 3-D image.

Chapter 2: introduces AGP with a description of the major features and a discussion of some of the fundamental system requirements to support the interface. A basic overview of AGP technology can be gained from this chapter.

Chapter 3: outlines the major signaling requirements of the AGP interface. The electrical AC and DC specifications are described. AGP driver and receiver characteristics are presented.

Chapter 4: defines the required and optional signals for AGP-compliant masters and targets. The signals are grouped by function and the purpose of each signal is described.

Chapter 5: focuses on the arbiter's role within the AGP interface. Optimization of grant pipelining is also discussed.

Chapter 6: defines all of the AGP commands, or transaction request types, that can be issued on the AGP bus. The rules associated with the ordering of these transactions by the core logic are explained through the use of examples.

Chapter 7: AGP transactions are broken into two distinct bus operations: the issuance of the transaction request by the AGP graphics accelerator (referred to as the AGP master), and the matching data transaction that is initiated later in time by the core logic (referred to as the AGP target). This chapter provides a detailed description of the issuance of transaction requests using the AD and C/BE busses, as well as the SBA port.

Chapter 8: There are two categories of transactions that can be performed on the AGP bus: AGP transactions and PCI transactions. This chapter explores the differences between the two.

Chapter 9: provides a detailed description of AGP data transactions in 1X, 2X, and 4X data transfer modes.

Chapter 10: provides a detailed description of Fast Write transactions in the 1X, 2X, and 4X data transfer modes.

Chapter 11: describes issues related to add-in cards, connectors, and the motherboard.

Chapter 12: describes the responsibilities of the software required for initializing and configuring AGP devices. The AGP-specific configuration registers used in the configuration process are described.

Who This Book Is For

This book is intended for use by hardware and software design and support personnel. Due to the clear, concise explanatory methods used to describe each subject, personnel outside of the design field may also find the text useful.

Prerequisite Knowledge

The reader should be familiar with PC and PCI System Architectures. Mind-Share's ISA System Architecture and PCI System Architecture books provide that foundation material.

Documentation Conventions

This document contains conventions for numeric values as follows.

Hexadecimal Notation

This section defines the typographical convention used throughout this book. Hex Notation: All hex numbers are followed by an "h." Examples:

```
9A4Eh
0100h
```

Binary Notation

All binary numbers are followed by a "b." Examples:

```
0001 0101b
01b
```

Decimal Notation

Numbers without any suffix are decimal. When required for clarity, decimal numbers are followed by a "d." The following examples each represent a decimal number:

```
16
255
256d
128d
```

Bits versus Byte Notation

This book employs the standard notation for differentiating bits versus bytes.

All abbreviations for "bits" use lower case. For example:

1.5Mb/s
2Mb

All references to "bytes" are specified in upper case. For example:

10MB/s
1KB

Identification of Bit Fields (logical groups of bits or signals)

All bit fields are designated in little-endian bit ordering:

[X::Y],

where "X" is the most-significant bit and "Y" is the least-significant bit of the field.

Visit Our Web Site

Our web site contains a listing of all of our courses and books. In addition, it contains errata for a number of the books, a hot link to our publisher's web site, and course outlines.

http://www.mindshare.com

Our publisher's web site contains a listing or our currently-available books and includes pricing and ordering information. Their home page is accessible at:

http://www.awl.com/cseng/series/mindshare

We Want Your Feedback

MindShare values your comments and suggestions. You can contact us via mail, phone, fax, or internet e-mail.

Phone: (972) 231-2216, and, in the U.S., (800) 633-1440

Fax: (972) 783-4715

E-mail: mindshar@interserv.com

For information on MindShare seminars, please check our website.

Mailing Address:

> MindShare, Inc.
> 2202 Buttercup Drive
> Richardson, Texas 75082

1 *The Need for AGP*

This Chapter

This chapter describes some of the motivating factors for the creation of the Accelerated Graphics Port (AGP). Some of the limitations of PCI graphics are discussed in the context of rendering a 3-D image.

The Next Chapter

The next chapter introduces AGP by making comparisons to the PCI bus. The major features of AGP are introduced. AGP texture mapping, AGP core logic requirements, and AGP basic operation are also discussed.

Introduction to the 3-D Graphics Pipeline

Please note that the discussion of the 3-D graphics pipeline should be considered an example. How the pipeline is actually constructed, i.e. what stages are involved and the order of the stages, is dependent on the system implementation. The pipeline can also be considered a moving target, meaning that the discussion that follows is relevant at this point in time. However, due to the rapid evolution of 3-D graphics technology, the pipeline itself is subject to change.

Producing a 3-D image is a multi-stage, pipelined process. No image can be displayed without completing each step in the pipeline. The pipeline has two groups of stages: geometry and rendering.

Geometry Calculations

The geometry calculations define the position of objects in a three-dimensional space. The distribution of work within the 3-D pipeline typically involves the host processor, or CPU, performing the geometry calculations. This is because the mathematics of the geometry stages is floating-point intensive. The host CPU is typically more adept at performing floating-point operations, compared to the graphics accelerator. The stages of the 3-D pipeline associated with geometry calculations include:

- Tessellation
- Transformation
- Lighting
- Setup

The output from the setup stage is fixed-point, vertex data. This data is in a format that the graphics accelerator can accept. The format is coordinate or pixel information of the scene that will be drawn, or rendered. The setup stage of the geometry calculations within the 3-D pipeline may actually be performed by the graphics accelerator.

Rendering Calculations

The work of rendering the scene is typically performed by the graphics accelerator. Rendering is the process of drawing a three dimensional object onto a two dimensional display, i.e., the monitor of the computer. Rendering calculations involve computing the surface qualities of the model prior to that model being displayed. The surface qualities associated with rendering include the color, smoothness, and texture of the object. Like the geometry portion of the 3-D pipeline, the rendering portion involves multiple stages. The stages of the 3-D pipeline for rendering are:

- Visibility
- Texture Mapping
- Shading
- Smoothing

The one stage of the rendering portion of the pipeline that is critical for efficient production of a 3-D image is texture mapping. One of the primary goals of AGP is to improve the ability of the graphics accelerator to map textures.

Texture Mapping

Texture mapping is the process of wrapping a pattern, referred to as a texture, around an object. Essentially, the mapping is done by overlaying a bitmap onto the surface that will be displayed. The bitmap, or texture, is typically a square array of pixels. Each pixel in the texture is called a texture element, or texel.

Texture mapping is a popular technique in 3-D graphics. The reason for the popularity is rooted in efficiency. By mapping a detailed texture onto an object, one can optimally develop detail. This detail is achieved without adding more fundamental geometry elements that would further complicate the geometry calculations. These fundamental geometry elements are either triangles or polygons.

By using detailed textures, a 3-D application developer can achieve a high degree of realism, especially over large surface areas. A flight simulator is a classic 3-D application that could immediately benefit from the added realism resulting from detailed texture mapping. A flight simulator is typically working with large surfaces (namely the terrain being flown over) and the sky. If the texture mapped onto the surface terrain were a bitmap taken from actual reconnaissance, the result would be photo-realism. The scene would look like the actual airport where one is attempting to land. The sky could also be made more realistic with textures that actually resemble clouds.

Although texture mapping sounds easy enough, the process is computationally intense. Textures must be applied to surfaces in a way that results in good image quality. To maintain good image quality, textures must be perspective correct. Due to the third dimension, polygons on which textures are mapped lie at different angles. In order to achieve perspective correctness, the texture map must be rotated to match the angle of the polygon. The texture map must be scaled to compensate for the depth of the polygon. Texture maps are typically filtered to further improve image quality.

All of the operations on the texture maps must be done rapidly in order to prevent this stage of the pipeline from becoming a bottleneck. The goal of 3-D graphics is to produce quality rendered images, while maintaining smooth animation. As the scene changes, the movement must be as natural and fluid as possible to achieve realism. A screen refresh rate of thirty frames per second is a minimum to achieve a flicker-free display. In order to meet the goals of an adequate frame rate and quality rendered images, the rendering engine within the graphics accelerator must quickly access the texture maps.

Processing of Texture Maps with PCI Graphics

On a PC platform without AGP, the graphics accelerator (and therefore the rendering engine) resides on the PCI bus. The geometry stages output data, generated by the host processor, is written to the graphics accelerator via the PCI bus. The pixel data representing the scene then resides in the local memory of the graphics accelerator. The size of the local memory of the graphics accelerator, or frame buffer, is relatively small. Usually, the frame buffer is comprised of two to eight megabytes of DRAM, VRAM (Video RAM), or SGRAM (Synchronous Graphics RAM) on PCs.

Figure 1-1: Block Diagram of a PC with PCI Graphics

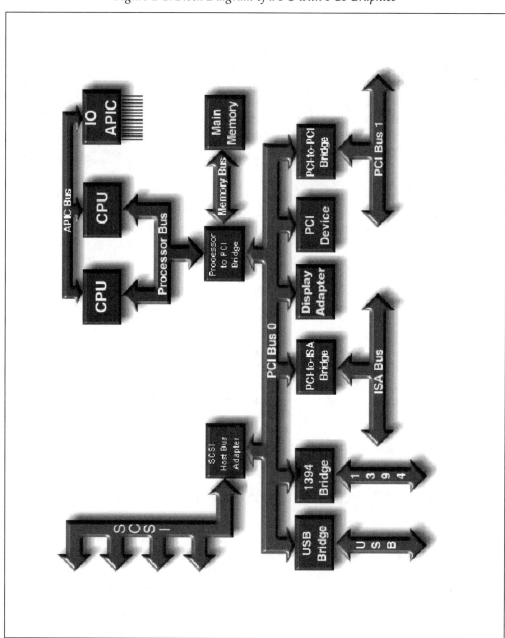

Textures, which are stored on the hard disk, are first written into main system DRAM memory via the PCI bus. This operation is usually performed by the hard disk controller, which is implemented as a PCI bus master. During this transfer, main memory is being accessed from the PCI bus. Memory must be coherent from the perspective of the internal caches of the processor. Any modifications to system memory by a PCI master require the invalidation of the corresponding processor cache lines. Any read transactions targeting main memory must not access stale data.

In Intel P6 processor-based platforms, the level one and level two caches are located in the processor. When PCI bus masters, like the hard disk controller, write to main memory, the host bus/PCI bridge must initiate invalidate transactions on the host bus. These transactions invalidate the cache lines within the processor that correspond to the memory locations being written to. The invalidation cycles on the host bus are necessary to maintain cache coherency. The invalidate transactions initiated on the host bus by the bridge are referred to as snoop cycles.

During the rendering process, the textures need to be transferred from main memory to the local memory of the graphics accelerator before the texture mapping can be performed. The graphics accelerator prefetches the needed textures from main memory in advance of the actual texture mapping operation. This is accomplished by the graphics accelerator by initiating memory read transactions on the PCI bus. The target of the memory read transaction is the host/PCI bridge. As with any PCI transaction targeting main memory, the host/PCI bridge will initiate snoop cycles on the host bus to maintain cache coherency.

It should be noted that the snoop cycles performed on the processor bus by the host bridge make the processor bus less available to the processor(s). To what degree this will impact the processor performance is application-specific.

Once the texture maps have been copied into the local memory of the graphics accelerator, the textures then reside both in main memory and in the accelerator's local memory. The graphics accelerator can now perform the texture processing required during the mapping process. This can include rotating, scaling, and filtering before the map is applied to the surface of the model.

How Much Local Memory is Dedicated to Textures?

Only a small percentage of the graphics accelerator's total local memory can be allocated to texture maps. The texture maps are in competition with the other buffers required for the rendering process. These buffers include a Z-buffer (for pixel depth information), the Alpha buffer (for pixel translucency information), a back buffer (to hold the information for the next frame to be displayed), and the front buffer (to hold the information for the frame currently being displayed).

How Much Texture Data for a Given Application?

How many textures are required for a particular application and the size of those textures is application implementation-specific. There is tremendous pressure to grow the size and number of the texture maps in 3-D applications in order to improve image quality. By improving image quality, the 3-D experience can be made more realistic.

The rendering engine must have fast access to the textures in order to maintain a high rendering rate. This frame rate is required for smooth movement and animation. The amount of textures required for a particular scene could exceed the amount of local frame buffer memory dedicated for texture maps. To compensate for this short coming, the size of the local memory of the graphics accelerator could be increased.

This solution is cost-prohibitive for commodity, desktop platforms. The SGRAMs used for graphics frame buffers are expensive. Increasing the size of the local memory on the graphics accelerator would result in a graphics subsystem that would be cost-prohibitive. There are 3-D graphics accelerators available today for several hundred dollars that have several megabytes of dedicated texture cache.

Local Frame Buffer is Not Large Enough

Assume that the 3-D graphics application is using texture maps that exceed the amount of the local frame buffer memory allocated for textures. Since the local frame buffer is not large enough to hold all of the textures needed to render a full scene, a portion of the frame buffer is used as a texture cache. The graphics accelerator prefetches the needed textures from main memory ahead of the rendering process using the PCI bus. Only a partial scene can be rendered at this time. The scene information is stored in the accelerator's local back buffer. Then the needed textures are brought into the texture cache and the scene is partially rendered again. This iterative process is repeated until the whole frame is rendered and the frame is then displayed by performing a transfer from the back buffer to the front buffer. This technique could yield a robust rendering rate if the graphics accelerator, acting as a PCI bus master, was granted adequate PCI bus bandwidth to fetch the needed textures quickly.

In most PCI-based platforms, PCI bus bandwidth is a resource under great demand. The PCI bus bandwidth is shared among multiple masters that may require service simultaneously. In other words, the 3-D graphics accelerator must share PCI bus bandwidth with other high-bandwidth peripherals. Examples of peripherals found in PCs that have large bandwidth requirements include: network adaptors, hard disk controllers, and high-speed serial bus controllers such as IEEE 1394 (i.e., FireWire).

DMA Texturing

The texture processing mechanism described earlier is referred to as DMA Texturing. This process is also referred to as local texturing. The term DMA comes from Direct Memory Access. A DMA transfer is involved in copying the textures from main memory to the local memory of the graphics accelerator. This is, traditionally, how PCI graphics accelerators have operated.

PCI Bus Limitations

Due to limitations of the PCI bus protocol, PCI DMA texturing can result in less than optimal 3-D rendering performance. The PCI bus is typically implemented with a 32-bit multiplexed Address/Data (AD) bus with a typical clock frequency of 33MHz. This frequency and bus width yields a theoretical maximum data transfer rate of 132MB/s. Although impressive compared to some bus transfer rates, it is difficult to achieve sufficient bus utilization, efficiency, and transfer rates required for 3-D graphics applications.

The Idle Clock

Because PCI is a shared bus environment, an idle tick (or clock period) is required between transactions initiated by different bus masters. This period is necessary to avoid contention on the shared or bussed signals. This idle time between bus transactions is one reason for diminished efficiency.

Time-Multiplexed Address/Data Bus

The multiplexed nature of the PCI bus is also a source of inefficiency. The PCI initiator must use the Address/Data bus to address the target of the transaction. At the start of every transaction, a PCI master must utilize the first clock cycle of the transaction to drive out the address onto the AD bus and the command (i.e., the transaction type) onto the C/BE bus. This one clock of overhead per transaction is one clock in which the AD bus cannot be used to transfer data.

Tightly Coupled Address and Data Phases

PCI transactions closely couple the data phase of the transaction with the address phase, leading to additional inefficiencies. Once the initiator of a PCI read transaction produces the address of the target on the AD bus, the initiator must wait for the target to respond with the data. It is common for the target to add wait states immediately after the address phase of a PCI read transaction due to memory latencies. During the clock cycles where wait states are added, there is no data transferred. Therefore, any wait states incurred on a PCI read transaction is wasted time on the bus.

Transactions May Be Retried

When a PCI bus master initiates a transaction that receives a Retry from the target of the transaction, the initiator must terminate the transaction with no data transferred. PCI transactions that are met with Retries are another source of inefficiency on the PCI bus.

Summary

AGP was designed to address the problems associated with DMA texturing in platforms running applications that use 3-D graphics. AGP was also architected to overcome the inefficiencies of the PCI bus. One of the primary goals of AGP is to yield higher performance 3-D graphics, relative to that achievable when the graphics accelerator resides on the PCI bus.

2 *The AGP Solution*

The Previous Chapter

The previous chapter described some of the motivating factors for the creation of AGP. Some of the limitations of the PCI bus, in terms of providing high performance for 3-D graphics, were discussed.

This Chapter

This chapter introduces AGP with a description of the major features and a discussion of some of the fundamental system requirements to support the interface. A basic overview of AGP technology can be gained from this chapter.

The Next Chapter

The next chapter outlines the major signaling requirements of the AGP interface. The electrical AC and DC specifications are described. AGP driver and receiver characteristics are presented.

Motivation for AGP

The primary motivation for the creation of AGP was to contain the cost of the 3-D graphics sub-system, while supplying a performance boost relative to PCI graphics. The cost containment results from reducing the amount of local memory necessary on the graphics accelerator even as 3-D graphical applications use larger and more detailed textures. This is accomplished through a technique known as AGP texturing. AGP texturing is described in this chapter.

The Revision 1.0 AGP specification was authored by Intel Corporation and released to the public on August 1, 1996. The Revision 2.0 specification was also written by Intel and released on May 4, 1998. As of this writing, the Revision 2.0 specification is the latest release and the one that this book is based on. The AGP specifications can be downloaded from the AGP Implementers Forum website at: www.agpforum.org.

AGP System Architecture

The AGP specification evolved from the Revision 2.1 PCI specification. AGP, however, implements some significant performance enhancements, relative to PCI. The AGP transfer mechanism is introduced in this chapter by examining the major AGP Revision 2.0 features.

AGP Revision 2.0 Features

Dynamic Memory Allocation

When needed by an application, the OS can dynamically allocate portions of main memory to an AGP graphics accelerator. That memory can then be used for storing texture maps or other data relevant to 3-D rendering. When running an application that is not graphically intensive, this memory can be dynamically deallocated by the OS. Deallocating this memory makes it available to increase the performance of the current application. Memory allocation is performed by the operating system.

This mechanism has a two-fold advantage over a graphics accelerator with a dedicated texture cache: decreased cost and increased flexibility. Consider the following example. A graphics accelerator card with a large on-board, dedicated texture cache consisting of 8MB of Synchronous Graphics RAM (SGRAM), will perform well when rendering 3-D graphics that use large and/or numerous textures. At the present time, however, this card will cost hundreds of dollars. When running an application that is not using 3-D rendering, the SGRAM on the card remains unused.

More information on AGP dynamic memory allocation is found later in this chapter in "AGP Memory Allocation" on page 24.

High Bandwidth Data Transfer Modes

AGP graphics accelerators can attain much higher data transfer rates than PCI graphics accelerators. This is because AGP is more efficient than PCI. AGP also offers modes of operation that result in higher data transfer rates relative to PCI. Like the vast majority of PCI implementations at this time, AGP is implemented as a 32-bit wide bus. PCI does offer an optional 64-bit wide extension, while AGP (in its current form) does not offer a data bus wider than 32 bits. The AGP bus clock is 66 MHz, while most PCI busses are clocked at 33 MHz at this time. There are currently three data transfer rates available on AGP:

- **AGP 1X Mode**: 4 Bytes per clock period are transferred, yielding 264 MB/s throughput.
- **AGP 2X Mode**: 8 Bytes per clock period are transferred, yielding 532 MB/s throughput.
- **AGP 4X Mode**: 16 Bytes per clock period are transferred, yielding 1 GB/s throughput.

The typical PCI bus is implemented with a bus width of 32 bits, clocked at 33 MHz. This combination yields a maximum data transfer rate of 132 MB/s. Due to inefficiencies of the PCI data transfer mechanism, it is impossible to realize this bandwidth. AGP, however, operating in the minimum, 1X data transfer mode, provides twice the bandwidth of PCI. Higher data transfer rates can be realized due to the efficient operation of AGP.

Core Logic = Target, AGP Accelerator = Master

Many designers use the term core logic when referring to the host/PCI bridge. Throughout this book, the host/PCI bridge is referred to as the core logic. The AGP accelerator (i.e., the 3-D graphics controller) acts as the master of AGP transactions, while the core logic acts as the target. The core logic contains the main memory controller and the accelerator initiates transactions to transfer data to or from main memory. When standard PCI transactions are performed on the AGP bus, however, either the graphics accelerator or the core logic may initiate the transaction, while the other device acts as the target of the transaction.

Bus Structure Similar to PCI

With a quick glance at the AGP specification signal list, AGP appears to be constructed similarly to the PCI bus. There is a 32-bit wide, multiplexed AD (Address/Data) bus, four C/BE (Command/Byte Enable) signals, a TRDY# (Target Ready) signal, an IRDY# (Initiator Ready) signal, and REQ# (Request) and GNT# (Grant) signals. In fact, the AGP interface does permit standard PCI transactions to be initiated by the core logic and optionally by the graphics accelerator. With a few exceptions, all of the PCI signals are implemented on the AGP interface. Some of the PCI signals are used for AGP transactions. These signals, however, have been redefined for AGP operations. AGP also implements additional signals, used for AGP transactions, which are not relevant for PCI transactions. Some of these signals are required for AGP operation, while some are optional.

Dedicated Interface for Graphics

Refer to Figure 2-1 on page 19. The name Accelerated Graphics Port implies a high-bandwidth data conduit, dedicated to the graphics device. The interface itself links the graphics accelerator to the core logic and therefore to main memory. There is only one bus master (the graphics accelerator) and one target device (the core logic or north bridge). Unlike PCI, there are no other bus masters to compete with the graphics accelerator for bus bandwidth.

With no competition for AGP bus bandwidth, the graphics accelerator encounters reduced arbitration latency relative to PCI. The graphics accelerator, acting as the AGP master, can immediately initiate a transaction when it needs to do so.

By removing the graphics accelerator from the PCI bus, more bandwidth is made available to other PCI bus masters, allowing higher overall system performance as well as higher performance for existing PCI peripherals. With the increasing popularity and bandwidth requirements of some disk and network interfaces, PCI busses can be heavily loaded. It is not uncommon to encounter Enhanced IDE, SCSI, 100 Mb/s Ethernet, ATM, Fiberchannel, and real-time video capture devices sharing the PCI bus. These high-bandwidth peripherals are causing the PCI bus to become congested.

In platforms such as servers where high performance graphics capability is not required, AGP may be used to provide disk and/or network peripherals with a 66 MHz PCI bus to main memory. This could be accomplished with a PCI-to-PCI bridge, where the graphics accelerator would normally reside, with a 66 MHz PCI bus subordinate to the PCI-to-PCI bridge.

Alternatively, the AGP master slot could house a single 66 MHz PCI peripheral that requires high bandwidth. Although these configurations are not within the spirit and scope of the AGP specification, there are few technical hurdles to overcome to implement such a system.

Figure 2-1: Block Diagram of a PC with AGP Graphics

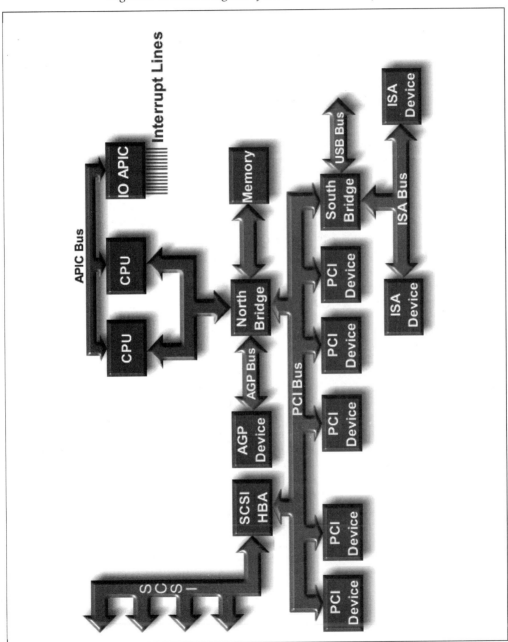

Transaction Pipelining

AGP allows the pipelining or enqueuing of transaction requests into the core logic by the graphics accelerator. When producing a transaction request, the AGP master delivers the start address to the core logic, as well as the amount of data to be transferred and the transaction type. This request transaction is a separate and distinct bus operation relative to the subsequent data transaction. In other words (to use PCI terminology), the request (or address) phase is decoupled from the data phase.

An AGP request transaction is analogous to the address phase of a PCI transaction. The matching, subsequent AGP data transaction is performed to transfer the data between the master (the graphics accelerator) and the target (the core logic). An AGP data transaction is analogous to the data phase, or phases, of a PCI transaction. The decoupling of the request and its associated data transfer allows the core logic to hide the memory access latency behind the issuance of additional requests by the master. This hiding of the memory latency is more efficient than PCI memory read transactions.

PCI Configuration Mechanism

AGP uses the well-defined PCI configuration space and PCI configuration mechanism for configuration. Both the AGP core logic and AGP graphic accelerator implement PCI configuration registers. When the host processor performs accesses to the core logic's configuration registers, the operation doesn't cause a PCI configuration transaction on the AGP bus. However, the core logic uses PCI configuration transactions to access the AGP master's PCI configuration registers when requested to do so by the processor.

The core logic includes a "virtual" PCI-to-PCI bridge that connects it to the AGP bus. For the purposes of configuration, the AGP interface is assigned a PCI bus number by the core logic designer. The AGP specification defines some enhancements to the PCI configuration registers. See Chapter 12, entitled "AGP Configuration," on page 235 for more information on AGP configuration.

Grant Pipelining

The AGP arbiter is physically located within the AGP target (i.e., the core logic). The role of the arbiter is to define how and when the AGP bus is used for the next transaction. The arbiter is designed to assert the GNT# (Grant) signal at the appropriate time to allow the next transaction to begin as soon as possible. This is referred to as grant pipelining. Using grant pipelining, the data bus can be used for back-to-back data transactions. This means that data transactions are performed without idle clocks inserted between them, maximizing AGP bus utilization. Additional information on Grant pipelining is in Chapter 5, entitled "AGP Arbitration," on page 91.

AGP Connector vs. PCI Connector

The AGP connector is physically different from a PCI connector. An add-in card designed for AGP is not mechanically compatible with a PCI connector and a PCI add-in card will not fit into an AGP connector. A description of the AGP connector can be found in Chapter 11, entitled "The Physical Environment," on page 225.

Optional Fast Write Transaction

AGP permits the rapid transfer of write data from the core logic device to the AGP graphics accelerator using the fast write transaction. The fast write transaction is initiated on the AGP bus by the core logic to write data to the graphics accelerator. The data is actually being written by one of the following devices:

- the **host processor**. The write data could be 3-D coordinate or vertex data supplied by the CPU.
- a **PCI master**. The data could be real-time video data supplied by a PCI bus master.

The core logic always initiates a PCI transaction when it must perform a transaction on the AGP bus that targets the graphics accelerator. If the AGP components are operating in either the 2X or 4X data transfer mode, PCI write transactions initiated by the core logic can take the form of a fast write transaction. The support for fast write transactions is optional for both the master and the target. A fast write transaction resembles a PCI write transaction to the graphics accelerator. The data, however, is transferred at the high data transfer rate (2X mode or 4X mode).

The Fast Write Transaction protocol is described in Chapter 10, entitled "Fast Write Transactions," on page 187.

Sideband Addressing

AGP permits the AGP master to send request information to the target over the Sideband Address Port, rather than over the AD bus. This feature is optional for masters, but all targets are required to support it. By using sideband addressing, the AD bus is no longer used to transfer request information, and, therefore, 100% of the bandwidth of the AD bus is available to transfer data.

Sideband addressing is described in "Enqueuing Transaction Requests via the Sideband Address Port" on page 118.

AGP Texturing: the "Execute" Model

Texture processing via the AGP bus is quite different than the DMA texture processing performed by PCI-based graphics accelerators. AGP texturing is referred to as the **execute model** in the AGP specification. When performing AGP texturing, the graphics accelerator executes the texture processing in place. In other words, when performing the texture manipulation required in texture mapping, the graphics accelerator reads the textures directly from main system memory using the AGP bus. This eliminates the need to copy the textures into the local memory of the graphics accelerator. This results in a three-fold benefit:

- The **cost** of the graphics accelerator **decreases** due to diminished on-board memory requirements.
- System **performance increases** due to the elimination of the need to transport the texture information to the local buffer before processing it.
- The reading and writing of the texture information now occurs over the AGP rather than the PCI bus, making the PCI bus more available to other PCI masters. This results in **increased** system **performance**.

Snoops of Texture Accesses Can Be Eliminated

Like PCI DMA texturing, AGP texturing begins with a transfer of the textures from disk into main memory. The texture information in memory is typically accessed by the graphics accelerator and not by the processor. This being the case, the OS will set up the area of memory containing the textures as uncacheable memory (in the case of a P6 processor, by programming the processor's

MTRR registers accordingly). The graphics accelerator must then access the texture information in main memory in order to manipulate the textures. There are two possible cases:

1. If the **graphics accelerator is implemented as a PCI bus master** and the textures are stored in main memory, the PCI master must access main memory via the host/PCI bridge. In this scenario, the bridge isn't aware of what area of memory contains the texture information versus areas of memory that contain other types of information. It therefore doesn't know that the processor isn't caching from the texture area. As a result, before permitting the PCI master to access the addressed memory area, the bridge must first use the processor bus to generate a snoop transaction. This causes the processors to latch the memory address, snoop it in their internal caches, and then report the snoop result back to the bridge. The bridge can only permit the PCI memory access to proceed after it has received a snoop result indicating that the cache line isn't modified. This snoop requirement has a negative impact on the PCI target (which must insert wait states into its transaction until the snoop result is received). In addition, it has a negative effect on the processors by diminishing the amount of time that the processor bus is available to the processors.

2. If the **graphics accelerator is implemented as an AGP device** and textures are stored in main memory, the AGP master must access main memory via the host/PCI bridge. In this scenario, however, the bridge is aware of what area of memory contains the texture information versus areas of memory that contain other types of information. The GART (Graphics Address Remapping Table) within the core logic has been programmed (by the OS) with this information. It knows that the processor isn't caching from the texture area. As a result, there is no need to stall the access to main memory while a snoop transaction is generated on the processor bus. This permits the AGP master faster access to memory and also diminishes the amount of traffic on the processor bus, making it more available to the processors.

Elimination of Texture Storage in Accelerator's Local Memory

AGP texturing eliminates the need to copy the texture maps into the local memory of the graphics accelerator. The texture maps therefore do not need to be stored redundantly in main system memory and in the graphics accelerator's local memory. This reduces the pressure to grow the size of the graphics accelerator's local memory as the amount of texture data grows. The size of the local graphics memory remains small, thereby reducing the cost of the graphics subsystem.

Textures Ideal Candidate to Move to Main Memory

Textures are ideal candidates to be placed in main memory rather than in the graphics accelerator's local memory. Texture processing requires a large amount of memory bus bandwidth compared to other stages of the rendering pipeline (e.g., compared to z-buffer and alpha buffer accesses). When running a 3-D intensive application on a CPU with a large cache, the CPU accesses main memory far less than the graphics accelerator.

The texture maps are generally not read, modified, and then written back into memory by the graphics accelerator. In general, the accesses into system memory by the AGP graphics accelerator tend to be short, random accesses.

As well as textures, there is an option to move other graphics data structures from the graphics accelerator's local memory to main memory. Good candidates for relocation would be the z-buffer (pixel depth), and the alpha buffer (pixel translucency). Doing so would further reduce the size requirements of local memory.

Performance Enhancements Relative to PCI DMA

In PCI DMA, the PCI-based graphics accelerator must transfer textures in blocks limited in size by the amount of local memory available for textures. PCI graphics accelerators must also assemble the frame from successive transfers from system memory. This causes the graphics accelerator to perform several transfers per frame over its local memory bus in order to assemble the frame prior to display. This procedure can be less efficient than AGP texturing (the execute model), because of the performance enhancements of AGP. In comparison, PCI transfers are much less efficient.

AGP Memory Allocation

An area of main memory can be dynamically allocated for the AGP graphics accelerator. AGP memory can then be deallocated, or returned to the free memory heap, when not needed for graphics. AGP memory is allocated by the operating system and is referred to as the **Graphics Aperture**. The graphics aperture is viewed by the graphics accelerator as a linear address space, but in reality, the graphics aperture can be spread across the physical address map of system memory by the operating system.

Applications using the DirectX5 (or higher) DirectDraw, Direct 3D Immediate Mode have access to AGP texturing support in Windows 95, Windows 98, and in Windows NT 5.0.

AGP system memory allocation is done on 4KB address boundaries and each 4KB block is known as a page. The core logic implements a mechanism to convert the linear address supplied by the graphics accelerator during the transaction request into a physical address in system memory. This remapping procedure is accomplished using a memory-based table known as the Graphics Address Remapping Table (GART). The GART could be located in system memory, or some dedicated memory. The actual implementation and structure of the GART is core logic specific. The core logic does a lookup in this table in order to perform the address translation.

The graphics accelerator views AGP memory as an extension of its local memory. The actual linear address range of the graphics aperture is not necessarily adjacent to the range of addresses assigned to the local frame buffer. The frame buffer address space is assigned through a PCI configuration base address register within the graphics accelerator. The graphics aperture is viewed as a contiguous block of memory addresses.

A Hardware Abstraction Layer (HAL) or a miniport driver provides a level of abstraction through a common Application Programmer's Interface (API), for accesses to the GART. The core logic vendor provides the HAL or miniport driver. This method allows flexibility in the implementation of the GART, from a hardware perspective, but avoids incompatibilities from a software perspective. In current AGP systems running Windows 95, the miniport driver is called VGARTD.VXD. This driver is provided by Intel.

Core Logic Requirements

The AGP specification identifies four specific requirements necessary in the implementation of an AGP target (i.e., core logic device). The four areas are:

- Cache Coherency
- PCI Bus Master Writes to the AGP Master
- AGP Remapping Support for PCI Masters
- Monochrome Display Adapter (MDA) Support

These topics are discussed in the sections that follow.

Cache Coherency Requirements

A PCI memory read is not permitted to return stale data. A PCI memory write must invalidate processor cache lines corresponding to the memory locations being updated. To enforce this coherency, the host/PCI bridge generates snoop transactions on the processor bus whenever a PCI master attempts to access main memory. As mentioned earlier, the snoop transaction can add wait states to the memory access latency of the PCI transaction (because the host/PCI bridge must wait for the snoop results before permitting the PCI memory access to proceed). These snoop transactions consume processor bus time that might otherwise be used by the processor.

However, as mentioned earlier ("Snoops of Texture Accesses Can Be Eliminated" on page 22) AGP transactions that target main memory do not have to be snooped by the processors. The area of main memory used by the AGP is designated as uncacheable. In P6 processor-based platforms, the processor has internal MTRRs (Memory Type and Range Registers) that are typically programmed by the operating system, so as to define the area of main memory used by the AGP as Write Combining (WC). WC memory is an uncacheable memory type that allows the processor to internally combine writes targeted to that space. For more information on the P6-family processors or on write combining memory, refer to the 2nd edition of *Pentium Pro and Pentium II System Architecture* by MindShare (published by Addison-Wesley).

The AGP specification allows AGP transactions to target cacheable areas of memory. If this is the case, it is the responsibility of the device driver for the AGP device, not the core logic, to guarantee cache coherency. How the device driver does that is outside of the scope of the specification. The behavior of the core logic when AGP transactions target cacheable memory is implementation-specific.

AGP transactions that target cacheable memory are outside of the GART range (the graphics aperture). GART addresses are always assigned an uncacheable memory type. A device driver can determine the ability of the core logic to support cache coherency by reading and interpreting the ID of the core logic. The ID is located in the Microsoft Windows 98 and Windows NT registries. Support for AGP accesses to cacheable areas of memory is currently under consideration for a future version of the specification.

PCI Bus Master Writes to the AGP Master

The core logic is required to support a PCI bus master writing to the AGP master, with the AGP graphics accelerator acting as the PCI target. This support is provided through a PCI-to-PCI bridge integrated within the core logic. PCI memory write and memory write and invalidate commands must be supported. This could potentially allow real-time video data captured by a PCI device to be streamed directly to the graphics accelerator. Any other PCI commands (e.g., memory reads, I/O reads, I/O writes, etc.) can optionally be supported by the core logic as well, but are generally not supported.

AGP Remapping Support for PCI Bus Masters

How the GART address remapping mechanism is implemented is core logic-specific. In addition to remapping memory addresses generated by the AGP accelerator, the core logic may optionally also provide remapping support for PCI bus masters that access AGP memory through the GART. For this option, the following rules apply:

- If address remapping is supported for accesses from the host processor to AGP memory through the GART, then the core logic must provide the identical support for PCI masters.
- If the core logic has no support for accesses from the host processor to AGP memory through the GART, then the core logic must not provide any address remapping support to PCI bus masters.
- In the latter case, if a PCI master were to initiate a transaction in which the address is within the GART range, it must be considered an error. The error handling mechanism is core logic-specific. Typically, a transaction on the PCI bus that targets the GART range will terminate with a master abort. This means the transaction will go unclaimed by the core logic, or by any other PCI target (in other words, the PCI DEVSEL# signal will not be asserted).

Monochrome Device Adapter (MDA) Support

Typically, PCI graphics adapters also support a second Monochrome Display Adapter (MDA) for software development and debug purposes. AGP core logic may also provide this support. Essentially, when the MDA is detected on the PCI bus, the core logic can route MDA accesses to the PCI bus instead of to the

AGP bus. When the MDA is detected present, the AGP graphics accelerator must not utilize the standard MDA memory and I/O addresses:

- Memory Addresses: 0B0000h to 0B7FFFh.
- I/O Addresses: 3B4h, 3B5h, 3B8h, 3BAh, and 3BFh, including the ISA aliases.

AGP graphics accelerators can utilize the MDA resources if an MDA is not present. Software will perform a test for the presence of the MDA before enabling the primary graphics device on the AGP. The test involves a write to a memory address within the MDA range, followed by a read from the same address. If the read results in the same data that was written, then the MDA is present.

AGP Transaction Queuing Models

When an AGP transaction request is sent to the core logic by the graphics accelerator, the core logic accepts it into a transaction request queue. This is referred to as enqueuing a transaction request into the core logic. An understanding of the model used when queueing transactions is fundamental to understanding how the AGP operates.

Decoupled Requests and Data

The AGP graphics accelerator initiates data transfers by enqueuing transactions requests into the AGP core logic. These transaction requests can take the form of:

- request transactions issued to the core logic over the AD bus, or
- commands issued to the core logic over the Sideband Address Port.

The core logic acts as the target of the request and responds by initiating a data transaction at a later point in time. In the case of an AGP read transaction, the core logic will source the data to the master at a later time, provided there is room for the data in the core logic's read data return queue. In the case of an AGP write transaction, the core logic will indicate to the master when it is ready to accept the write data into its write data queue.

The delivery of the request and the transfer of the data are decoupled from one another and are performed as separate transactions on the AGP bus. The master can continue to enqueue, or pipeline, multiple transaction requests into the core logic while there are outstanding data transfers pending completion. The core logic will buffer the outstanding requests in a request queue.

The request queue is divided into two sub-queues:

- a low-priority request sub-queue, and
- a high-priority request sub-queue.

Each sub-queue has its own transaction ordering rules. The transaction ordering rules for each sub-queue are described in the section entitled "AGP Ordering Rules" on page 102. The master may continue to issue requests as long as there is room remaining in the core logic's request queue. The depth of the request queue is determined by the core logic designer and its depth is communicated to the AGP master by software during configuration.

PCI Transaction Enqueuing on AGP

PCI transactions initiated on the AGP bus have a separate queue within the AGP master and the AGP target. These transactions are initiated on the AGP bus, but are completed as non-pipelined transactions.

Performance Considerations

With the implementation of pipelining and queuing of transactions, read transactions can be as efficient as write transactions. Write data is typically buffered into a posted memory write buffer and the write transaction therefore completes quickly on the AGP bus. Read transactions require the data to be accessed from system memory, usually incurring wait states on the bus due to the latency of main memory. By pipelining read transactions, this latency can be masked with additional transaction requests.

As a comparison of PCI memory read transactions and AGP memory read transactions, consider the example in Figure 2-2 on page 30. Please note that the representation of the AGP transactions in the example is conceptual and is not intended to represent compliant AGP protocol.

Figure 2-2: PCI Read Transactions versus AGP Read Transactions

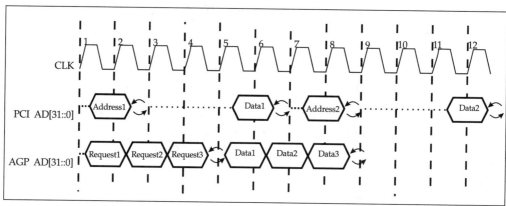

PCI Read Transactions

Clock 1. PCI initiator drives address of target (Address1).

Clock 2. Target latches and decodes Address1. Memory access begins. This clock is a required wait state. It allows the bus to change ownership, from the master to the target.

Clock 3. For this example, memory access time is assumed to be three clock periods. Therefore, this clock is a wait state. No data is transferred.

Clock 4. This clock is the third and final wait state for this transaction.

Clock 5. Memory target responds with Data1. First transaction completes.

Clock 6. This clock is a required turn-around clock in between read transactions. During this clock, the memory target of the first transaction floats the AD bus.

Clock 7. PCI master initiates the second transaction. This clock is the PCI address phase. Same as Clock 1.

Clock 8. PCI memory target latches and decodes Address2. Required wait state. Same as Clock 2.

Clock 9. This clock represents a wait state due to memory access latency time.

Clock 10. Third and final wait state for Data2.

Clock 11. Memory target responds with Data2. Second transaction ends.

Clock 12. Master latches Data2 on the rising edge of the clock. Memory target floats the AD bus.

AGP Read Transactions

Clock 1. AGP master drives Request1.

Clock 2. AGP master drives Request2. First wait state for Data1.

Clock 3. AGP master drives Request3. First wait state for Data2. Second wait state for Data1.

Clock 4. Required turn-around clock. AGP master floats the AD bus. First wait state for Data3. Second wait state for Data2. Third and final wait state for Data1.

Clock 5. AGP target sources Data1. First data transaction is over. Final wait state for Data2. Second wait state for Data3.

Clock 6. AGP target sources Data2. Second data transaction is over. Final wait state for Data3.

Clock 7. AGP target sources Data3. Third data transaction is over.

Clock 8. AGP target floats the AD bus. Returns bus to a high-impedance state.

This example illustrates the power of pipelined transactions. By overlapping the memory access time of Data1 with the issuance of Requests 2 and 3, three doublewords were transferred in 8 clock periods. On the other hand, each PCI transaction incurred the memory access latency. It took 12 clocks to transfer only two doublewords and would be an additional six clocks to transfer another doubleword.

Due to insufficient memory bandwidth, most platforms will not realize the full utilization of AGP. For the purpose of optimizing AGP, the specification recommends that core logic vendors provide the information identified in the sections that follow.

Guaranteed Latency

Guaranteed Latency is defined as the worst-case memory access latency when performing main memory accesses through the AGP high-priority request sub-queue. It is defined as the number of clocks from the clock in which the REQ# signal is asserted to the first clock in which data is transferred. This assumes that the AGP pipeline is empty and that no wait states are inserted by the master.

Typical Latency

Typical Latency is defined as the typical memory latency when accessing main memory through the AGP low-priority request sub-queue. It is defined as the number of clocks from the clock in which the REQ# signal is asserted to the first clock in which data is transferred. This assumes that the AGP pipeline is empty and that no wait states are inserted by the master.

Mean Bandwidth

Mean Bandwidth is defined as the AGP memory bandwidth that can be delivered through the low-priority request sub-queue, averaged over the period of the display of one frame. This time is typically 10ms, at a refresh rate of 100Hz. The following assumptions apply:

- No wait states inserted by the master.
- No accesses to the high-priority request sub-queue.
- The graphics master maintains an optimal pipeline depth of X.
- The average access length is Y.

"X" and "Y" are defined by the core logic manufacturer.

Number of Devices

More than two devices may be attached to the AGP, but only two devices (one master and one target) are allowed to be enabled at one time. It is up to the motherboard designer to verify that the system operates correctly if more than two devices are attached. The challenge is from an electrical perspective. The specification states that no electrical specifications can be violated by adding additional devices.

The most common example where more than two devices are attached is a three-load bus that includes the following devices:

- core logic device
- planar motherboard graphics accelerator
- card slot

This could be an area of differentiation for a system or motherboard OEM. The card slot gives the end user an upgrade path. When the card slot is unoccupied, there exists one electrical environment. When an add-in card is installed, the electrical environment is changed. Intel has published a paper detailing the electrical requirements associated with this scenario (the paper can be downloaded from the AGP forum web site).

When the add-in card is installed, the embedded graphics accelerator must be disabled. How this is accomplished is outside the scope of the specification.

Enqueuing Requests and Delivering Data in 1X Mode

This section introduces the timing and protocol required used by an AGP master and AGP target transferring read data in 1X data transfer mode. As an example, the AGP master could be reading texture maps from main memory to performing AGP texturing. The graphics accelerator is always the AGP master, and the core logic is always the AGP target. This section provides an introduction. More detailed examples follow in subsequent chapters.

Drawing Convention Used

The drawing convention is consistent for all the timing diagrams in the book.

In AGP 1X data transfer mode, all signals are synchronized to the rising edge of the AGP clock. This means that when an AGP device drives a signal inactive or active, the output driver is enabled on the rising edge of the AGP clock. The signals in the examples that follow transition near the middle of the clock period. By transitioning mid-period, a realistic, non-zero "output valid" delay and signal propagation delay is represented.

Input signals are sampled on the rising edge of the clock signal. In the illustrations, the output signals transition during the clock period, and are valid from the perspective of any inputs that sample the signals, on the next rising edge of the clock.

At some times, a signal is actively driven while at other times it isn't. When an AGP device is actively driving a signal, the signal is depicted as a solid line. When a signal is not being actively driven, it may be pulled high, or low, by a resistor, or simply be allowed to float. Whenever a signal is not actively driven, the timing diagram depicts it as a dashed line. If the dashed line is high or low, assume that a pull up or pull down resistor is maintaining the state of that signal. When a signal is in a float state, the dashed line will be mid-way between the active high and low voltage levels.

The turn-around symbol, represented by two curved arrows pointing to each other's tails, indicates that a signal is being returned to the float state by its current owner. The current owner is backing off its output driver from this signal in preparation for another device taking ownership and turning on its output driver.

Any signal name with a pound sign (#) suffix following it is asserted when driven low. Signal names lacking the pound sign suffix are asserted when high.

Enqueuing Multiple Requests Using AD and C/BE Busses

There are two mechanisms that may be used to enqueue requests over the AGP bus:

- the Sideband Address (SBA) Port
- the AD bus

An AGP master can use either method. However, when one method is used the other is never used. This decision is typically made during the design of the master. Bit 9 of the master's AGP status register (Refer to Table 2-1 on page 35) indicates the mechanism that is employed by the master. Bit 9 in the target's command register (refer to Table 2-2 on page 36) must be programmed to indicate the mechanism that the master uses. For more information on AGP device configuration, refer to Chapter 12, entitled "AGP Configuration," on page 235.

When the SBA port is not used for enqueuing requests, the AGP transaction is split into two transactions performed on the AD bus:

- The first transaction takes place when the request is enqueued into the target. This transaction is analogous to the address phase of a PCI transaction.
- The second transaction occurs at a later time when the data is actually transferred.

The start address driven onto the AD bus during the request transaction is always aligned on an address divisible by eight (in other words, it's a quadword-aligned address) and is delivered on AD[31::3]. AD[2::0] convey the transaction length. AGP transactions always have an explicit size. Eight bytes is the minimum transfer size, while 256 bytes is the maximum. The encoding on AD[2::0] indicates the transfer size either as a number of quadwords or as a number of 32-byte blocks. The transfer length encodings are found in the sections entitled, "Read Commands and Transfer Length" on page 98 and "Long Read Commands and Transfer Length" on page 100.

Table 2-1: AGP Status Register (Offset CAP_PTR + 4)

Bits	Field	Description
31:24	RQ	The RQ field contains the maximum depth of the AGP request queue. Therefore, this number is the maximum number of command requests this device can manage. A "0" is interpreted as a depth of one, while FFh is interpreted as a depth of 256.
23:10	Reserved	Writes have no affect. Reads return zeros.
9	SBA	If set, this device supports sideband addressing.
8:6	Reserved	Writes have no affect. Reads return zeros.
5	4G	If set, this device supports addresses greater than 4 GB.
4	FW	If set, this device supports Fast Write transactions.
3	Reserved	Writes have no affect. Reads return a zero
2:0	RATE	The RATE field is a bit map that indicates the data transfer rates supported by this device. AGP devices must report all that apply. The RATE field applies to AD, C/BE#, and SBA busses. **Bit Set** **Transfer Rate** 0 1X 1 2X 2 4X

Table 2-2: AGP Command Register (Offset CAP_PTR + 8)

Bits	Field	Description
31:24	RQ_DEPTH	**Master**: The RQ_DEPTH field must be programmed with the maximum number of requests the master is allowed to enqueue into the target. The value programmed into this field must be equal to or less than the value reported by the target in the RQ field of its AGP Status Register. A "0" value indicates a request queue depth of one entry, while a value of FFh indicates a request queue depth of 256. **Target**: The RQ_DEPTH field is reserved.
23:10	Reserved	Writes have no affect. Reads return zeros.
9	SBA_ENABLE	When set, the sideband address mechanism is enabled in this device.
8	AGP_ENABLE	**Master**: Setting the AGP_ENABLE bit allows the master to initiate AGP operations. When cleared, the master cannot initiate AGP operations. Also when cleared, the master is allowed to stop driving the SBA port. If bits 1 or 2 are set, the master must perform a re-synch cycle, before initiating a new request. **Target**: Setting the AGP_ENABLE bit allows the target to accept AGP operations. When cleared, the target ignores incoming AGP operations. The target must be completely configured and enabled before the master is enabled. The AGP_ENABLE bit is the last to be set. Reset clears this bit.
7:6	Reserved	Writes have no affect. Reads return zeros.

Table 2-2: AGP Command Register (Offset CAP_P??

Bits	Field	De...
5	4G	**Master**: Setting the 4G bit a... AGP requests to addresses at o... boundary. When cleared, the mast... access addresses in the lower 4 GB of ... **Target**: Setting the 4G bit enables the target ... DAC commands, when bit 9 is cleared. When b... are set, the target can accept a Type 4 SBA comman... utilize A[35::32] of the Type 3 SBA command.
4	FW_ENABLE	When this bit is set, memory write transactions initiated by the core logic will follow the fast write protocol. When this bit is cleared, memory write transactions initiated by the core logic will follow the PCI protocol.
3	Reserved	Writes have no affect. Reads return zeros.
2:0	DATA_RATE	Only one bit in the DATA_RATE field must be set to indicate the maximum data transfer rate supported. The same bit must be set in both the master and the target. **Bit Set** **Transfer Rate** 0 1X 1 2X 2 4X

Figure 2-3 on page 38 illustrates the enqueuing of multiple requests (five, to be precise). The bus command (i.e., the transaction type) is encoded on the C/BE# bus. For the sake of discussion, assume that the transaction types are all low-priority reads. This means that the master wants to read data from AGP memory through the low-priority request sub-queue. High-priority and low-priority transactions are compared in Chapter 6, entitled "AGP Commands and Ordering Rules," on page 97.

All signals in this example are driven and sampled at the rising edge of the AGP clock. Since the frequency of the clock signal is 66 MHz, the clock period is 15ns.

Figure 2-3: Enqueuing Multiple Requests on the AD Bus

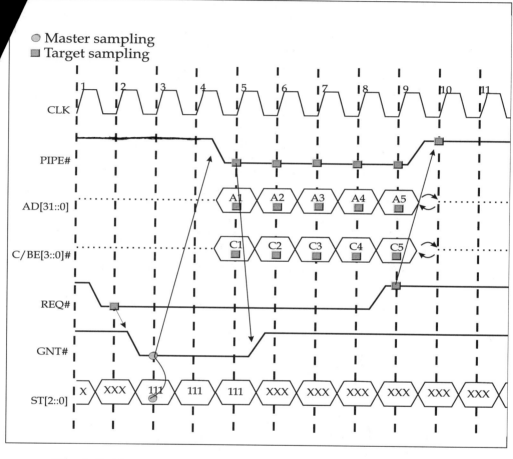

Clock 1. The AGP master begins this transaction by asserting the REQ# signal to request access to the bus. The master is requesting the bus to initiate the transaction.

Clock 2. The arbiter within the target (i.e., the core logic) responds to the bus master's request by asserting GNT#. The GNT# assertion gives the master permission to start the transaction, and indicates that the content of the status bus (ST[2::0]) is valid. A status of 111b indicates that the arbiter is granting bus ownership to the master to start a request transaction. Note that this is the fastest that the arbiter can assert GNT# in response to sampling REQ# asserted.

The arbitration algorithm employed by the core logic is implementation-specific and outside the scope of the specification. Arbitration is discussed in more detail in Chapter 5, entitled "AGP Arbitration," on page 91.

Clock 3. The master samples GNT# and the Status bus and recognizes that it has been granted bus ownership to issue one or more transaction requests to the target.

Clock 4. The master responds to GNT# by asserting the PIPE# signal. PIPE# stands for "pipelined." When asserted, it indicates that the master is enqueuing, or pipelining, transaction requests into the target. When PIPE# is asserted, a full-width transaction request is driven by the master onto the AD and C/BE# busses.

A full-width transaction request consists of:

- **AD[31::3]** contain a **start address** that is divisible by eight.
- **AD[2::0]** contain the transaction length. The length is indicated in either quadwords or in 32-byte blocks (as qualified by the transaction type).
- The bus command, or transaction type, is encoded on the **C/BE#** bus.

Note that the example illustrates the maximum latency that the master can exhibit when asserting PIPE#, relative to sampling GNT# asserted. The minimum latency would result in PIPE# assertion in Clock 3. While PIPE# remains asserted (clocks 4 through 9), the target enqueues one request on each rising edge of the clock on which PIPE# is sampled asserted.

Clock 5. Once the PIPE# signal is detected asserted, the arbiter can deassert the GNT# signal. With the deassertion of GNT#, the status bus contents goes to "XXX," which means "don't care" or an invalid state. The first request (A1) is latched by the core logic on the rising edge of clock 5 and the second request is then driven.

Clock 6. The PIPE# and REQ# signals remain asserted as the master continues enqueuing requests. With PIPE# and REQ# both asserted, the master indicates that it intends to continue enqueuing requests. In addition, this also indicates that this is not the last request to be enqueued. The core logic latches the second request (A2) on the rising edge of clock 6 and the master then drives out the third request (A3).

Clock 7. The core logic latches the third request (A3) on the rising edge of clock 7 and then the master drives out the fourth request (A4). Note that the master cannot add any wait states while enqueuing requests. Requests must be enqueued at the rate of one per clock (in other words, at full speed).

Clock 8. The core logic latches the fourth request (A4) and then the master drives out the fifth request (A5). The master deasserts the REQ# signal to indicate that the next request to be enqueued is the last request in this series. The master could continue enqueuing requests, if so desired, by keeping PIPE# and REQ# low. Once the master has filled all of the available slots in the request queue of the target, the master must terminate this bus transaction. The depth of the request queue in the core logic can be found in the AGP target's configuration status register (see the RQ field in Table 2-1 on page 35). The master knows the depth of the target's queue from the value programmed into the master's AGP configuration command register (see the RQ_DEPTH field in Table 2-2 on page 36) during configuration.

Clock 9. The master enqueues the last request of this series. The master is required to deassert PIPE# one clock after deasserting REQ#. The master returns the AD and C/BE# busses to idle by tri-stating the output drivers.

Back-to-Back Read Data Transactions

Figure 2-4 on page 41 illustrates the target device (i.e., the core logic) responding with the read data requested by transaction requests issued earlier by the AGP master (i.e., the graphics accelerator). The data is sourced to the master using a series of back-to-back read data transactions.

The data rate for this example is 1X mode, meaning that four bytes of data can be transferred on each rising edge of the AGP clock. The data transfer rate is established during configuration. Each transaction request was for eight bytes of data. Low-priority read data is always returned to the master in the order that it was requested (relative to other low-priority read transactions). More information on AGP transaction ordering can be found in Chapter 6, entitled "AGP Commands and Ordering Rules," on page 97.

Figure 2-4: Back-to-Back Read Data Transactions in 1X Mode

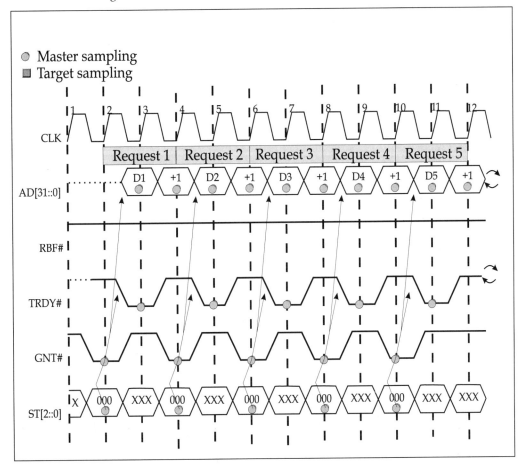

Clock 1. The target (i.e., the core logic) begins the first data transaction by asserting the GNT# signal. The assertion of GNT# qualifies the status bus content as valid. A status of 000b indicates that previously requested low-priority read data is being returned to the master (i.e., the accelerator). Once GNT# is sampled asserted by the master on the rising edge of clock 2, the master begins latching data from the AD bus on each rising edge of the clock. The latched data is qualified as valid by the assertion of TRDY#.

Clock 2. The target drives out the first dword and asserts TRDY# to indicate that the data on the AD bus is valid. TRDY# is only asserted for one clock. The assertion of TRDY# indicates that the target is ready to transfer all of the data. In this example, the total amount of data transferred for each previously-issued transaction request is eight bytes. When a data transaction can be completed in four clocks or less, there is only one assertion of TRDY#.

This example shows the minimum delay between GNT# sampled asserted and the assertion of TRDY#. The maximum delay permissible would be if TRDY# were asserted in Clock 3. This would indicate that the target is adding one wait state prior to the data transfer. A maximum of one wait state is allowed for this type of transaction. There is more information on data throttling in Chapters 8 and 9.

GNT# is deasserted in this clock to prepare for the pipelining of the GNT# signal, in Clock 3, for the next transaction.

Clock 3. Four bytes of valid data (dword D1) are latched by the master on the rising edge of Clock 3. The target then sources the next four bytes of valid data (dword D1 + 1) in this clock, for a total of eight bytes for this data transaction. These bytes are the final four bytes of the first transaction. The TRDY# signal is deasserted by the target in this clock.

The GNT# for the second transaction is asserted in this clock. The arbiter is allowed to assert GNT# for a new transaction in the final clock of the current transaction. This is referred to as GNT# pipelining. The pipelining of the GNT# signal allows back-to-back read transactions to proceed without idle clocks on the AD bus between the data transactions. This permits the most efficient use of AD bus bandwidth. When GNT# is asserted, the arbiter also sources valid status on the status bus. The status again indicates low-priority read data is being returned (status = 000b).

Clock 4. On the rising edge, the master latches the last four bytes of data for the first transaction (dword D1 + 1). The "+1" indicates that an additional doubleword is transferred, relative to the first doubleword. Wait states are not allowed to be added by either master or target between dword transfers. For more information on the rules for adding wait states, see "Three Times Where Data Can Be Delayed" on page 134.

During this clock, the target sources the first four bytes (dword D2) for the second transaction and asserts TRDY# to indicate that all eight bytes are ready to be transferred.

The arbiter deasserts GNT# and GNT# becomes available for pipelining in the next clock. When GNT# is deasserted, the status bus becomes invalid ("don't care" state).

Clock 5. The master latches the first four bytes of the second transaction (D2) on the rising edge of the clock. The target sources the next four bytes, for a total of eight bytes for this transaction. TRDY# is deasserted by the target and GNT# is asserted, or pipelined, for the third transaction. The status bus indicates low-priority read data will be returned during the next transaction (status = 000b).

Clock 6. The final four bytes of the second transaction (dword D2 + 1) are latched by the bus master on the rising edge of the clock. The target sources the first four bytes for the third transaction (D3). The target indicates that the data on the AD bus is valid by asserting TRDY# (the target is operating with zero wait states added). GNT# is deasserted in preparation for grant pipelining in the next clock. With the deassertion of GNT#, the status bus becomes a "don't care."

Clock 7. The master latches the first four valid bytes of the third transaction (D3) on the rising edge of the clock. During this clock, the target sources the next four bytes (dword D3 + 1), for a total of eight bytes for this transaction. TRDY# is deasserted by the target and GNT# is asserted, pipelining it for the fourth transaction. The status bus indicates low-priority read data will be returned for the next transaction (status = 000b).

Clock 8. The final four bytes of the third transaction (dword D3 + 1) are latched by the bus master on the rising edge of the clock. The target sources the first four bytes for the fourth transaction (dword D4) during this clock. The target indicates that the data on the AD bus is valid by asserting TRDY#, and GNT# is deasserted in preparation for GNT# pipelining in the next clock. With the deassertion of GNT#, the status bus becomes a "don't care."

Clock 9. The master latches the first four valid bytes of the fourth transaction (dword D4) on the rising edge of the clock. The target sources the next four bytes (dword D4 + 1), for a total of eight bytes for this transaction. TRDY# is deasserted by the target, and GNT# is asserted (pipelined) for the fifth transaction. The status bus indicates low-priority read data is being returned for the next transaction (status = 000b).

Clock 10. The final four bytes of the fourth transaction (dword D4 + 1) are latched by the master on the rising edge of the clock. The target sources the first four bytes for the fifth transaction (dword D5). The target indicates that the data is valid by asserting TRDY#. GNT# is deasserted, and the status bus becomes a "don't care."

Clock 11. The master latches the first four bytes of the fifth transaction (dword D5) on the rising edge of the clock. The target sources the next four bytes (dword D5 + 1), for a total of eight bytes for this transaction. TRDY# is deasserted by the target. GNT# remains deasserted, ending this series of data transactions.

Clock 12. The final four bytes of data for the fifth transaction (dword D5 + 1) are latched by the bus master on the rising edge of the clock. TRDY# is floated during the turn-around cycle. This means that the target is backing off its output driver from the TRDY# signal. The AD bus also goes into a turn-around state as the core logic ceases to drive the final data item.

This completes the return of the data for the five transaction requests that were previously enqueued.

3

The Signaling Environment

The Previous Chapter

The previous chapter introduced AGP with a description of the major features and a discussion of some of the fundamental system requirements to support the interface. A basic overview of AGP technology can be gained from this chapter.

This Chapter

This chapter outlines the major signaling requirements of the AGP interface. The electrical AC and DC specifications are described. AGP driver and receiver characteristics are presented.

The Next Chapter

The next chapter defines the required and optional signals for AGP-compliant masters and targets. The signals are grouped by function and the purpose of each signal is described.

AGP Voltage Characteristics

For a complete list of the DC and AC specifications, refer to the AGP specification.

AGP uses either a 1.5V or 3.3V signaling environment. The signaling level actually used depends on the value of the Vddq pins. Vddq is the I/O voltage. This voltage is not the component supply voltage. The component supply voltage is implementation specific. Vddq must be sourced to the master and the target from the same supply line.

AGP plug-in cards are keyed to operate at one voltage or the other. The motherboard connectors are keyed accordingly, to source a particular value of Vddq. A 1.5V card will not fit into a 3.3V connector, and a 3.3V card will not fit into a 1.5V connector. A universal connector can accept graphics cards that operate at either voltage level. The universal connector does not have a keyway. Motherboards that support the universal connector must implement core logic devices that can support either voltage. The system board must source the appropriate Vddq voltage indicated by the value sampled on the TYPDET# pin of a universal connector.

There are 3 data transfer rates: 1X mode, 2X mode, and 4X mode. Due to signal integrity issues associated with high-frequency and high-voltage operation, 4X mode can only operate at the 1.5V signaling levels. 1X and 2X operation can occur at either the 1.5V or 3.3V signaling levels. The signaling rates for the core logic and the graphics accelerators are communicated to the system via their respective PCI configuration registers. The transfer rate selected must be the highest rate supported by both master and target. The selection of the transfer rate is accomplished during configuration.

DC Specifications

3.3 Volt Signaling

Although modified for the point-to-point AGP environment, the 3.3V specifications are based on the revision 2.1 66 MHz PCI specifications. These specifications are relevant regardless of the selected transfer mode (1X or 2X mode operation).

- Vddq (I/O supply voltage) is specified as 3.3V +/- 0.15V.
- The input and output voltages are specified relative to Vddq.
- When it appears in the text that follows, the "*" symbol represents the multiplication symbol.
- VILmax (Maximum input low voltage) = 0.3 * Vddq. As an example, if Vddq is 3.3V, then for an input to be detected as low, the voltage must be a maximum of 0.99V.
- VILmin (Minimum input low voltage) is - 0.5V.
- VIHmin (Minimum input high voltage) = 0.5 * Vddq. As an example, if Vddq is 3.3V, then for an input to be detected as high, the voltage must be a minimum of 1.65V.
- VIHmax is Vddq + 0.5V.
- VOLmax (Maximum output low voltage) = 0.1 * Vddq. For example, if

Vddq is 3.3V, then for an output to be a valid low voltage, the voltage must be a maximum of 0.33V.

- VOHmin (Minimum output high voltage) = 0.9 * Vddq. For example, if Vddq is 3.3V, then for an output to be a valid high voltage, the voltage must be a minimum of 2.97V.
- The maximum input pin capacitance = 8 pF, compared to 10 pF for PCI devices. As in the PCI specification, the AGP specification allows a maximum input capacitance of 16 pF for planar devices (to allow for the use of pin grid array (PGA) packaging).

1.5 Volt Signaling

1.5V specifications are based on a scaling of the 3.3V signaling specifications. These specifications are relevant, regardless of transfer mode (1X, 2X, or 4X mode operation).

- Vddq (I/O supply voltage) is specified as 1.5V +/- 0.075V.
- The input and output voltages are specified relative to Vddq.
- VILmax (Maximum input low voltage) = 0.4 * Vddq. As an example, if Vddq is 1.5V, then for an input to be detected as low, the voltage must be a maximum of 0.6V.
- VILmin (Minimum input low voltage) = - 0.5V.
- VIHmin (Minimum input high voltage) = 0.6 * Vddq. As an example, if Vddq is 1.5V, then for an input to be detected as high, the voltage must be a minimum of 0.9V.
- VIHmax is Vddq + 0.5V.
- VOLmax (Maximum output low voltage) = 0.15 * Vddq. For example, if Vddq is 1.5V, then for an output to be a valid low voltage, the voltage must be a maximum of 0.225V.
- VOHmin (Minimum output high voltage) = 0.85 * Vddq. For example, if Vddq is 1.5V, then for an output to be a valid high voltage, the voltage must be a minimum of 1.275V.

Incremental Requirements for 2X and 4X Mode Operation

The primary addition to the DC specifications for 2X and 4X mode operation is a **common reference voltage (Vref)**. The Vref specification permits a differential input buffer design. Although the differential input buffer is not required, its implementation is strongly recommended by the specification when operating

at the higher data transfer rates. For AGP (1.5V or 3.3V) motherboard-only implementations, a common reference circuit is also strongly recommended by the specification. The Vref is not supplied through the 3.3V connector, therefore a common reference voltage is not applicable to add-in cards that are operating at 3.3V. Add-in cards with a 1.5V Vddq have two voltage reference pins (Vref) available on the connector.

The reference voltage is intended to be the mid-point of the VOL/VIH range. Therefore the reference voltage, like the VIL/VIH voltages, is specified relative to Vddq. For 2X mode operation at 3.3V, the minimum reference voltage = 0.39 * Vddq, and the maximum reference voltage = 0.41 * Vddq. As an example, if Vddq is 3.3V, then Vref must be within a range of 1.287V to 1.353V.

For 2X and 4X mode operation at 1.5V Vddq, the minimum reference voltage = 0.48 * Vddq, and the maximum reference voltage = 0.52 * Vddq. As an example, if Vddq is 1.5V, then Vref must be within a range of 0.72V to 0.78V.

1X Transfer Mode Timing Model

Critical 1X Mode Timings

The critical 1X mode timing relationships can be broken up into four categories:

- Clocks
- Outputs
- Inputs
- Reset

Each category is discussed individually in the sections that follow.

Clocks

The clock cycle has a minimum cycle time of 15ns, indicating a **maximum frequency** of **66.66MHz**. A maximum clock cycle time of 30ns is also specified, therefore, the **minimum** clock **frequency** is **33.33MHz**. AGP devices may operate at any stable frequency from 33 to 66MHz. A **minimum clock high and low time** of **6ns** must be met at all times.

To keep devices out of an indeterminate range, a **minimum clock slew rate** of **1.5V/ns** is specified. To ensure signal integrity, a **maximum clock slew rate** of

4V/ns is also specified. This slew rate must be maintained across the minimum peak-to-peak portion of the clock waveform, which has a minimum voltage swing of 0.4 * Vddq.

In all data transfer modes, the **maximum clock skew** is **1ns** and represents the difference between the rising edge of the AGP clock at the input of the master and the target. The 1ns specification includes skew and jitter that may originate on the motherboard, add-in card, and clock generator.

Outputs

The clock-to-control signal valid delay is a minimum of 1.0ns and a maximum of 5.5ns. For 3.3V operation, the relative test points are based on a 0.4 * Vddq point on the clock and signals. The test points for 1.5V operation are on the 0.5 * Vddq point on the clock and signals. Clock-to-data valid delay is a minimum of 1.0ns and a maximum of 6.0ns.

Clock-to-float delay (from active) is a minimum of 1.0ns and a maximum of 14ns. The output slew rate specification is identical to the clock slew rate specification. Keep in mind that the faster the output transitions, the more time is allowed for logic delays within the device. For signal integrity reasons, however, the maximum output slew rate cannot be violated.

Maximum propagation delay is 2.5ns. This flight time is broken down as follows:

- a maximum of 1.65ns for the motherboard trace,
- 0.7ns for the add-in card trace
- 0.15ns for the connector

Inputs

Control signals have a **minimum input setup time to clock** of **6.0ns**. Minimum **data setup time-to-clock** is **5.5ns**. The **minimum hold time** is **0ns**.

Reset

The reset timings on the AGP interface are **identical to the PCI reset timings**. Reset must be held active a minimum of 1ms after power is stable, and a minimum of 100us after the clock is stable. Reset assertion and deassertion may be asynchronous to the AGP clock. After reset is detected active, all devices have a maximum of 40ns to tri-state their output buffers. There is a reset minimum slew rate of 50 mV/ns, specified for the rising edge (deassertion) of reset.

2X and 4X Transfer Mode Timing Model

When transferring data in either the 2X or 4X modes, data strobes are supplied by the agent that is sourcing the data. These strobes indicate when the data can be latched. The receiver of the data uses the edges of the strobes to latch the data. As used in this context, the word "data" refers to anything transmitted over the AD bus, the C/BE# bus, as well as request information sourced over the SBA port. The same transfer mode is used by these three signal groups. Usage of different transfer modes for these signal groups is not supported.

As an example, if the data transfer rate on the AD bus is 2X, then the data transfer rate used over the SBA port and C/BE# bus is also 2X. The transfer rate is selected at configuration time.

Definition of the Outer Loop

The outer loop signals consists of:

- the AGP clock signal
- the control signals that are used for bus arbitration
- the control signals that indicate the readiness of the master and target to transfer data (such as IRDY# and TRDY#, respectively)

These signals are all synchronized to the rising edge of the AGP clock and control the overall data transfer. In 1X mode, the outer loop signals control the overall data transfer as well as the transfer of each individual data item.

In 2X and 4X mode, while they control the overall data transfer, they are not used to drive and receive each individual data item.

Definition of the Inner Loop

Outer Loop Controls Overall Data Transfer

Figure 3-1 on page 52 illustrates the relationship of the inner and outer timing loops. During a data transfer in 2X or 4X mode, the outer loop signals still control the overall data transfer, but the transfer of each individual data item is controlled by a separate group of signals (referred to as the inner loop).

Inner Loop Controls Transfer of Each Data Item

Rather than using the next rising-edge of the clock to latch the data, a separate signal is provided to the receiving device by the transmitter of the data. When the transmitter drives the data onto the bus, it also generates a transition on a strobe signal that is sourced to the receiver along with the data. The strobe is derived from the AGP clock, but is deliberately delayed so as to transition (high-to-low, or low-to-high) at about the mid-point of the data valid time. Transmit strobe edges are positioned near the center of the minimum data valid window to give the receiver a good input data sampling window for all the various system timing skew cases. A minimum data valid before strobe edge (tDvb) and a minimum data valid after strobe edge (tDva) are specified.

Figure 3-1: Relationship of Outer and Inner Timing Loops

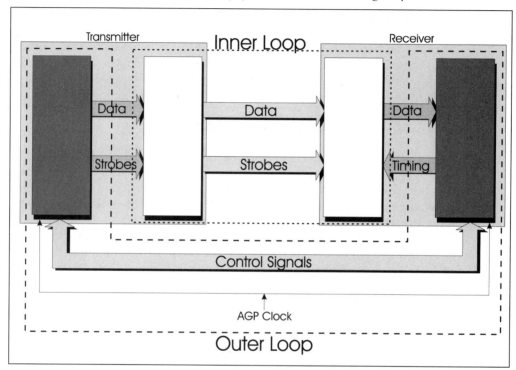

Strobe/Data Relationship in 2X Mode

In 2X mode, three strobes are used to strobe the data into the receiver's input latches: two are used to strobe data, while the other is used to strobe requests. AD_STB[1::0] are the two data strobes. Data is latched on both edges of the strobes and a total of eight bytes are transferred per AGP clock cycle.

The sampling point is specified relative to a specific voltage level on the strobe edge. The voltage level that defines the sampling point is referred to as Vtest. This test voltage is specified as 0.4 * Vddq when Vddq is 3.3V, while it is 0.5 * Vddq when Vddq is 1.5V.

Chapter 3: The Signaling Environment

Refer to Figur 3-2 below. The two data strobes are supplied by the same device that sources the data. The strobes are timed to change state approximately in the middle of the data valid window.

- **AD_STB0**: The receiving device latches the content of AD[15::0] and C/BE[1::0]# on the falling edge of the AD_STB0 signal. This is the lower two bytes of the first dword and their respective byte enables. **AD_STB1**: The receiving device latches the content of AD[31::16] and C/BE[3::2]# on the falling edge of the AD_STB1 signal. This is the upper two bytes of the first dword and their respective byte enables.
- **AD_STB0**: The receiving device latches the content of AD[15::0] and C/BE[1::0]# on the rising edge of the AD_STB0 signal. This is the lower two bytes of the second dword and their respective byte enables. **AD_STB1**: The receiving device latches the content of AD[31::16] and C/BE[3::2]# on the rising edge of the AD_STB1 signal. This is the upper two bytes of the second dword and their respective byte enables.

SB_STB: Refer to Figure 3-3 on page 54. When operating at the 2X data rate and issuing requests using the SBA bus, the receiving device latches the content of SBA[7::0] on the falling and then again on the rising edge of the SB_STB signal. As with the data strobes, the SideBand strobe is timed to change state approximately in the middle of the data valid window. Two 8-bit requests can be transferred per clock cycle.

Figure 3-2: Strobe/Data Relationship in 2X Mode

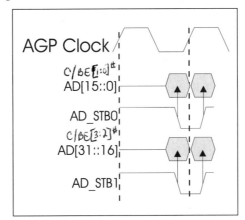

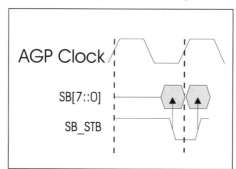

Figure 3-3: Strobe/Request Relationship in 2X Mode

Strobe/Data Relationship in 4X Mode

In 4X mode, six strobes are used to strobe the data into the receiver's input latches: four are used to strobe data, while the other two are used to strobe requests. AD_STB[1::0] have the same timing, while AD_STB[1::0]# are the complements of AD_STB[1::0]. Data is only latched on the falling edge of the strobe. A total of 16 bytes (four dwords) is transferred in each AGP clock. Refer to Figure 3-4 on page 56.

- **AD_STB0**: The receiving device latches the content of AD[15::0] and C/BE[1::0]# on the first falling edge of the AD_STB0 signal. This is the lower two bytes of the first dword and their respective byte enables. **AD_STB1**: The receiving device latches the content of AD[31::16] and C/BE[3::2]# on the first falling edge of the AD_STB1 signal. This is the upper two bytes of the first dword and their respective byte enables.
- **AD_STB0#** is the **complement of AD_STB0**. The receiving device latches the content of AD[15::0] and C/BE[1::0]# on the first falling edge of the AD_STB0# signal. This is the lower two bytes of the second dword and their respective byte enables. **AD_STB1#** is the **complement of AD_STB1**. The receiving device latches the content of AD[31::16] and C/BE[3::2]# on the first falling edge of the AD_STB1# signal. This is the upper two bytes of the second dword and their respective byte enables.
- **AD_STB0**: The receiving device latches the content of AD[15::0] and C/BE[1::0]# on the second falling edge of the AD_STB0 signal. This is the lower two bytes of the third dword and their respective byte enables. **AD_STB1**: The receiving device latches the content of AD[31::16] and C/BE[3::2]# on the second falling edge of the AD_STB1 signal. This is the upper two bytes of the third dword and their respective byte enables.

- **AD_STB0#** is the **complement of AD_STB0**. The receiving device latches AD[15::0] and C/BE[1::0]# on the second falling edge of AD_STB0#. This is the lower two bytes of the fourth dword and their respective byte enables. **AD_STB1#** is the **complement of AD_STB1**. The receiving device latches AD[31::16] and C/BE[3::2]# on the second falling edge of AD_STB1#. This is the upper two bytes of the fourth dword and their respective byte enables.

SB_STB and SB_STB#: Refer to Figure 3-5 on page 56. When operating at the 4X data rate and issuing requests using the SBA bus, the receiving device latches SBA[7::0] on the falling edge of SB_STB and then again on the falling edge of SB_STB#. An additional request is latched on the second falling edge of SB_STB, and a final request on the second falling edge of SB_STB#. Four 8-bit requests can be transferred per clock cycle.

Using Strobes as Differential Signal Pairs in 4X Mode

The 4X strobe signals are complements of each other and may optionally be implemented as differential signal pairs. The differential strobes are produced at a frequency of 133 MHz and are 180 degrees out of phase relative to their respective complement strobe. The 4X timings are based on the crossover point of the differential strobes. The crossover point is at the 50% point on the rising or falling edges of the strobes. The only Vddq value applicable in 4X mode is 1.5V, due to signal integrity issues. Therefore, the crossover point is, nominally, 0.75 V.

- Using **AD_STB0 and AD_STB0#**, the receiving device latches the content of AD[15::0] and C/BE[1::0]# on the first crossover point of the differential signal pair. This is the lower two bytes of the first dword and their respective byte enables. Using **AD_STB1 and AD_STB1#**, the receiving device latches the content of AD[31::16] and C/BE[3::2]# on the first crossover point of the differential signal pair. This is the upper two bytes of the first dword and their respective byte enables.
- Using **AD_STB0 and AD_STB0#**, the receiving device latches the content of AD[15::0] and C/BE[1::0]# on the second crossover point of the differential signal pair. This is the lower two bytes of the second dword and their respective byte enables. Using **AD_STB1 and AD_STB1#**, the receiving device latches the content of AD[31::16] and C/BE[3::2]# on the second crossover point of the differential signal pair. This is the upper two bytes of the second dword and their respective byte enables.
- Using **AD_STB0 and AD_STB0#**, the receiving device latches the content of AD[15::0] and C/BE[1::0]# on the third crossover point of the differential signal pair. This is the lower two bytes of the third dword and their respective byte enables. Using **AD_STB1 and AD_STB1#**, the receiving device latches the content of AD[31::16] and C/BE[3::2]# on the third crossover

point of the differential signal pair. This is the upper two bytes of the third dword and their respective byte enables.

- Using **AD_STB0 and AD_STB0#**, the receiving device latches the content of AD[15::0] and C/BE[1::0]# on the fourth crossover point of the differential signal pair. This is the lower two bytes of the fourth dword and their respective byte enables. Using **AD_STB1 and AD_STB1#**, the receiving device latches the content of AD[31::16] and C/BE[3::2]# on the fourth crossover point of the differential signal pair. This is the upper two bytes of the fourth dword and their respective byte enables.

Figure 3-4: Strobe/Data Relationship in 4X Mode

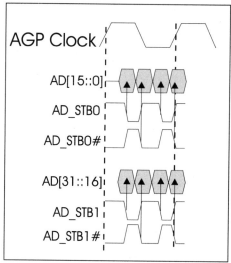

Figure 3-5: Strobe/Request Relationship in 4X Mode

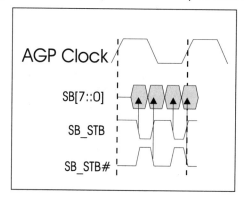

Four Time Domains

The discussion of the relationship of the Inner Loop signals and the Outer Loop signals is divided into four sections.

- **Relationship of the Outer Loop signals at the Transmitter and the Receiver.** This defines the timing relationship between the AGP clock and the outer loop transfer control signals at both the Transmitter and the Receiver.
- **Data/strobe timing relationship at the Transmitter and the Receiver.** This is the timing relationship between the data and its respective data strobes as they are driven by the Transmitter and when they arrive at the receiving device's inputs.
- **Relationship of the Outer Loop to the Inner Loop signals at the Transmitter.** In the outer loop, the AGP clock in concert with signals such as IRDY# TRDY, WBF# and RBF# are used to control the overall flow of data over the bus. In the inner loop, the data and its respective strobes are used to actually deliver the data from one device to the other. This area defines the timing relationship of the outer loop and inner loop signals to each other at the Transmitter.
- **Relationship of the Inner Loop and Outer Loop signals at the Receiver.**

Each is discussed in the sections that follow.

Relationship of Outer Loop Signals at Transmitter and Receiver

The timings employed in the outer loop are the AGP 1X mode timings. All control signals are synchronized to the rising edge of the 66MHz AGP clock. The receiver and transmitter of control signals share this common clock input signal. The transfer on the control signals is bidirectional. Examples of Outer Loop signals are: REQ# and GNT#, IRDY# and TRDY#.

Data/Strobe Timing Relationship at Transmitter and Receiver

This is the timing relationship between the data and its respective data strobes as they are driven by the transmitting device and when they arrive at the receiving device's inputs.

Within the inner loop, the "data" that is being transferred, could be:

- Data on the AD[31::0] bus
- Byte enables on the C/BE[3::0]# bus
- Request commands on the SBA[7::0] port

Transmitter-sourced strobes are used by the receiver to latch the data. In 2X mode, data is transferred on both edges of the strobes. The falling edges of the strobes are used to latch the first dword of the data, and the rising edges are used to latch the second dword of the data. The transmitter positions the strobes approximately in the center of the minimum window in which the data is valid. This positioning provides a good sampling window for the receiver, allowing for margin at all the timing skew corners.

For the transmitter, there are two timing specifications:

- **tDvb**. Minimum data valid before strobe edge.
- **tDva**. Minimum data valid after strobe edge.

For the receiver, there are also two specifications for latching the data:

- **tDsu**. Minimum setup time relative to the input strobe edge.
- **tDh**. Minimum hold time relative to the input strobe edge.

The data sent by the transmitter must meet these specifications at the receiver.

Relationship of Outer Loop to Inner Loop Signals at Transmitter

At the transmitter, the outer to inner loop timing relationship is characterized by three specifications relating the output strobe to the AGP clock:

- **tTSfmin**. Minimum time from the rising edge of the clock to the falling strobe edge.
- **tTSfmax**. Maximum time from the rising edge of the clock to the falling strobe edge.
- **tTSr**. Maximum time from the rising edge of the clock to the rising strobe edge.

These specifications are necessary to define a deterministic relationship between the outer loop flow control signals, like IRDY# and TRDY#, and the inner loop data transfers. A strobe pulse is allowed to cross an AGP clock boundary. Therefore, two clock periods (called T1 and T2) are required to illustrate the three specifications. Although two clock periods are required, all three specifications are relative to the rising edge of the first clock period (T1). The falling edge of the strobe comes first and is required to occur within the T1 clock period. Therefore, there is a minimum and maximum time specified for the falling strobe edge, relative to the rising edge of the T1 clock.

The rising edge of the strobe may come within the T1 or T2 clock period. There is a maximum, but no minimum time specified for the rising strobe edge, relative to the falling edge of the T1 clock. Each new xRDY# event (i.e., sampling TRDY# or IRDY# asserted on the rising edge of the clock) represents a new T1 clock period.

Relationship of Inner Loop and Outer Loop Signals at Receiver

The most complicated set of timings to comprehend is the relationship of the inner loop and outer loop signals at the receiver.

In 2X Mode. When transferring data in 2X mode, a dword is latched on the falling edges of the strobes, and another on the rising edges of the strobes. This is a total of eight bytes per AGP clock. The question is: "In what clock period does this quadword actually transfer: T1 or T2?" There is an uncertainty in the positioning of the rising edges of the strobes. At the latest, these strobes can occur at the receiver in clock T2, and, at the earliest, in clock T1. Therefore, the only reliable place to transfer a quadword of data from the inner loop to the outer loop is on the AGP clock edge at the end of T2.

There is another thing to consider when building the receive circuitry. If data is transferred in 2X mode with the minimum strobe transmit timings, then the entire transfer can occur in T1. A second quadword could be transferred in T2. To avoid a buffer overflow condition within the inner loop receive circuitry, the designer must provide, at a minimum, two quadword-wide latches that are edge-triggered.

In 4X Mode. In 4X mode, the amount of data transferred per clock doubles relative to 2X mode. When transferring data in 4X mode:

- A dword is latched on the first falling edges of the strobes.
- A dword is latched on the first falling edges of the compliment strobes.
- A dword is latched on the second falling edges of the strobes.
- A dword is latched on the second falling edges of the compliment strobes.

This is a total of 16 bytes per AGP clock. The question is: "In what clock period does this two quadword block actually transfer: T1 or T2? "

There is an uncertainty in the positioning of the falling edges of the second set of strobes. At the latest, these strobes can occur at the receiver in clock T2, and, at the earliest, in clock T1. The safe place to transfer two quadwords of data is on the rising edge of the clock at the end of T2. If data is transferred in 4X mode with the minimum strobe transmit timings, then the entire transfer can occur in T1. A second pair of quadwords could be transferred in T2. To avoid a buffer overflow condition within the inner loop receive circuitry, the designer must provide, at a minimum, two double quadword-wide latches that are edge-triggered.

Regardless of the data transfer mode, 2X or 4X, the data from the inner loop will transfer to the outer loop based on the AGP clock. Therefore, there is a minimum setup and a minimum hold specification for the receive strobes, relative to the AGP clock. The rising strobe edges are specified for 2X mode. This guarantees deterministic data transfer from the output of the inner loop latch to the input of the outer loop latch. These specifications, tRSsu (Receive Strobe setup) and tRSh (Receive Strobe hold), are relative to the T1 edge for the previous set of strobes.

Driver Characteristics

In both PCI and AGP, each trace is treated as a transmission line. PCI and AGP specify no external transmission line termination. Therefore, reflections are expected on the lines. The drivers must be designed to compensate for this reflection. In order to maintain good signal integrity, overshoot beyond Vddq and undershoot beyond Vss must be minimized. To ensure this, the AGP spec defines the maximum output slew rate, overshoot, undershoot, and ringback.

Comparing the output drive strength of a driver in a terminated incident wave bus environment to that of PCI, it is found that the PCI driver is much weaker. The weakness of the PCI driver compensates for the reflective wave switching that occurs in PCI. PCI, however, supports multiple electrical loads on the trace, while AGP, on the other hand, permits only one electrical load (beyond the characteristic impedance of the trace itself) to be presented to the output driver. The point-to-point nature of AGP permits the AGP driver to be weak when compared to PCI output buffers. The AGP specification estimates that the AGP driver be "roughly half the strength of the PCI buffer." Unlike PCI outputs, which typically rely on reflections to switch the state of input receivers, AGP output buffers are required to source an initial voltage swing to the input of either VIL or VIH (through some known characteristic trace impedance).

When designing for 2X and 4X operation, the specification strongly recommends that the output buffers for "data" and strobes match the rise and fall time delays across all process, voltage, and temperature variations. The term "data" refers to any signal latched using the strobes. For 2X operation, the specification recommends matching rise and fall time delays to within 1ns. For 4X operation, the specification recommends matching rise and fall time delays to within 100ps. In AGP 4X mode, there are 266 Mega-transfers per second. In order to provide adequate setup and hold times for these signals at this high data transfer rate, the tight matching specification is required.

For all data transfer modes, the output driver characteristics are defined in the AGP specification using V/I curves. Those figures are not duplicated here. Inputs to the output driver are required to be clamped to both ground and Vddq. The characteristics of the diodes that are used to clamp these inputs are also specified.

Receiver Characteristics

In 2X and 4X data transfer modes, the implementation of differential input receivers is strongly recommended. The reference voltages for the receivers are specified for both values of Vddq (1.5Vdc and 3.3Vdc). Using the differential inputs and the specified reference voltages can lead to increased input timing margins and better noise immunity. These are critical system parameters, given that this is a reduced voltage swing environment.

To reduce the current consumption of the Vref supply, the differential input buffer must be designed with low input leakage current. The combined load of all inputs on Vref must be less than 10uA. The differential input voltage is approximately 100 mV, so the differential input buffer must have sufficient gain to convert the differential input voltage to internal, CMOS voltage levels. When performing this amplification, introduction of additional timing skews is prohibited.

Changes to Clock Frequencies in Mobile Designs

In order to save power in mobile designs, changes to the AGP clock frequency are allowed. However, the only change allowed is from a normal operating state to a clock stopped state. If the clock is stopped, it must be stopped in the low state. When the clock is stopped, the AGP devices must maintain their software-visible configuration state. Also, AGP devices must exhibit pin control as defined in the PCI Power Management Specification. Refer to the MindShare book entitled *PCI System Architecture, Fourth Edition (published by Addison-Wesley)* for more information on PCI power management.

Once the clock is restarted from a stopped state, mobile AGP devices must lock their phase lock loops (PLLs) within 1ms, relative to the stable clock. An AGP master cannot issue a new transaction until the 1ms period has elapsed. This period is necessary to allow the target device's PLL to re-synchronize.

4 *The Signal Groups*

The Previous Chapter

The previous chapter outlined the major signaling requirements of the AGP interface. The electrical AC and DC specifications were described. AGP driver and receiver characteristics were presented.

This Chapter

This chapter defines the required and optional signals for AGP-compliant masters and targets. The signals are grouped by function and the purpose of each signal is described.

The Next Chapter

The next chapter focuses on the arbiter's role within the AGP interface. Optimization of grant pipelining is also discussed.

The Required and Optional Signals for AGP Masters

It is required that the AGP master (i.e., the graphics accelerator) also be a compliant PCI target device. This is necessary because the core logic may initiate, on behalf of the processor or a PCI bus master, a PCI transaction on the AGP bus to access the graphics accelerator. The AGP master may, optionally, be capable of acting as a PCI master. Also, the AGP master may optionally support fast write transactions (when acting as the target of a PCI memory write or memory write and invalidate transaction initiated by the core logic).

Figure 4-1 on page 64 illustrates the required versus optional signals for an AGP master device (i.e., the graphics accelerator).

AGP System Architecture

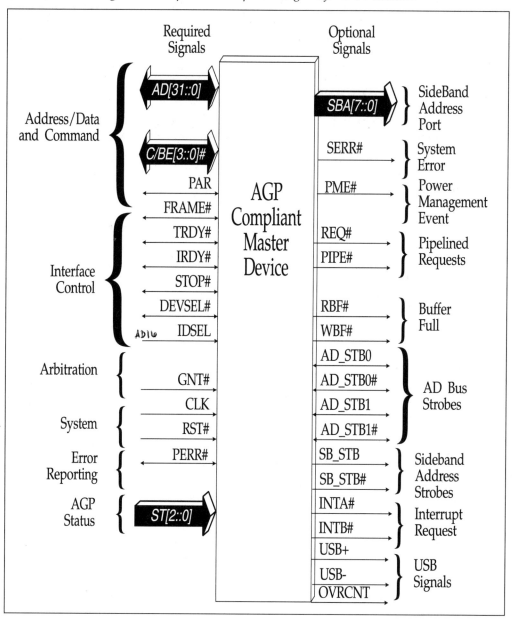

The Required and Optional Signals for AGP Targets

It is required that the AGP target (i.e., the core logic) also be a PCI-compliant initiator and PCI target. When acting as a PCI target, the core logic is not required to comply with the PCI Revision 2.1 rules that govern the maximum permissible latency in the initial (16 PCI clocks) and subsequent (eight PCI clocks) data phases.

The AGP target may optionally implement the ability to initiate fast write transactions when performing PCI memory write or memory write and invalidate transactions on behalf of the processor or a PCI bus master.

Figure 4-2 on page 66 illustrates the required versus optional signals for an AGP-compliant target device (i.e., the core logic).

AGP System Architecture

Figure 4-2: Required and Optional Signals for AGP Targets

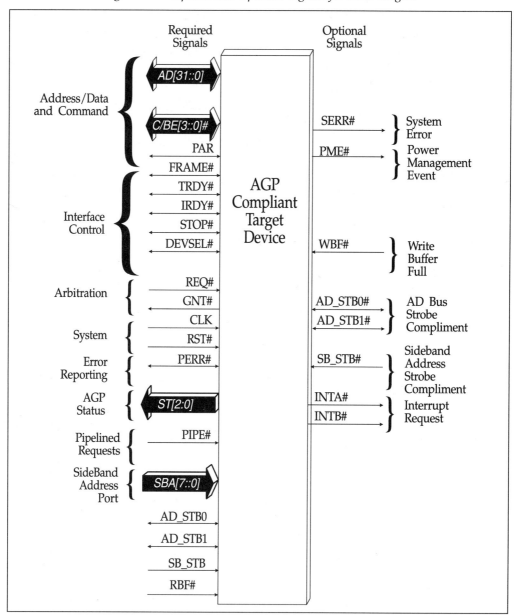

Chapter 4: The Signal Groups

Description of Signals

The descriptions that follow focus exclusively on the use of signals while operating in AGP (rather than PCI) operating mode. This includes the use of these signals for Fast Write transactions. Signals that are exclusive to PCI are identified as such. For more information about PCI, refer to the MindShare book entitled *PCI System Architecture, 4th Edition* (published by Addison-Wesley).

When signals require a pull-up or pull-down resistor, the specification states that it must be between 4K and 16K Ohm, with 8.2K Ohm being a typical value.

Address/Data and Command

AD[31::0] — Address/Data Bus

When using a multiplexed Address/Data bus (rather than issuing requests over the SideBand Address bus), the 32-bit Address/Data bus is used to transfer both request information as well as data. When issuing requests over the Sideband Address bus, SBA[7::0], the AD bus is dedicated to the transfer of data between the master and the target.

When the SBA has not been implemented, the AD bus is used for transferring request information. During a request transaction, the AD bus contains a quadword-aligned start address (an address divisible by eight) for the transfer. The least-significant three AD bus pins, AD[2::0], contain the data transfer length encoded either as a group of quadwords or a group of 32-byte blocks. A binary encoded value of 000b indicates a transfer length of one quadword (eight bytes) or one 32-byte block, while a value of 111b indicates a transfer length of either eight quadwords or eight 32-byte blocks. The transaction type defines the interpretation of the length field. As an example, for long read commands, the length indicates the number of 32-byte blocks, while for read commands it specifies the number of quadwords.

The AD bus is the physical data conduit between master and target during data transactions. In write data transactions, the master sources the data on the AD bus, while in read transactions, the target sources the data on the AD bus. In fast write transactions, the target (core logic) sources the data to the master (graphics accelerator) on the AD bus.

C/BE[3::0]# — Command/Byte Enable Bus

The command/byte enable bus has two purposes:

- When a transaction request is being issued using the AD and C/BE busses (rather than the SBA port), the four-bit transaction type is placed on C/BE[3::0]#.
- During a data transaction, the state of C/BE[3::0]# indicates which bytes within the current dword are being transferred (read or written). The byte enable signals are driven low if the associated byte within the current dword is being transferred.

During read data transactions, the target drives the C/BE[3::0]# bus to 0000b and it is ignored by the master. For read transactions, all data lanes contain valid data. In other words, it is a rule that the entire dword must be returned.

During write data transactions, the master sources byte enables with the data. The byte enables indicate which bytes are being written to within the currently addressed dword. The byte enables also indicate the data lane that contains the valid data:

- C/BE[0]# corresponds to data lane 0, or AD[7::0].
- C/BE[1]# corresponds to data lane 1, or AD[15::8].
- C/BE[2]# corresponds to data lane 2, or AD[23::16].
- C/BE[3]# corresponds to data lane 3, or AD[31::24].

As in PCI, any combination of byte enables is considered valid. The byte enables may change from one doubleword to the next.

In fast write transactions, the core logic is the initiator of the transaction and the source of the data. Therefore, the core logic sources the byte enables, as well as the data. The AGP master sources the byte enables during AGP write transactions.

PAR — Parity Bit

The PCI Parity signal is not valid for AGP transactions. It must, however, be actively driven by the agent that sources the data for the transaction. In this case, the term "data" could be request information (start address, transfer length, and command) sourced by the master when asserting the PIPE# signal.

In compliance with the PCI 2.1 specification, the PAR signal must be driven when PCI transactions are performed on the AGP bus. For more information on

PCI parity, refer to *PCI System Architecture, Fourth Edition* by MindShare (published by Addison-Wesley). The generation of parity is not supported during Fast Write transactions.

AGP Requests

PIPE# — Request Pipelined

The Pipeline signal is asserted by the AGP master when the arbiter grants the master permission to enqueue transaction requests. The PIPE# signal is only used when transaction requests are issued over the AD and C/BE busses, rather than over the SBA port. When PIPE# is asserted, this indicates that the AD bus contains a valid start address and transfer length, and the C/BE bus contains a valid command. This is referred to as a full-width transaction request. While PIPE# remains asserted, the target enqueues one transaction request on each rising edge of the AGP clock.

Since only the master can enqueue requests, PIPE# is an output from the master and an input to the target. The AGP master must either implement PIPE# and enqueue requests over the AD and C/BE busses, or implement the SBA port. The AGP target must support both mechanisms (because the master may use either).

SBA[7::0] — SideBand Address Bus

Rather than issuing transaction requests over the AD and C/BE busses, the SideBand Address Port (SBA) can be used by the AGP master to issue requests to the AGP target. Enabling the SBA port permits the AD and C/BE busses to be dedicated to data transmission. The target ignores the SBA unless this feature is enabled in bit nine of its AGP PCI command register (refer to Table 4-1 on page 70). A value of FFh on the SBA[7::0] indicates a NOP, and indicates to the target that no command is currently present on the SBA port.

Either PIPE# and the AD and C/BE busses are used to issue transaction requests, or the SBA, but never both. If a master implements the SBA, there is no need to implement the PIPE# mechanism. Dynamic switching between mechanisms during run time is not permitted. The selection of transaction issuance mechanism is typically made during the design of the master.

Table 4-1: AGP Command Register (Offset CAP_PTR + 8)

Bits	Field	Description
31:24	RQ_DEPTH	**Master**: The RQ_DEPTH field must be programmed with the maximum number of requests the master is allowed to enqueue into the target. The value programmed into this field must be equal to or less than the value reported by the target in the RQ field of its AGP Status Register. A "0" value indicates a request queue depth of one entry, while a value of FFh indicates a request queue depth of 256. **Target**: The RQ_DEPTH field is reserved.
23:10	Reserved	Writes have no effect. Reads return zeros.
9	SBA_ENABLE	When set, the sideband address mechanism is enabled in this device.
8	AGP_ENABLE	**Master**: Setting the AGP_ENABLE bit allows the master to initiate AGP operations. When cleared, the master cannot initiate AGP operations. Also when cleared, the master is allowed to stop driving the SBA port. If bits 1 or 2 are set, the master must perform a re-synch cycle, before initiating a new request. **Target**: Setting the AGP_ENABLE bit allows the target to accept AGP operations. When cleared, the target ignores incoming AGP operations. The target must be completely configured and enabled before the master is enabled. The AGP_ENABLE bit is the last to be set. Reset clears this bit.
7:6	Reserved	Writes have no effect. Reads return zeros.

Table 4-1: AGP Command Register (Offset CAP_PTR + 8) (Continued)

Bits	Field	Description
5	4G	**Master**: Setting the 4G bit allows the master to initiate AGP requests to addresses at or above the 4GB address boundary. When cleared, the master is only allowed to access addresses in the lower 4 GB of addressable space. **Target**: Setting the 4G bit enables the target to accept AGP DAC commands, when bit 9 is cleared. When bits 5 and 9 are set, the target can accept a Type 4 SBA command and utilize A[35::32] of the Type 3 SBA command.
4	FW_ENABLE	When this bit is set, memory write transactions initiated by the core logic will follow the fast write protocol. When this bit is cleared, memory write transactions initiated by the core logic will follow the PCI protocol.
3	Reserved	Writes have no affect. Reads return zeros.
2:0	DATA_RATE	Only one bit in the DATA_RATE field must be set to indicate the maximum data transfer rate supported. The same bit must be set in both the master and the target. **Bit Set** **Transfer Rate** 0 1X 1 2X 2 4X

Interface and Flow Control

FRAME# — (PCI-only signal)

FRAME# is a PCI signal and is not used during AGP transactions. It is kept deasserted by a central resource (typically a pull-up resistor on the motherboard or inside the core logic). Refer to *PCI System Architecture, Fourth Edition* by MindShare (published by Addison-Wesley) for a description of FRAME# usage in PCI transactions.

FRAME# is asserted by the initiator (the core logic) of a Fast Write transaction to indicate the beginning and duration of a fast write transaction. When FRAME#

is sampled asserted on the rising edge of the clock, the AGP master (acting as the target of the fast write transaction) latches the start address and command. Refer to Chapter 10, entitled "Fast Write Transactions," on page 187 for more information on Fast Write transactions.

IRDY# — Initiator Ready

In write data transactions, Initiator Ready (IRDY#) is asserted by the AGP master to indicate that it is ready to provide all of the data to the target. In a read data transaction, IRDY# asserted indicates that the master is ready to accept a subsequent block of previously-requested read data from the target. In a read data transaction, the master cannot throttle (i.e., add wait states to) the transfer of the initial data block.

In the PCI protocol, there is a fundamental relationship between FRAME# and IRDY#. FRAME# can only be deasserted by the initiator in the clock when it becomes ready to transfer the final data item of the transaction. In other words, it can only deassert FRAME# in the clock when it asserts IRDY# to indicate its readiness to transfer the final data item. FRAME# and IRDY# are never deasserted simultaneously (during the same clock). FRAME# will be deasserted when IRDY# is asserted to indicate that the master is ready to transfer the final data item. The master then subsequently deasserts IRDY# when the transfer of the final data item has completed (i.e., TRDY# has been sampled asserted indicating that the target was also ready to transfer the final data item). FRAME# and IRDY# are then both sampled deasserted on the next rising edge of the clock, indicating a bus idle condition.

FRAME# is not used in AGP transactions, and there is no relationship between FRAME# and IRDY#. In fast write transactions, data is transferred to the graphics accelerator by the core logic (acting as the PCI master). The core logic asserts IRDY# to indicate its readiness to transfer valid write data. The initiator of a fast write can insert wait states prior to the transfer of a data block other than the first, but not on individual dword boundaries, as in PCI.

This is one, but not the only difference between AGP fast write transactions and PCI write transactions. For more information on fast write transactions, refer to Chapter 10, entitled "Fast Write Transactions," on page 187.

TRDY# — Target Ready

In a read data transaction that completes in 4 AGP clocks or less, TRDY# is asserted by the AGP target when it's ready to source all of the data. In longer read data transactions, TRDY# assertion indicates that the target is ready to source the initial or a subsequent block of data. In write data transactions, TRDY# is asserted by the target to indicate its readiness to accept a subsequent block of data. In both read and write transactions, the target may add wait states prior to the transfer of a block of data by deasserting TRDY# at the throttle point for that data block. For more information on adding wait states, refer to "Three Times Where Data Can Be Delayed" on page 134. In fast write transactions, the graphics accelerator is the target of the transaction and the core logic is the initiator. The graphics accelerator asserts TRDY# to indicate to the core logic its readiness to accept a subsequent block of data.

DEVSEL# — Device Select (PCI-only signal)

Like the FRAME# signal, Device Select (DEVSEL#) is a PCI signal and is not used during AGP transactions. When not in use, it is kept deasserted by a pull-up resistor on the motherboard or inside the core logic. Refer to the MindShare book entitled *PCI System Architecture, Fourth Edition* by MindShare, for more information on the use of DEVSEL#.

In a fast write transaction, DEVSEL# is asserted by the target (the graphics accelerator) to indicate to the initiator that it is claiming the transaction. In other words, it has decoded the address and transaction type and is recognizing that it is the target of the transaction. DEVSEL# remains asserted for the duration of the transaction. If DEVSEL# is not asserted within the appropriate period of time, the initiator terminates the transaction by performing a master abort. Refer to "Master-Initiated Premature Transaction Termination" on page 210 for more information on fast writes and master abort.

STOP# (PCI-only signal)

Like the FRAME# and DEVSEL# signals, STOP# is a PCI signal and is not used during AGP transactions. When not in use, it is kept deasserted by a pull-up resistor on the motherboard or in the core logic.

STOP# is asserted by the target of a Fast Write transaction (the graphics accelerator) to prematurely terminate the transaction (before all the data has been transferred). Using the STOP# signal in concert with TRDY# and DEVSEL#, the target can terminate fast write transactions prematurely by signaling a disconnect or a target abort. The protocol for these terminations is described in "Target-Initiated Premature Transaction Termination" on page 210.

The PCI Retry mechanism is not supported in fast write transactions on the AGP bus. Instead, the target uses WBF# (Write Buffer Full) to prevent the core logic from initiating fast write transactions when the graphics accelerator is unable to accept the first block of data.

WBF# — Write Buffer Full (Optional)

Write Buffer Full (WBF#) can be used as an output by the target of a fast write transaction (the graphics accelerator) to prevent the core logic from initiating a fast write transaction. WBF# is an input to the arbiter in the core logic. While WBF# is asserted, the core logic is prohibited from initiating a fast write transaction. WBF# is an optional signal. An AGP master is not required to support acting as the target of fast write transactions. The master indicates whether or not it supports fast write transactions with bit four in its AGP status configuration register (refer to Table 4-2). WBF# is also an optional signal with respect to the core logic, but is required to be implemented as an input on all core logic devices that are capable of initiating fast write transactions. After determining via bit four of the graphics accelerator's status configuration register that the accelerator supports the fast write transaction, software can set bit four in the core logic's AGP command configuration register (refer to Table 4-3 on page 75). WBF# requires a central resource pull-up resistor. More information on WBF# can be found in the section entitled "Use of the WBF# Signal" on page 218.

Table 4-2: AGP Status Register (Offset CAP_PTR + 4)

Bits	Field	Description
31:24	RQ	The RQ field contains the maximum depth of the AGP request queue. Therefore, this number is the maximum number of command requests this device can manage. A "0" is interpreted as a depth of one, while FFh is interpreted as a depth of 256.
23:10	Reserved	Writes have no effect. Reads return zeros.
9	SBA	If set, this device supports sideband addressing.
8:6	Reserved	Writes have no effect. Reads return zeros.
5	4G	If set, this device supports addresses greater than 4 GB.
4	FW	If set, this device supports Fast Write transactions.
3	Reserved	Writes have no effect. Reads return a zero.

Table 4-2: AGP Status Register (Offset CAP_PTR + 4) (Continued)

Bits	Field	Description
2:0	RATE	The RATE field is a bit map that indicates the data transfer rates supported by this device. AGP devices must report all that apply. The RATE field applies to AD, C/BE#, and SBA busses. **Bit Set** **Transfer Rate** 0 1X 1 2X 2 4X

Table 4-3: AGP Command Register (Offset CAP_PTR + 8)

Bits	Field	Description
31:24	RQ_DEPTH	**Master**: The RQ_DEPTH field must be programmed with the maximum number of requests the master is allowed to enqueue into the target. The value programmed into this field must be equal to or less than the value reported by the target in the RQ field of its AGP Status Register. A "0" value indicates a request queue depth of one entry, while a value of FFh indicates a request queue depth of 256. **Target**: The RQ_DEPTH field is reserved.
23:10	Reserved	Writes have no effect. Reads return zeros.
9	SBA_ENABLE	When set, the sideband address mechanism is enabled in this device.

Table 4-3: AGP Command Register (Offset CAP_PTR + 8) (Continued)

Bits	Field	Description
8	AGP_ENABLE	**Master**: Setting the AGP_ENABLE bit allows the master to initiate AGP operations. When cleared, the master cannot initiate AGP operations. Also when cleared, the master is allowed to stop driving the SBA port. If bits 1 or 2 are set, the master must perform a re-synch cycle, before initiating a new request.
		Target: Setting the AGP_ENABLE bit allows the target to accept AGP operations. When cleared, the target ignores incoming AGP operations. The target must be completely configured and enabled before the master is enabled.
		The AGP_ENABLE bit is the last to be set. Reset clears this bit.
7:6	Reserved	Writes have no affect. Reads return zeros.
5	4G	**Master**: Setting the 4G bit allows the master to initiate AGP requests to addresses at or above the 4GB address boundary. When cleared, the master is only allowed to access addresses in the lower 4 GB of addressable space.
		Target: Setting the 4G bit enables the target to accept AGP DAC commands, when bit 9 is cleared. When bits 5 and 9 are set, the target can accept a Type 4 SBA command and utilize A[35::32] of the Type 3 SBA command.
4	FW_ENABLE	When this bit is set, memory write transactions, initiated by the core logic will follow the fast write protocol. When this bit is cleared, memory write transactions, initiated by the core logic will follow the PCI protocol.
3	Reserved	Writes have no affect. Reads return zeros.

Table 4-3: AGP Command Register (Offset CAP_PTR + 8) (Continued)

Bits	Field	Description
2:0	DATA_RATE	Only one bit in the DATA_RATE field must be set to indicate the maximum data transfer rate supported. The same bit must be set in both the master and the target. **Bit Set** **Transfer Rate** 0 1X 1 2X 2 4X

RBF# — Read Buffer Full

The AGP master asserts RBF# when unable to accept previously requested, low-priority read data. The target, therefore, is prevented from initiating the return of the data while RBF# remains asserted. Like WBF#, RBF# is an input to the core logic arbiter and requires a central resource pull-up. RBF# is an optional output signal on the graphics accelerator. If an AGP master is always ready to accept the first block of a low-priority read transaction, then RBF# need not be implemented on the graphics accelerator.

Proper use of RBF# will minimize the amount of low-priority read data buffering that is required in the master. The specification strongly recommends that the master not use RBF# as part of normal operation. Normally, the master should be able to consume low-priority read data faster than the target can produce the data. However, in those rare situations when the master cannot consume the data fast enough, the RBF# signal could then be used to throttle data traffic.

Once the arbiter asserts GNT# with a status of 000b, the assertion of RBF# doesn't affect the current transaction. The assertion of RBF#, however, prevents the next transaction from being a return of low-priority read data. RBF# must be implemented on all core logic devices. For more information on RBF# and AGP low priority read flow control, see "Use of the RBF# Signal" on page 138.

Arbitration and Status

REQ# — Bus Request

The Request (REQ#) signal is asserted by the AGP master when it requires ownership of the AD and C/BE busses in order to issue one or more transaction requests to the target (i.e., the core logic). REQ# is deasserted in the clock during which the final request is issued. When REQ# is deasserted, it must remain so for a minimum of one clock. REQ# is not used when issuing requests via the SBA port, so REQ# can be considered an optional output from the perspective of the AGP master. REQ# is a required input signal to all AGP target devices, and is integral to specifying core logic latencies.

If the AGP master is also capable of acting as a PCI master, then REQ# is required to be implemented as an output from the master. To initiate a PCI transaction, the AGP master first asserts REQ# to request use of the AD and C/BE busses. For more information on the PCI use of the REQ# signal, refer to the MindShare book entitled *PCI System Architecture, Fourth Edition* (published by Addison-Wesley).

If the core logic is capable of initiating fast write transactions, then the REQ# signal may be implemented internally (the arbiter for the AGP interface is internal to the core logic device). The core logic may require a weak pull-up on the REQ# signal. If so, the core logic manufacturer must specify the value of the pull-up.

GNT# and ST[2::0] — Bus Grant and the Status Bus

In concert with ST[2::0], the arbiter uses the GNT# signal to grant AD bus ownership to the graphics accelerator for one of a number of reasons. The reason is encoded on the Status Bus (ST[2::0]). ST[2::0] only has meaning to the master when GNT# is sampled asserted. Table 4-4 on page 79 lists the Status bus encodings.

Once asserted, the arbiter may deassert GNT# at any time to avoid a deadlock condition. By keeping GNT# deasserted, the core logic can delay the transfer of the initial data block of a pending read or write data transfer.

When pipelining read data transactions together, GNT# can only be asserted for the next transaction during the clock in which the final data is transferred for the current transaction. This requirement minimizes the amount of read buffering required by the master. By pipelining transactions, the arbiter can avoid any idle clocks between transactions, thus eliminating "dead" or wasted time on the AD bus. The arbiter is not allowed to assert GNT# for a low-priority read transaction when the RBF# signal is asserted (indicating that the master is not prepared to accept the read data). If GNT# is sampled asserted on the same clock that RBF# is sampled asserted, RBF# has no affect on the current transaction.

For write data transactions, the arbiter asserts GNT# when the target is ready to accept the initial block of data. To minimize the grant tracking logic of the master, the arbiter limits the number of outstanding grants it issues. The master is required to support up to five outstanding grants for write data transactions. When pipelining grants for writes, the arbiter must not assert GNT# if there are already five grants outstanding. For more information on GNT# pipelining, refer to Chapter 5.

GNT# is a required input for all AGP masters and a required output for all AGP targets. GNT# is treated as an internal signal within a core logic device when it initiates fast write transactions. For more information on the PCI use of GNT#, refer to the MindShare book entitled *PCI System Architecture, Fourth Edition* (published by Addison-Wesley).

The status bus signals are required inputs for masters. The status bus signals are required outputs for targets. The status bus in not used for fast write transactions.

Table 4-4: AGP Status Bus Encodings

ST[2::0]	Description
000	Indicates that the previously requested, low priority read or flush data is being returned to the AGP master.
001	Indicates that the previously requested, high priority read data is being returned to the AGP master
010	Indicates that the AGP target is ready for the AGP master to provide the data for a previously enqueued, low priority write command.
011	Indicates that the AGP target is ready for the AGP master to provide the data for a previously enqueued, high priority write command.
100	Reserved. May not be used. May be defined in the future by Intel.
101	Reserved. May not be used. May be defined in the future by Intel.
110	Reserved. May not be used. May be defined in the future by Intel.
111	Indicates that the AGP master has permission to begin enqueuing transaction requests with PIPE#, or start a PCI transaction by asserting FRAME#.

AGP Clock, Data Strobes, and Request Strobes

CLK — AGP Clock

The 66 MHz AGP clock signal (CLK) provides the fundamental timing for all transfer control signals. When issuing transaction requests over the AD bus, the start address, transfer length, and command information are latched on the rising edge of the clock. When operating in AGP 1X mode, data is also latched on the rising edge of the clock. Finally, when operating in 1X mode and issuing transaction requests over the SBA port, the SBA commands are latched by the target on the rising edge of the clock.

Although the clock signal is used as the timebase for the overall transaction in all transfer modes, it is not used to latch data in AGP 2X and 4X modes. Rather, the AD_STB[1::0] strobe signals are used to latch data in 2X mode, and the AD_STB[1::0] and AD_STB[1::0]# strobe signals are used in 4X mode. The timing of these strobes is derived from the clock.

The CLK signal is a required input for both the master and the target, and is a 3.3V signal. The CLK frequency must be within the range of 33 to 66MHz.

AD_STB0 and AD_STB1 — Data Strobes

In AGP 2X and 4X modes, AD Bus Strobe 0 (AD_STB0) is used to latch the two bytes of data on AD[15::0], while AD Bus Strobe 1 (AD_STB1) is used to latch the two bytes of data on AD[31::16]. These signals are always sourced by the agent that is sourcing the data. Data is valid on the rising and falling edges of the two strobes in 2X mode, and eight bytes of data are transferred during each AGP clock period. The first four bytes are latched on the falling edges of the two strobes, and the next four bytes are latched on the rising edges of the two strobes.

AD_STB0 and AD_STB1 are required signals for all AGP target devices (because the graphics accelerator may be capable of using these modes). The strobes are required signals for all AGP master devices that operate in 2X or 4X modes. During fast write transactions, the strobes are also used to latch data from the AD bus. These signals require central resource pull-up resistors.

AD_STB0# and AD_STB1# — Data Strobe Complements

In AGP 4X mode, AD Bus Strobe 0 Complement (AD_STB0#) and AD_STB0 together provide timing for data transfers on AD[15::0], and AD Bus Strobe 1 Complement (AD_STB1#) and AD_STB1 together provide timing for data transfers on AD[31::16]. The agent receiving data in 4X mode uses the falling edges of the strobes and the falling edges of the strobe complements to latch data.

AD_STB0# and AD_STB1# are required signals for all AGP target and master devices that support 4X mode operation. During fast write transactions in 4X mode, AD_STB0# and AD_STB1# are used to latch data on the AD bus.

When transferring data in 4X mode, 16 bytes of data are transferred during each AGP clock period:

- The first four bytes are latched on the first falling edge of the strobes.
- The second four bytes are latched on the first falling edge of the complement strobes.
- The third four bytes are latched on the second falling edge of the strobes.
- The fourth four bytes are latched on the second falling edge of the compeiment strobes.

The rising edges of the strobes are never used to latch data in 4X mode.

A strobe and its respective complement signal may be used as a differential pair to create an internal latch signal within the receiving device. Data is then latched by the receiving device at the cross-over point of strobe and complement strobe signals. By using these signals as a differential pair, increased timing margin and noise immunity is gained. The cross-over point occurs earlier in time relative to the VILmax voltage threshold, than if just using the falling edges to latch. The noise immunity comes from the fact that as noise is introduced into the strobes, the noise typically affects both strobes equally. Ground bounce, cross talk, or jitter may affect both strobes, but the difference between the two strobes remains equal and cancels the noise out within the receiver. These signals require a pull-down resistor.

SB_STB — Sideband Strobe (2X and 4X modes)

When operating in AGP 2X mode, the SideBand Strobe signal (SB_STB) is used to latch transaction requests issued by the graphics accelerator over the SBA port. The source of SB_STB is always the AGP master. When the SBA port has been idle, including after reset, the master must send a synchronization cycle over the SBA port before sending any SBA commands. SB_STB may be stopped for power management purposes. SB_STB is required of any AGP master that supports the SBA and AGP 2X mode operation. SB_STB is required of all AGP target devices.

In 2X mode, 16 bits of request information, called an SBA command, is transferred across the SBA port in one AGP clock period. The falling edge of the SB_STB is used to latch the high byte of the two byte command, while the rising edge of the SB_STB is used to latch the lower byte. SB_STB timing is specified relative to the rising edge of the AGP CLK. This signal requires a central resource pull-up resistor.

SB_STB# — Sideband Strobe Complement (4X Mode)

In AGP 4X mode, SideBand Strobe Complement (SB_STB#) and SB_STB together provide timing for the transfer of transaction requests over the SBA port. Like SB_STB, SB_STB# is always sourced by the AGP master along with a command on the SBA port. SB_STB# is required on any master that supports the SBA and AGP 4X mode operation. SB_STB# is required on all AGP target devices that support AGP 4X mode operation. In 4X mode, 32 bits of request information, consisting of two SBA commands, are transferred across the SBA port during one AGP clock period. Of those two commands, only one may be a Type 1 command. For more information on the SBA command types, refer to "Four SBA Command Types" on page 119.

In 4X mode, only the falling edges of the strobes are used to latch request information. The high byte of the first two-byte command is latched on the first falling edge of SB_STB, and the low byte is latched on the first falling edge of SB_STB#. The high byte of the second two-byte command is latched on the second falling edge of SB_STB, and the low byte on the second falling edge of SB_STB#. SB_STB# requires a central resource pull-down resistor.

System

RST#

AGP Reset (RST#) has the same characteristics as RST# on the PCI bus:

- The assertion and deassertion of RST# can be asynchronous to the AGP clock.
- RST# must remain asserted for an minimum of 1ms after system power has become stable.

- RST# must remain asserted for a minimum of 100us after the AGP CLK has become stable.
- After the assertion of RST#, all devices must float their outputs within 40ns.
- The assertion of RST# forces devices to their initial state. The default state after reset is disabled.

To provide noise immunity, there is a minimum slew rate specification of 50 mV/ns for the rising edge (or deassertion) of the reset signal. System reset logic is required to assert reset during power-up, and when a power failure has occurred. A power failure is specified as any power rail (12V, 5V, or 3.3V) exceeding the specified tolerances by more than 500mV. Reset must be asserted within 500ns of this event. If the system 5V supply should fall below the 3.3V supply by more than 300mV, then reset must be asserted within 100ns. Reset is a 3.3V signal.

INTA# and INTB# — Interrupt Pins

In function and usage, the AGP Interrupt Request pins, INTA# and INTB#, adhere to the PCI specification. The INTA# and INTB# signals are outputs used by a device to request servicing by its device driver. The INTx# signals are level-sensitive inputs to the interrupt controller. These signals are an open drain signal type, asserted when low. They cannot be actively driven from the asserted to the deasserted state. Rather, a weak pull-up resistor returns the signal to the deasserted state once all devices that were asserting it turn off their output drivers. Because the signals are open drain, they are sharable. This means that they may be asserted by multiple agents simultaneously, without adverse side effects.

The interrupt signals are 3.3V signals. The assertion and deassertion of these signals can be asynchronous to the AGP clock. A single function AGP device that generates interrupt requests must do so on the INTA# pin. A multifunction AGP device, in which more than one function is capable of generating interrupt requests, may implement INTB#, in addition to INTA#. Then the multi-function AGP device could distribute the interrupt requests from the various functions across the two interrupt request pins. PCI interrupt request signals INTC# and INTD# are not implemented on the AGP connector.

The AGP interrupts must be routed to the system interrupt controller, which typically resides within a component on the PCI bus (typically, it resides within the South bridge; i.e., the PCI-to-ISA bridge). It is possible that the AGP and PCI interrupt signal lines utilize different voltages for signaling. An example would be a 3.3V AGP system with a 5V PCI signaling environment. If the PCI interrupt request signals were pulled up to 5V, then the AGP interrupt request signals could not be directly connected to the PCI interrupt request signals.

AGP interrupt requests can be directly connected to PCI interrupts. If PCI is a 5V signaling environment, then the motherboard designer could tie all PCI interrupts to 3.3V. This would supply a 5V-compliant high voltage, but would be 3.3V tolerant, allowing the AGP interrupt signals to be directly connected to PCI interrupt signals. In the case of a 5V PCI bus and 3.3V AGP interrupt request signals, the core logic could provide buffering. The AGP interrupt request signals could be inputs to the core logic. The core logic could then assert 5V interrupt outputs to the PCI interrupt request signals. External buffering outside of the core logic could be provided by the motherboard to buffer the 3.3V AGP signals to the 5V PCI environment.

The interrupt request signals are optional for an AGP master.

USB

USB+ and USB- — Universal Serial Bus Data Lines

The USB Positive and Negative Differential Data Lines are used for transmitting and receiving serial data that conforms to the Universal Serial Bus protocol. Typically, the device that would participate in this serial communication would be a USB-controlled monitor. Although implemented on the AGP connector, these signals are not required to be implemented by an AGP master or target. When included on the add-in card or motherboard, the USB signal traces must be designed with an impedance of 45 Ohms, +/-5%. This is in order to match impedances with the USB driver and the USB cable. These traces must be routed carefully to avoid high-frequency noise coming from the monitor cable. This is necessary to maintain signal integrity. A 15K Ohm, +/-5%, pull-down resistor must be provided on the motherboard on these signals. For more information on USB, refer to the MindShare book entitled *USB System Architecture* (published by Addison-Wesley).

OVRCNT# — USB OverCurrent

This signal is the USB Over-Current indicator. It is an active low signal, indicating that a USB over-current condition has been detected by the AGP/USB add-in card. This would typically occur when the USB monitor/hub is drawing too much current. This condition could also occur when the USB hub/monitor has detected an over-current condition on one of its down-stream ports.

Power Management

PME# — Power Management Event

The PCI Power Management Event (PME#) signal is an output used to request a change in the device with respect to power. It is an optional signal for both the AGP master and target. Typically, this signal is used to initiate a wake-up from a powered-down state. Like the interrupt signals, the assertion and deassertion of this signal can be asynchronous to the AGP clock. PME# is architected as an open drain output and requires a pull-up resistor. PME# is a 3.3V signal. For more information on the PME# signal, refer to the MindShare book entitled *PCI System Architecture, Fourth Edition* (published by Addison-Wesley).

Special

TYPDET# — Vddq Type Detect

The Type Detect (TYPDET#) signal indicates the Vddq (I/O interface) voltage level required by the add-in card.

- If the TYPDET# signal is low, then the interface voltage level required is 1.5V.
- If the TYPDET# signal is an open circuit, then the interface voltage level required is 3.3V.

On the universal connector, which can accept either a 3.3V or 1.5V card, the TYPDET# signal is intended to be part of a voltage regulator circuit. TYPDET# could be connected to a resistor that makes up a voltage divider circuit for a linear voltage regulator. If the resistor connected to TYPDET# is open, then the output of the regulator is 3.3V. If the resistor is connected to ground, then the output of the regulator would be 1.5V.

Error Reporting

PERR# — Parity Error (PCI-only signal)

The PCI Parity Error signal (PERR#) is used to signal the detection of a data phase parity error during PCI transactions. This signal is not used during AGP transactions. During an AGP transaction, the PERR# signal is kept high (deasserted) by a pull-up resistor located either in the core logic or on the mother-board. During PCI transactions performed on the AGP bus, PERR# may or may not be used. The PCI 2.1 specification allows graphics devices to be exempt from reporting data phase parity errors. The designer could choose to not report corrupted video data because the data being accessed or received is not criti-cally affecting the residual state of the device, application, or system.

For example, if pixel information is being written into the frame buffer of the graphics controller and a data phase parity error occurs, then the pixel associ-ated with the location is corrupted. However, if this error were to go undetected and unreported, the operation of the machine would proceed, probably without the end user noticing the bad pixel. The typical recovery from PCI data phase parity errors is to attempt to re-send the data. The theory is that the cause of the data phase parity error is transient in nature. Therefore, re-sending the data with good parity fixes the problem. There is not time to re-send the pixel infor-mation in this application, even if the graphics accelerator were to detect and report the data phase parity error.

Devices that are integrated onto the system board (like core logic devices) are also exempt from reporting data phase parity errors that occur in PCI transac-tions. The PERR# signal is not supported for fast write transactions.

SERR# — System Error

The PCI System Error signal (SERR#) is used to signal the detection of an address phase parity error during PCI transactions, or any other critical error not associated with parity. The assertion of SERR# is considered fatal and is therefore unrecoverable. The implementation of SERR# for AGP masters and targets is optional. If implemented, SERR# could be used by the AGP master to alert the core logic to some catastrophic failure. Like the PERR# signal, the PCI 2.1 specification allows exemptions from reporting errors with SERR#.

SERR#, like the optional interrupt request signals, INTA# and INTB#, is an open drain output signal. The motherboard designer should note that the AGP SERR# signal must be asserted synchronized to the 66MHz AGP clock, meaning that the signal meets setup and hold times relative to that clock. If the PCI bus is being clocked at a different frequency (e.g., 33MHz), the AGP SERR# and the PCI SERR# signal could not be directly connected. Even if the PCI clock fre-quency were the same as the AGP clock (e.g., 66MHz), the SERR# signals from the two domains could only be coupled if the two clocks were in sync.

PCI Signals Not Supported

LOCK#

The PCI LOCK# signal is used to maintain exclusive ownership of the bus during an operation that requires multiple transactions to complete. The AGP interface does not support the LOCK# signal. This is true for both AGP and PCI transactions.

IDSEL — Initialization Device Select

Initialization Device Select (IDSEL) is a PCI signal that is used during a type 0 PCI configuration transaction to select a PCI target device as the target of the transaction. IDSEL is not implemented on the AGP connector. When the graphics accelerator is the target of a PCI configuration transaction initiated on the AGP bus, IDSEL must be generated internal to the graphics accelerator. For the graphics accelerator, IDSEL must be generated from AD16 at the component. When the core logic is the target of a PCI configuration transaction on the AGP bus, then IDSEL is typically generated internally within the core logic.

If the graphics accelerator has been designed to operate solely in the AGP environment, then the graphic chip will not have an external IDSEL pin. In this case, IDSEL will be generated internal to the component, from the AD16 pin for PCI type 0 configuration transactions.

Signal Types

Refer to Table 4-5 on page 89 for a listing of all signals and their type. For all signals, the type is defined either from the perspective of the core logic, or the AGP target device. For the T/S and S/T/S signals, the direction is also from the perspective of the core logic.

IN — Input

This signal type is input-only. Examples include RBF# and WBF#. These signals are inputs from the perspective of the core logic.

OUT — Output

This signal type is a totem pole output-only and is actively driven. Examples include: the three status bus (ST[2::0]) pins. These signals are only outputs from the perspective of the core logic.

T/S — Tri-State

This signal type is a bidirectional, input/output signal that can be tri-stated (placed in the high-impedance state). An example would be the AD bus, AD[31::0]. These signals can carry data in both directions and can be floated.

S/T/S — Sustained Tri-State

This signal type is a Sustained Tri-State. S/T/S signals are active low, are able to be tri-stated, and can only be driven by one agent at a time. An agent that drives an S/T/S signal low returns the signal to the deasserted state by driving the signal high for one clock before turning the driver off, and then floating the signal. A pull-up resistor sustains the inactive state of the S/T/S signal until another agent takes ownership of the signal and begins to drive it. All S/T/S signals require pull-up resistors.

The next owner cannot start driving the S/T/S signal any sooner than one clock after it is released by the previous owner. This one clock is known as a turn-around cycle. The AD bus strobe signals, AD_STB0 and AD_STB1, follow the S/T/S protocol. The AD bus complement strobes, AD_STB0# and AD_STB1#, are also S/T/S signals, but these signals have pull-down resistors. Therefore, the complementary strobe signals need to be driven low for one clock before being floated.

O/D — Open Drain Output

This signal type is an open-drain output. To assert the signal, the signaling agent drives the signal low. To deassert it, the output driver stops driving the signal low and a weak pull-up resistor pulls the signal back to the deasserted state (high). Be aware that this will take several clocks and the signal will ring before settling. During periods of time when the signal isn't being used, the deasserted state is maintained by the pull-up resistor. The INTx# and SERR# signals are examples of open drains.

Table 4-5: AGP Signal Types

Signal Name	Signal Type
PIPE#	S/T/S (IN)
SBA[7::0]	IN
RBF#	IN
WBF#	IN
ST[2::0]	OUT
AD_STB0	S/T/S
AD_STB1	S/T/S
AD_STB0#	S/T/S
AD_STB1#	S/T/S
SB_STB	S/T/S (IN)
SB_STB#	S/T/S (IN)
CLK	IN*
USB+	T/S
USB-	T/S
OVRCNT#	OUT*
PME#	OUT*
FRAME#	S/T/S
IRDY#	S/T/S
TRDY#	S/T/S
STOP#	S/T/S
DEVSEL#	S/T/S
PERR#	S/T/S

Table 4-5: AGP Signal Types (Continued)

Signal Name	Signal Type
SERR#	O/D*
REQ#	IN
GNT#	OUT
RST#	OUT
AD[31::0]	T/S
C/BE[3::0]#	T/S
PAR	T/S
INTA#	O/D*
INTB#	O/D*

The type indicated in parentheses indicates the direction from the perspective of the core logic. Signal types with an asterisk (*) indicate the signal type from the perspective of the graphics accelerator.

5 *AGP Arbitration*

The Previous Chapter

The previous chapter defined the required and optional signals for AGP-compliant masters and targets. The signals were grouped by function and the purpose of each signal was described.

This Chapter

This chapter focuses on the arbiter's role within the AGP interface. Optimization of grant pipelining is also discussed.

The Next Chapter

The next chapter defines all of the AGP commands, or transaction request types, that can be issued on the AGP bus. The rules associated with the ordering of these transactions by the core logic are explained through the use of examples.

Introduction to the AGP Arbiter

Master Needs to Issue Transaction Request

The AGP arbiter is physically located within the core logic. Acting as the AGP master, the graphics accelerator issues memory read or write transaction requests to the core logic (the AGP target). The master uses one of two mechanisms to issue these requests:

- the AD bus and the C/BE bus
- the SideBand Address port

If it uses the SBA port to issue requests, it doesn't need to ask for ownership of the SBA port before using it (because the SBA port is dedicated to this purpose). On the other hand, if it uses the AD and C/BE busses to issue requests, then it must assert the REQ# signal to request ownership of the bus before using it to issue a request. It must then wait for the arbiter within the core logic to indicate that it has been granted bus ownership for the purpose of issuing one or more transaction requests.

Target Needs to Initiate a Data Transfer

When the target (the core logic) is ready to transfer previously requested read data or to accept the write data for a previously requested memory write transaction, the arbiter within the core logic must grant ownership of the bus to the master to perform that type of data transfer.

GNT# and the Status Bus (ST[2::0])

In response to the master's assertion of REQ# to issue a transaction request, or because the core logic is ready to perform a previously-requested data transfer, the arbiter within the core logic issues the following to the master:

- **GNT#** is asserted to indicate to the master that it being granted bus ownership.
- At the same time that GNT# is asserted, a three-bit value is driven onto the **Status bus, ST[2::0]**. This value indicates for what purpose the bus is being granted to the master.

AGP Master's Request Signal

An AGP master that enqueues transaction requests using the AD and C/BE busses must assert REQ# to request ownership of the bus (i.e., AD[31::0] and C/BE[3::0]#). AGP masters that can initiate PCI as well as AGP transactions are also required to implement REQ#. The master asserts REQ# to request permission to use the bus to begin enqueuing requests or to start a PCI transaction.

In response (when the master wishes to issue an AGP transaction request), the master waits for the arbiter to respond with GNT# and a status of 111b. This indicates that the arbiter has granted the master permission to start issuing a transaction request to the core logic. REQ# must deasserted for a minimum of one clock between back-to-back request transactions. However, to minimize bus idle time it is strongly recommended that the master concatenate as many requests into a single request transaction.

When the AGP master is also capable of initiating PCI transactions on the AGP bus, the master must comply with the rules defined in the PCI specification with respect to the REQ# and GNT# signals. A grant issue to a PCI master will also include the status value 111b.

When the Core Logic Must Start a Data Transfer

As indicated earlier, when the target (the core logic) is ready to transfer previously-requested read data or to accept the write data for a previously-requested memory write transaction, the arbiter within the core logic must grant ownership of the bus to the master to perform that type of data transfer.

To do this, the arbiter within the core logic does the following:

- It asserts GNT# to the master to indicate that it is being granted ownership of the bus (i.e., AD bus and C/BE bus).
- It drives a three-bit value onto the Status bus, ST[2::0], to indicate the reason for the grant. Table 5-1 indicates the Status bus encodings.

In response to sampling GNT# asserted and based on the Status code, the master and target take the appropriate actions.

Table 5-1: AGP Status Bus Encodings

ST[2::0]	Description
000	Indicates that previously requested low-priority read or flush data is being returned to the AGP master. The target then starts sourcing the read data to the master.
001	Indicates that previously requested high priority read data is being returned to the AGP master. The target then starts sourcing the read data to the master.
010	Indicates that the AGP target is ready for the AGP master to provide the data for a previously enqueued low-priority write command. The master then starts sourcing the write data and byte enables to the target.
011	Indicates that the AGP target is ready for the AGP master to provide the data for a previously enqueued high-priority write command. The master then starts sourcing the write data and byte enables to the target.

Table 5-1: AGP Status Bus Encodings (Continued)

ST[2::0]	Description
100	Reserved for future use.
101	Reserved for future use.
110	Reserved for future use.
111	Indicates that the AGP master has permission to begin issuing transaction requests using the bus, or to start a PCI transaction by asserting FRAME#.

GNT# Pipelining

The rules associated with GNT# pipelining have two goals:

- Allow back-to-back data transactions to occur without idle clocks in between transactions.
- Minimize the complexity of the AGP master design.

In order to achieve the first goal, the arbiter must pipeline grants to the master. In other words, it must grant the master ownership for the next transaction before the current transaction has completed. In this way, the master can immediately start a new transaction upon completion of the current one. The master must therefore be able to accept pipelined grants.

In order to achieve the second goal, the rules dictate when the arbiter can assert the grant signal for a subsequent transaction, and limit the number of outstanding grants that the arbiter may issue to the master for subsequent transactions. As in the PCI specification, the arbitration algorithm used by the AGP arbiter is not specified—it is chipset-specific.

The specification permits the arbiter to remove the GNT# signal at any time in order to prevent deadlocks. When it has removed grant from a master, the arbiter must wait a sufficient number of clocks to allow the master to start a transaction before the GNT# signal is reasserted to a new master. The minimum number of clocks that GNT# must be deasserted in this case is two.

When pipelining GNT# to the AGP master, the arbiter must limit the number of outstanding GNT#'s. This rule exists to minimize the grant tracking logic implemented in the master. It is recommended that the arbiter assert the next GNT# at the earliest time possible, to allow the agent sourcing the data in that next transaction as much time as possible to avoid idle clocks between transactions.

There are some cases when idle clocks on the interface cannot be avoided. This can occur when

- there is a change in ownership of the AD bus or any control signals from one transaction to another. An example is when an AGP read data transaction follows an AGP write data transaction or AGP request transaction, or vice versa. In this case, one device is driving the AD bus at the end of the first transaction and another must start driving it at the start of the next transaction.
- there is a change in bus protocol. An example is when the first transaction is a PCI transaction and the next is an AGP transaction.

It is the new driver of the bussed signals that is responsible for guaranteeing the idle clock so that bus contention is avoided

If the current transaction is a write data transaction, GNT# can be pipelined immediately for the next transaction (while there are four or fewer outstanding grants queued for write data). Said another way, on writes, up to five grants can be pipelined and the master must be able to handle five pipelined grants. The arbiter tracks the number of outstanding grants for writes. The master increments its grant counter when it samples GNT# issued for an outstanding write data transaction. The arbiter decrements its grant counter when the master asserts IRDY# for an outstanding write (indicating that it's ready to start delivery of the first write data block for that transaction). The master considers a GNT# canceled when the data transaction finishes.

If the current transaction is a transaction request or a PCI transaction, then GNT# for a data transaction can be asserted immediately after GNT# for the current transaction. In fact, up to four grants for write data transactions, or three writes and one additional transaction, could be pipelined.

In order to issue an AGP transaction request using the AD and C/BE busses, the master must sample GNT# asserted with a Status of 111b in order to start the transaction. If the arbiter pipelined the GNT# signal before the master started the request transaction, but deasserted GNT# before the master started, the master cannot start the request transaction. The master is prohibited from memorizing its GNT# in this case.

During AGP read data transactions, the arbiter is only allowed to assert GNT# for the next transaction in the final clock of the read data transaction. The arbiter is not allowed to assert GNT# for a low-priority read data transaction while RBF# (Read Buffer Full) remains asserted. GNT# must be deasserted when RBF# is detected asserted to prevent the low-priority read data transaction from starting. Other transactions types (high-priority reads, writes, etc.) may start while RBF# is asserted.

6 *AGP Commands and Ordering Rules*

The Previous Chapter

The previous chapter focused on the arbiter's role within the AGP interface. Optimization of grant pipelining was also discussed.

This Chapter

This chapter defines all of the AGP commands, or transaction request types, that can be issued on the AGP bus. The rules associated with the ordering of these transactions by the core logic are explained through the use of examples.

The Next Chapter

AGP transactions are broken into two distinct bus operations: the issuance of the transaction request and the matching data transaction that occurs later in time. The next chapter provides a detailed description of the issuance of transaction requests using the AD and C/BE busses as well as the SBA port.

Command Types and the Transfer Length

When transaction requests are issued using the AD and C/BE busses, the transaction type, also referred to as the command, is issued over C/BE[3::0]#, and the transaction length is issued on AD[2::0]. When transaction requests are issued using the SBA port, the command is contained in the Type 2 Command packet, and the transfer length is contained in the Type 1 Command packet. For a detailed description of how transaction requests are issued, refer to Chapter 7, entitled "AGP Request Transactions," on page 109. AGP commands only access main system memory. The start address is always quadword-aligned (an address divisible by eight). The total number of data bytes transferred is always a quantity divisible by eight.

Table 6-1: AGP Bus Commands

CCCC	AGP Operation
0000	Low-Priority Read
0001	High-Priority Read
0010	Reserved
0011	Reserved
0100	Low-Priority Write
0101	High-Priority Write
0110	Reserved
0111	Reserved
1000	Long Low-Priority Read
1001	Long High-Priority Read
1010	Flush
1011	Reserved
1100	Fence
1101	Dual Address Cycle (DAC)
1110	Reserved
1111	Reserved

Read Commands and Transfer Length

Read commands (low- or high-priority read, or long low- or high-priority read) request that memory read data be sent from the AGP target to the AGP master. The target will respond at a later time by performing a read data transaction to return the requested data. Data is transferred sequentially, beginning at the specified start address. The transfer size is the number of quadwords that was indicated in the length field of the transaction request. Table 6-2 on page 99 lists the transfer length values. Note that the LLL field represents the transfer length field encoding. When transaction requests are issued over the AD and C/BE busses, the length field is contained in AD[2::0], while it is contained in the Type 1 Command packet when requests are issued using the SBA port.

Table 6-2: Data Transfer Length Field Encodings for Read and Write Commands

LLL	Number of Bytes
000	8
001	16
010	24
011	32
100	40
101	48
110	56
111	64

There are two priority levels for read commands, low-priority and high-priority.

Low-Priority Reads

Low-priority reads are processed through the low-priority request sub-queue, and obey the ordering rules associated with that queue (see "AGP Ordering Rules" on page 102). The data is sent through the read data return queue. An example of when the master would issue low-priority reads could be when reading texture maps from main memory.

High-Priority Reads

High-priority reads are processed through the high-priority request sub-queue, and obey the ordering rules associated with that queue (see "AGP Ordering Rules" on page 102). High-priority reads complete within a maximum latency window guaranteed by the core logic. The data is sent through the read data return queue. This command is used in any access where the data has a real-time deadline. Examples would be video capture, video display, or video editing applications.

Long Read Commands and Transfer Length

Long read commands can transfer up to 256 bytes of data (versus a maximum of 64 for the regular read commands). 256 bytes is the maximum transfer length on the AGP bus. The transfer length field (LLL) indicates the number of 32-byte blocks that are to be read. Long reads offer low- and high-priority options, just like the read commands. Table 6-3 indicates the encoding of the length field.

Table 6-3: Data Transfer Length Encodings for Long Read Commands

LLL	Number of Bytes
000	32
001	64
010	96
011	128
100	160
101	192
110	224
111	256

Write Commands

A Write command requests that the target accept write data from the AGP master to the AGP target. As in read commands, the transfer size is contained either on AD[2::0] or in the Type 1 Command packet, depending on the request enqueuing method. Table 6-2 on page 99 lists the transfer length encodings. The target will respond at a later time by performing a write data transaction to accept the write data from the master. Data is transferred sequentially, beginning at the start address that was specified in the transaction request. During the subsequent write data transaction, the master will use C/BE[3::0]# to indicate which bytes are being written within the current dword.

Chapter 6: AGP Commands and Ordering Rules

Low-Priority Writes

Low-priority writes are processed through the low-priority request sub-queue and obey the ordering rules associated with that queue (see "AGP Ordering Rules" on page 102). The data is sent through the write data queue.

High-Priority Writes

High-priority writes are processed through the high-priority request sub-queue and obey the ordering rules associated with that queue (see "AGP Ordering Rules" on page 102). High-priority writes complete within a maximum latency window. An example usage would be when the graphics accelerator is updating a unified memory architecture (UMA) frame buffer. Any application that is dealing with real-time critical data would use high-priority transactions.

Dual-Address Cycle

When the AGP master is using the AD bus to enqueue transaction requests and must access a memory location at or above the 4GB address boundary, a 64-bit memory address must be produced. As in the PCI bus protocol, the dual-address cycle (DAC) command is used. The dual-address cycle command indicates that the master requires two AGP clock ticks to produce a valid request on the AD[31::0] bus.

- In the first clock of the dual-address cycle, the master provides the lower 32 bits of the 64-bit memory address on AD[31::3] (remember that the transaction length is encoded on AD[2::0]). C/BE[3::0]# contains the dual-address command.
- In the second clock cycle, AD[31::0] contains the upper 32 bits of the 64-bit memory address. C/BE[3::0]# contains the normal command (e.g., read, long read, write, etc.).

The dual-address command is not valid and is a reserved command when the master is using the SBA to enqueue transaction requests. With the SBA, the master can produce a 48-bit wide address with the Type 4 command. This is covered in more detail in "Enqueuing Transaction Requests via the Sideband Address Port" on page 118.

Flush and Fence Commands

The Flush and Fence commands are explained after a discussion of the ordering rules (see "Fence Command" on page 106 and "Flush Command" on page 107).

Reserved Commands

Any reserved command encodings must never be used by an AGP master that is compliant with the revision 2.0 specification. These command encodings are reserved for future use.

AGP Ordering Rules

The ordering rules documented in the PCI specification for PCI transactions and the ordering of transactions on the host CPU bus, are different than the AGP transaction ordering rules. It is important to examine the ordering of AGP transactions relative to:

- CPU- and PCI-initiated transactions.
- High-Priority versus Low-Priority AGP transaction streams.
- Same Priority AGP streams (Reads versus Writes).

Relationship of AGP and CPU or PCI Transactions

No ordering relationship exists between AGP transactions and transactions initiated on another system bus (e.g., PCI and CPU). AGP transactions are only required to follow the AGP ordering rules even when crossing into the domain of another system component. As an example, when an AGP master is accessing a locked memory location in system memory (locked from the perspective of the CPU), the AGP master does not have to honor the lock. If this is an error, then it is a software error, not a hardware error.

AGP transactions do not have to ensure that cache consistency is maintained when accessing main memory. In other words, the AGP target (the core logic) is not required to stall the memory access while a transaction is generated on the processor bus to snoop the processor's internal caches. The BIOS or OS should make all memory accessed by the AGP graphics accelerator uncacheable from the perspective of the processor.

Chapter 6: AGP Commands and Ordering Rules

In platforms based on P6 family processors, the memory type used for AGP memory is typically set up as write-combining (WC) by programing the processor's internal MTRR registers. The WC memory type is uncachable, so the processor will not copy lines from AGP-accessed memory into its internal caches. There is therefore no need for the core logic to send snoop transactions back to the processor before permitting AGP accesses to memory to proceed. The WC memory type allows writes initiated by the CPU core to be merged into write buffers internal to the CPU. Due to the reduction of host bus traffic, this combining of writes increases overall performance.

No ordering rules exist between AGP and PCI transactions, even PCI transactions initiated on the AGP bus itself. If the AGP master is also capable of acting as a PCI master on the AGP bus, no ordering relationship exists between AGP and PCI transactions it initiates. The AGP target may process different transaction request types (AGP versus PCI) in any order with respect to each other. PCI masters and targets on the AGP bus must be compliant with the ordering rules described in the PCI 2.1 specification. For more information on PCI ordering rules, refer to the MindShare book entitled *PCI System Architecture, Fourth Edition* (published by Addison-Wesley).

Relationship of High- and Low-Priority AGP Transaction Streams

No ordering relationship exists between AGP high- and low-priority transactions. As an example, if the transaction requests were enqueued in the following order:

HPA, HPB, HPC, LPD, LPE

where HPA = High-Priority transaction A, and LPD = Low-Priority transaction D, etc., the transactions could complete:

- HPA, HPB, HPC, LPD, LPE, or
- LPD, LPE, HPA, HPB, HPC, or
- HPA, LPD, HPB, LPE, HPC

just to give three valid permutations.

High-priority requests have a maximum latency that is guaranteed by the core logic and this guarantee may effect transaction ordering. As an example, if the transaction requests were enqueued in the following order:

LPD, LPE, HPA, HPB, HPC

the core logic could order and complete the transactions:

HPA, HPB, HPC, LPD, LPE

to meet the latency requirements of HPA, HPB, and HPC.

Relationship of Same Priority AGP Streams (Reads and Writes)

Ordering of Same Command Types

Requests of the same command type must complete on the AGP bus in the same order as requested.

Ordering of Multiple Memory Read Requests. As an example, assuming that transactions A, B, C, and D, were all low-priority reads enqueued in alphabetical order, the core logic must return the data in the order A, B, C, then D. This does not necessarily mean that the reads are performed at the destination (system memory) in the same order as requested. The core logic may reorder the transactions on the memory bus for performance reasons.

As an example, consider low-priority read transactions enqueued in the order A, B, C, then D. The core logic might initiate and complete the transactions on the system memory bus in the order D, C, B, then A. However, the data must be returned in the original order on the AGP interface: A, B, C, then D.

Ordering of Multiple Memory Write Requests. Writes must complete to the destination (system memory) in the same order as requested. This is referred to as strong write ordering. As an example, assume that four low-priority write transactions were enqueued: A, B, C, and D. The data must be delivered across the AGP bus in the original order: A, B, C, then D. This order must be maintained by the memory controller when updating main memory. If A and D were to the same memory location, then this would mean that D would overwrite A.

Chapter 6: AGP Commands and Ordering Rules

Ordering of High-Priority Reads and High-Priority Writes

No ordering relationship exists between high-priority reads and high-priority writes. As as example, assume two high-priority transactions were enqueued in the following order: HPA (a read), then HPB (a write). Also assume that transaction A and B target the same memory location. The write may be re-ordered around the read (in other words, be performed before the read) by the core logic. The transactions could complete as the write B followed by read A, such that read A returns "new" data. "New" data is this case is the data written by write B. Alternatively, the transactions could complete in the order A followed by B, such that the read returns "old" data.

Ordering of Low-Priority Reads and Low-Priority Writes

There is an ordering relationship between low-priority reads and low-priority writes. Low-priority reads will push low-priority writes ahead of them. In other words, any previously initiated low-priority memory write will be performed to memory before a subsequently issued low-priority memory read. This ensures that the read will return the updated data (if the write updates any of the locations targeted by the read).

As an example, assume transaction A is a low-priority write and transaction B is a low-priority read targeting the same memory location. The order that the transactions are enqueued is A (the low-priority write) then B (the low-priority read). The read transaction, B, will return the data written by A.

Low-priority write transactions may pass (i.e., be re-ordered around) previously enqueued low-priority reads. Therefore, reads may return either "old" data or "new" data. As an example, assume that four low-priority transactions are enqueued and they all target the same memory location (the first letter denotes the transaction type (W= write, R = read), while the second letter is a unique transaction identifier):

WA, RB, WC, and RD.

The data returned for RD will always be WC, because reads push writes. The data returned for RB may be WA or WC. If the data returned for RB is WC, then WC was re-ordered around RB.

If it is imperative that the old data is returned, the master either waits to enqueue new writes until the read data is returned, or issues a fence command between the RB and the WC. The fence command is only applicable to low-priority commands. The fence command has no effect on high-priority commands.

For a detailed description of the fence command, refer to "Fence Command" on page 106. The first solution, waiting to issue the write, has the potential for creating a deadlock. When delaying a write, the data engine of the master may "back up" and stall. If the data engine of the master is stalled, it cannot remove read data from the read data buffer in the master. If the read data buffers are full, then "old" data cannot be returned. The write transaction continues to be delayed. This situation creates a deadlock.

As a rule, deadlocks must be avoided. Therefore, the AGP master cannot make the data transfer of a previously enqueued request dependent on the completion of any other transaction targeting the same device. This rule is applicable for AGP transactions where the graphics accelerator is the master, or PCI transactions performed on the AGP bus where the graphics accelerator is the target or the master.

To ensure that new data, rather than old data, is returned for a low-priority read, the master that initiates both transactions could detect the conflict. In the previous example, to ensure that RB returns WC, the master could detect the condition that RB must return WC. After detecting this condition, the master could internally merge, or substitute, the new write data (WC) with the old read data (RB).

Alternatively, the master could delay the read (RB) until the write (WC) is enqueued. This second solution may be difficult to detect. In addition, delaying the read may cause the pipeline to stall, having a negative impact on performance.

Fence Command

The fence command provides a transaction demarcation, or road block, in the low-priority request stream. This demarcation indicates where low-priority write commands are prohibited from passing previously enqueued low-priority read commands. The use of the fence command can guarantee the return of old data when a low-priority read transaction is followed with subsequent low-priority write transactions. Using the previous example, the four low-priority transactions enqueued were: WA, RB, WC, and RD, in that order, targeting the exact same memory location.

The data returned for RB could be WA or WC. If the data returned for RB is WC, then WC was re-ordered around RB. If it is important that RB returns WA, then a fence command must be inserted in the transaction stream immediately after RB and before WC. The new transaction sequence would be:

WA, RB, **Fence**, WC, RD

The data returned for RB is WA, because, after the fence, no re-ordering of writes is permitted around reads prior to the fence. The fence command is the only AGP command that does not occupy a slot in the low-priority request sub-queue, in either the master or the target. AGP ordering rules govern the processing of transactions on either side of the fence.

Flush Command

What's the Problem?

When the master issues low-priority (LP) write commands, the writes may be latched into posted memory write buffers within the core logic. From the perspective of the AGP master, it looks as if the LP writes have completed to memory (because those write transactions have completed on the AGP bus). In reality, however, the LP writes have not yet arrived in main memory. In most cases, it is not important that the LP writes have not completed to the final system location. However, when the graphics accelerator is generating an interrupt request, the device and the device driver may, for proper operation, require that those buffered LP writes complete to the final system destination before the interrupt service routine is executed.

As an example, the device driver might check device status by performing a memory read on the CPU bus (the AGP graphics accelerator's control registers are implemented as memory-mapped IO ports). The core logic translates the memory read on the processor bus into a PCI memory read on the AGP bus. As a result of the apparent completion of the LP write transactions on the AGP bus, the device reports that there is new data in memory. The PCI and CPU read transactions do not force the core logic to flush the posted write buffers (because AGP transactions are not related to the CPU or PCI transactions). There is no ordering relationship and no rules exist, when crossing domains. If the device driver executing on the host CPU were to read those memory locations, the memory controller could return stale data (because the data is still posted in the posted write buffers within the core logic).

PCI-Based Graphics Accelerator Solution

If the posted write buffers were filled from the PCI bus rather than the AGP bus, a **read presented to the bridge** by either the processor or a PCI bus master **forces** a **flush of** the **posted write buffers** to memory before the read could be passed through the bridge to memory. This is a transaction ordering rule associated with the PCI specification. In general, this rule has a negative impact on performance. In most cases, the read will not be dependent on the previously posted writes.

AGP-Based Graphics Accelerator Solution

In this case, the generation of the interrupt request is known as a synchronizing event. It is important that the device driver being contacted through the interrupt be in sync with the hardware generating the interrupt. In this example, the synchronization includes having all posted writes be made visible to the final system memory location. Therefore, in order to guarantee that all LP posted writes have completed prior to generating the interrupt request, the master issues the Flush command to the core logic.

The flush command forces the AGP target to flush (i.e., empty) all LP write transactions currently latched in the posted write buffers to main memory. After the flush is complete, the interrupt request can then be generated.

The flush command resembles an LP read command. In response to the flush command, the AGP target returns a single quadword of data to the master. The contents of the quadword is a "don't care" and is an acknowledgment that the flushing of the buffers has completed. The address and length fields of the flush command are "don't care." The flush command is not applicable to high-priority write commands.

7 *AGP Request Transactions*

The Previous Chapter

The previous chapter defined all of the AGP commands, or transaction request types, that can be issued on the AGP bus. The rules associated with the ordering of these transactions by the core logic were explained through the use of examples.

This Chapter

AGP transactions are broken into two distinct bus operations: the issuance of the transaction request by the AGP graphics accelerator (referred to as the AGP master), and the matching data transaction that is initiated later in time by the core logic (referred to as the AGP target). This chapter provides a detailed description of the issuance of transaction requests using the AD and C/BE busses, as well as the SBA port.

The Next Chapter

There are two categories of transactions that can be performed on the AGP bus: AGP transactions and PCI transactions. The next chapter explores the differences between the two.

Two Request Enqueuing Mechanisms

The architect of an AGP master has two mechanisms to choose from when designing the master to enqueue requests:

- Transaction requests can be issued to the core logic using AD[31::0] and C/BE[3::0]# and the PIPE# and REQ# signals, or
- Requests can be issued to the core logic using the Sideband Address Port, SBA[7::0].

Either mechanism can be used, but the mechanism cannot be changed during runtime. The mechanism is typically selected at design time. The master communicates the method that it uses to configuration software via bit nine in its AGP status configuration register (see Table 7-1). This bit is read-only. The AGP target is required to support both mechanisms. The configuration software programs bit nine of the AGP target's AGP command configuration register (see Table 7-2 on page 111) to reflect the mechanism used by the master.

Table 7-1: AGP Status Register (Offset CAP_PTR + 4)

Bits	Field	Description
31:24	RQ	The RQ field contains the maximum depth of the AGP request queue. Therefore, this number is the maximum number of command requests this device can manage. A "0" is interpreted as a depth of one, while FFh is interpreted as a depth of 256.
23:10	Reserved	Writes have no effect. Reads return zeros.
9	SBA	If set, this device supports sideband addressing.
8:6	Reserved	Writes have no effect. Reads return zeros.
5	4G	If set, this device supports addresses greater than 4 GB.
4	FW	If set, this device supports Fast Write transactions.
3	Reserved	Writes have no effect. Reads return a zero.
2:0	RATE	The RATE field is a bit map that indicates the data transfer rates supported by this device. AGP devices must report all that apply. The RATE field applies to AD, C/BE#, and SBA busses. **Bit Set** **Transfer Rate** 0 1X 1 2X 2 4X

Table 7-2: AGP Command Register (Offset CAP_PTR + 8)

Bits	Field	Description
31:24	RQ_DEPTH	**Master**: The RQ_DEPTH field must be programmed with the maximum number of requests the master is allowed to enqueue into the target. The value programmed into this field must be equal to or less than the value reported by the target in the RQ field of its AGP Status Register. A "0" value indicates a request queue depth of one entry, while a value of FFh indicates a request queue depth of 256. **Target**: The RQ_DEPTH field is reserved.
23:10	Reserved	Writes have no effect. Reads return zeros.
9	SBA_ENABLE	When set, the sideband address mechanism is enabled in this device.
8	AGP_ENABLE	**Master**: Setting the AGP_ENABLE bit allows the master to initiate AGP operations. When cleared, the master cannot initiate AGP operations. Also when cleared, the master is allowed to stop driving the SBA port. If bits 1 or 2 are set, the master must perform a re-synch cycle, before initiating a new request. **Target**: Setting the AGP_ENABLE bit allows the target to accept AGP operations. When cleared, the target ignores incoming AGP operations. The target must be completely configured and enabled before the master is enabled. The AGP_ENABLE bit is the last to be set. Reset clears this bit.
7:6	Reserved	Writes have no effect. Reads return zeros.

Table 7-2: AGP Command Register (Offset CAP_PTR + 8) (Continued)

Bits	Field	Description
5	4G	**Master**: Setting the 4G bit allows the master to initiate AGP requests to addresses at or above the 4GB address boundary. When cleared, the master is only allowed to access addresses in the lower 4 GB of addressable space. **Target**: Setting the 4G bit enables the target to accept AGP DAC commands, when bit 9 is cleared. When bits 5 and 9 are set, the target can accept a Type 4 SBA command and utilize A[35::32] of the Type 3 SBA command.
4	FW_ENABLE	When this bit is set, memory write transactions, initiated by the core logic will follow the fast write protocol. When this bit is cleared, memory write transactions, initiated by the core logic will follow the PCI protocol.
3	Reserved	Writes have no effect. Reads return zeros.
2:0	DATA_RATE	Only one bit in the DATA_RATE field must be set to indicate the maximum data transfer rate supported. The same bit must be set in both the master and the target. Bit Set Transfer Rate 0 1X 1 2X 2 4X

Enqueuing Transaction Requests via AD and C/BE Busses

To make the most efficient use of the AD bus, a SideBand Address (SBA) port should be implemented. By implementing an SBA, 100% of the AD bus bandwidth is available to transfer data. There are cases, however, where, due to pin count, component complexity, or performance constraints, implementing the SBA port may not be feasible. In these cases, enqueuing requests via the AD and C/BE busses would be the preferred mechanism.

When enqueuing requests over the AD and C/BE busses in all transfer modes (1X, 2X, or 4X), a new request is enqueued on each rising edge of the AGP clock, as long as the PIPE# signal remains asserted. The enqueuing of transaction requests via the AD and C/BE busses are therefore governed by outer loop timings.

Example Request Enqueued Using AD and C/BE Busses

Refer to Figure 7-1 on page 114. The start address is driven onto AD[31::3] and is aligned on an address divisible by eight. The transfer length is contained on AD[2::0]. AGP data transfers always have an explicit size. Eight bytes is the minimum transfer size and the maximum transfer size is 256 bytes.

This example illustrates the enqueuing of a single transaction request using the AD and C/BE busses. For an example of enqueuing multiple requests, refer to "Enqueuing Multiple Requests on the AD Bus" on page 38. The bus command (i.e., the transaction type) is contained on C/BE[3::0]#. All signals are driven and sampled on the rising edge of the AGP clock.

AGP System Architecture

Figure 7-1: Enqueuing a Single Transaction Request on AD and C/BE Busses

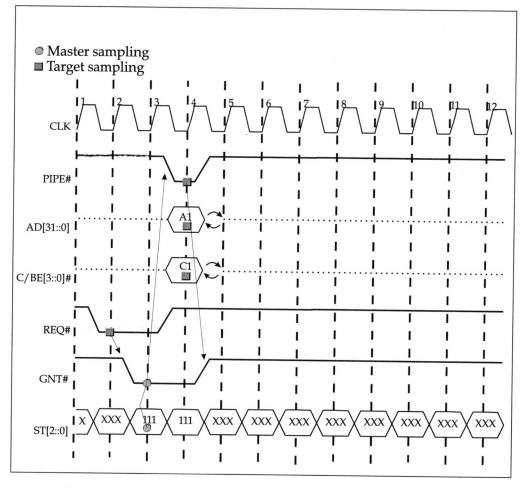

Clock 1. This example begins with the AGP master asserting the REQ# signal to request access to the bus in order to initiate the request transaction.

Clock 2. The arbiter (within the core logic) responds by asserting GNT#, thereby giving the master permission to start the transaction. GNT# asserted qualifies the status bus (ST[2::0]) content as valid. A status of 111b indicates that the arbiter is giving permission to the master to start the transaction. Note that this is the fastest the arbiter could respond to the assertion of REQ#.

Clock 3. The master responds to GNT# by asserting the PIPE# signal (PIPE# = "pipelined"). The assertion of PIPE# indicates that the master is enqueuing or pipelining a transaction request into the target. In other words, the assertion of PIPE# indicates that the start address is on AD[31::3], the transfer length is on AD[2::0], and the command is on C/BE[3::0]#. This is referred to as a full-width transaction request.

Note that the figure shows the minimum latency that the master can exhibit when asserting PIPE# in response to GNT# from the arbiter. The maximum latency, or worst-case delay, would be for the master to assert PIPE# during Clock 4. In the example, the target enqueues one transaction request on the rising edge of Clock 4 when PIPE# is sampled asserted.

The master deasserts the REQ# signal in this clock, indicating that this is the last request to be enqueued for this assertion of REQ# and PIPE#. The master could continue enqueuing requests, if it so desired, by keeping PIPE# and REQ# asserted. REQ# must be deasserted for a minimum of two clocks before the master can reassert it for a new transaction.

Clock 4. Once the PIPE# signal is sampled asserted, the arbiter can deassert the GNT# signal. With the deassertion of GNT#, the status bus contents goes to a "don't care" state. The master is required to deassert the PIPE# signal in this clock. PIPE# is always deasserted one clock after REQ# is deasserted. The master returns the AD and C/BE bus output drivers to a high-impedance state.

64-Bit Memory Addressing

If bit five in the master's AGP status configuration register (see Table 7-1 on page 110) is set to one, this indicates that the master supports extended addressing (the ability to use memory addresses wider than 32 bits to address memory that resides above the 4GB address boundary). Bit five in the master's AGP command configuration register can then be set to one by software (see Table 7-2 on page 111), thereby enabling the master to issue requests using 64-bit memory addressing.

Two AGP clocks are required to enqueue a transaction request that uses a 64-bit memory address. In the first clock of the dual-address cycle, the master provides the lower 32 bits of the 64-bit memory address on AD[31::3]. The transfer length is encoded on AD[2::0]. C/BE[3::0]# contains the dual-address cycle (DAC) command. In the second clock cycle, AD[31::0] contains the upper 32 bits of the 64-bit memory address. C/BE[3::0]# contains the normal command (e.g., read, long read, write, etc.). When using 64-bit memory addressing, it is a rule that the memory address must reside above the 4GB address boundary. This means that the upper 32 address bits of the 64-bit memory address cannot be all zeros.

Multiple Requests Being Enqueued Using 64-Bit Addressing

Refer to Figure 7-2. All signals in this example are driven and sampled on the rising edge of the AGP clock.

Figure 7-2: Multiple Requests Using 64-Bit Addressing

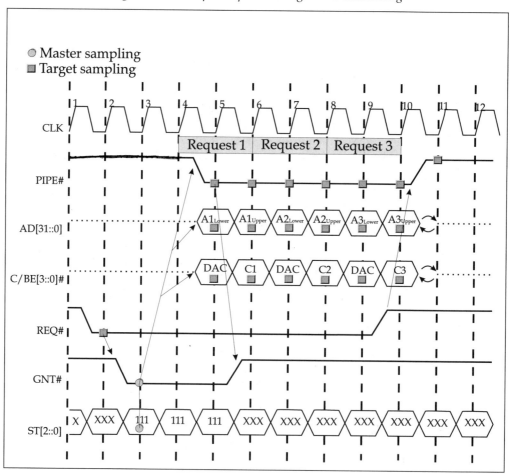

Clock 1. This example begins when the AGP master asserts REQ# to request access to the bus to initiate the transaction.

Clock 2. The arbiter (within the core logic) samples REQ# asserted on the rising edge of the clock and responds by asserting GNT#. GNT# gives the master permission to start the transaction and qualifies the status bus (ST[2::0]) content as valid. A status of 111b indicates that the arbiter is granting bus ownership to the master. As pictured in the example, this is the fastest that the arbiter could respond to REQ# assertion.

Clock 3. The master samples GNT# asserted, indicating that it may begin to enqueue requests now.

Clock 4. The master responds to GNT# by asserting PIPE#. In addition, the master drives the lower 32 bits of the 64-bit address onto AD[31::3], and AD[2::0] contains the transfer length. The dual-address command is encoded on C/BE[3::0]#. The assertion of PIPE# qualifies the content of the AD and C/BE busses as valid. As pictured in the figure, this is the maximum latency that the master can exhibit when asserting PIPE# in response to GNT#. The minimum latency would be to assert PIPE# in Clock 3.

Clock 5. The core logic samples PIPE# asserted on the rising edge of the clock. Once PIPE# is sampled asserted, the arbiter deasserts GNT#. With the deassertion of GNT#, the status bus contents goes to a "don't care" state. The target latches and decodes the contents of the AD and C/BE busses. Since the command is the DAC, the target must wait for the remainder of the request (upper 32 address bits and the command) before it can enqueue the request. The master drives the upper 32 bits of the 64-bit memory request onto AD[31::0] during this clock, as well as the normal command (e.g., long read, read, etc.).

Clock 6. On the rising edge of the clock, the target latches the upper 32 bits of the address and also latches the normal command. The target can now enqueue the first transaction request in this examples series of transaction requests. The PIPE# and REQ# signals remain asserted, indicating that the master intends to continue enqueuing additional transaction requests. By keeping both PIPE# and REQ# asserted, the master indicates that this is not the last request to be enqueued. Neither the master nor the target can add any wait states while enqueuing requests. In other words, requests must be enqueued at full speed. There is no mechanism for the target to terminate the request transaction.

During this clock, the master drives the lower 32 bits of the 64-bit memory address as well as the transfer length for the second transaction request onto the AD bus. The dual-address cycle command is driven onto C/BE bus.

Clock 7. On the rising edge of the clock, the target latches and attempts to decode the start address, length and command. Since the command is the DAC command, however, the target must wait for the remainder of the request information to be delivered in the next clock cycle.

During this clock, the master drives the upper 32-bits of the 64-bit memory address onto the AD bus, and the normal command onto C/BE[3::0]#.

Clock 8. On the rising edge of the clock, the target receives the remainder of the transaction request information and enqueues the second transaction request in this request series. PIPE# and REQ# remain asserted, indicating that the master intends to continue enqueuing requests. During this clock, the master drives the lower 32-bits of the 64-bit memory address, the transaction length and the DAC command for the third transaction request.

Clock 9. During this clock, the master deasserts REQ#, indicating that this request shall be the last request to be enqueued in this series of requests. The master could continue enqueuing requests, if it so desired, by keeping PIPE# and REQ# asserted. The target latches the lower portion of the address, the transaction length, and the DAC command on the rising edge of the clock. The master drives out the upper 32 bits of the address and the normal command during this clock.

Clock 10. On the rising edge of the clock, the target latches the final portion of the 64-bit address and the command for the third transaction request and it enqueues the third transaction request. The master is required to deassert PIPE# one clock after deasserting REQ#. The master returns the AD and C/BE busses to idle by tri-stating the respective output drivers during this clock. This is represented by the turn-around symbol.

Enqueuing Transaction Requests via the Sideband Address Port

Rather than using the AD and C/BE busses to enqueue transaction requests, the Sideband Address (SBA) port may be used. The AD bus is then dedicated to performing data transfers. The SBA port consists of SBA[7::0]. The SBA port is kept to a low pin count to keep the pin and trace count down. This means low cost. The SBA is unidirectional: it is always an output from the master (the AGP graphics accelerator) and an input to the target (the core logic).

When the master implements the SBA port, there is no need to implement the PIPE# or REQ# signals. The REQ# signal, however, must be implemented, if the AGP master is also capable of acting as a PCI master.

Since a transaction request is wider than 8-bits (the width of the SBA port), the request must be sent to the target in a series of one or more packets. Each packet consists of 16 bits and is referred to as an SBA command. Two transfers of eight bits each are required to send one SBA command across the SBA from master to target. The upper byte of the command is transferred first, followed by the lower byte. These two transfers across the SBA comprise an SBA operation:

- In 1X data transfer mode, the operation of the SBA port is synchronized to the AGP clock and it requires two ticks of the AGP clock to transfer a command. The upper eight bits of the command are latched on the first rising edge of the clock, and the lower eight bits on the next rising edge.
- In 2X data transfer mode, the operation of the SBA port is synchronized to the Sideband Address Strobe (SB_STB) signal. The upper eight bits of the command are latched by the target on the falling edge of SB_STB, and the lower eight bits on the strobe's rising edge. The transmission of the entire 16-bit command takes one tick of the AGP clock. This is double the throughput achievable when transmitting multiple requests via the port in 1X mode.
- In 4X data transfer mode, the operation of the SBA is synchronized to SB_STB and the Sideband Address Strobe Complement (SB_STB#) signal. The upper byte of the command are latched by the target on the first falling edge of SB_STB, and the lower byte on SB_STB#'s first falling edge. The transmission of the entire command takes one half of an AGP clock cycle. The two bytes of a second command are latched on the second falling edges of SB_STB and SB_STB#, respectively. Two complete 16-bit commands can be transmitted in one AGP clock cycle. This doubles the throughput achievable when transmitting multiple requests via the port in 2X mode, and is four times the throughput achievable in 1X mode.

Four SBA Command Types

There are four different types of SBA commands, each of which is 16-bit wide. The command type can be can be determined by decoding the most significant nibble (i.e., the upper four bits) of the upper byte in the 16-bit command. This nibble is referred to as the opcode. Refer to Table 7-3 on page 121 for the encodings of the SBA commands.

Type 1 Command — A[15::0]

The Type 1 SBA command contains the least significant 15 address bits, A[14::3] and the three-bit transfer length field. Since the address must be aligned on an address divisible by eight, the least-significant three address bits are always presumed to be zeros.

Type 2 Command — Command + A[23::15]

The Type 2 SBA command contains the four-bit bus command and the middle nine address bits of the full length address, A[23::15].

Type 3 Command — A[35::24]

The Type 3 SBA command contains the upper 12 bits of the full length address, A[35::24].

Bit five in both the master's and the target's AGP command registers (see Table 7-2 on page 111) is used to enable or disable extended addressing (addressing above the 4GB address boundary). When bit five is set to one, A[35::24] supplied in the type 3 command are valid. The type 4 command could also be optionally generated (see the next section).

If bit five of the master's AGP command configuration register is zero, then address bits A[35::32] in the type 3 command must be driven to zeros by the master. In other words, it is illegal to generate an address above the 4GB address boundary. When bit five of the target's AGP command configuration register is zero, then address bits A[35::32] in the type 3 command must be ignored by the target.

Type 4 Command — A[47::36]

The Type 4 SBA command is optional. If issued, the type 4 command contains the upper 12 address bits, A[47::36], of a 48-bit memory address. The type 4 command is only valid when bit five in the master's and the target's AGP command configuration registers are set to one.

Reserved Bits

Reserved bits within the command encodings (see Table 7-3 on page 121) must be driven to zero by the master and must be ignored by the target. Reserved command encodings must never be used by an AGP master. These command encodings are reserved for future use. When the SBA port is used to enqueue requests, the DAC is a reserved command.

Table 7-3: SBA Port Command Encodings

$S_7S_6S_5S_4$ $S_3S_2S_1S_0$	Description
1 1 1 1 1 1 1 1 1 1 1 1 1 1 1 1	**NOP, or Bus Idle**. When in 1X mode, a NOP is one byte in length. In 2X or 4X mode, a NOP is two bytes in length.
0 A A A A A A A 14 · · · · · 08 A A A A A L L L 07 · · · · 03	**Type 1 SBA Command**. The AGP data transfer length (LLL) and lower 12 address bits (A[14::3]) are encoded in this command. The lower three address bits are assumed to be zero. The most-significant bit of the most-significant byte (MSB) is the one-bit opcode used to identify this as the type 1 SBA command.
1 0 C C C C R A · · · · · · · 15 A A A A A A A A 23 · · · · · · 16	**Type 2 SBA Command**. The AGP bus command (CCCC) and middle 9 address bits (A[23::15]) are encoded in this command. The most-significant two bits of the MSB is the two-bit opcode used to identify this as the type 2 SBA command. R is a reserved bit.
1 1 0 R A A A A · · · · 35 · · · 32 A A A A A A A A 31 · · · · · · 24	**Type 3 SBA Command**. The upper 12 bits (A[35::24]) are encoded in this command. The most-significant three bits of the MSB is the three-bit opcode used to identify this as the type 3 SBA command. R is a reserved bit.
1 1 1 0 A A A A · · · · 39 · · · 36 A A A A A A A A 47 · · · · · · 40	**Type 4 SBA Command**. Address bits (A[47::36]) are encoded in this command. The most-significant nibble of the MSB is the four-bit opcode used to identify this as the type 4 SBA command.
1 1 1 1 0 * * * * * * * * * * *	**Reserved**. Must not be issued by an AGP master complying to the Revision 2.0 specification. These encodings may be defined by Intel in the future. A "*" indicates that the bit location could be a 0 or a 1. Any encoding where SBA[7::4] is 1111b and any bit location S2, S1, or S0 is a 0, is considered reserved.

Sideband Address Port Operation

There are no restrictions as to the relative order in which the types of SBA commands are issued by the master. A transaction request is only considered enqueued when a type 1 command is issued, so the type 1 should be the last one issued to the target. The SBA command types 2, 3, and 4 are sticky, meaning that, once issued, these commands only need to be updated when that part of request information needs to be changed. Subsequent requests with the same transaction type (that was issued in the type 2 command) that target a memory location within the same 32KB block of memory as the previous request can be enqueued by issuing only a new type 1 command (to change the lower 12 bits of the address and the transfer length).

Because only a new type 1 command is needed to enqueue a new transaction request, the latency to enqueue a subsequent request is reduced to 2 clocks (in 1X mode). This technique leverages the principle of spatial locality of reference: data in memory is typically accessed in a linear fashion. Said another way, there is a high probability that subsequent accesses will be in close proximity to the address of the current access. The core logic memorizes the information supplied in the type 4, 3, and 2 commands, and assumes that information remains true until receiving new ones. Upon receiving a subsequent type 1 command without receiving new type 4, 3, or 2 commands, the target enqueues a new transaction request. The target uses the previously memorized information to build the new full-length transaction request.

Example

For this example scenario, the following assumptions are made:

- The graphics controller is required to access a 256KB texture map in AGP memory and the start address of the texture map is aligned on a 256KB address boundary.
- Using the AGP long read command with a transaction length of 256 bytes per transaction, the transfer of the 256KB texture would take 1024 data transactions. Therefore, 1024 requests would need to be enqueued by the target in order to complete the entire transfer.
- The machine is limited to 4GB of memory space, and only 32-bit addressing is therefore required.

The AGP graphics accelerator would issue the following series of transaction requests via the SBA port:

1. Enqueuing the first transaction request requires three SBA operations, the first of which is a type 3 command indicating (using A[35::24]) the 16MB block of memory within the 4GB address space that contains the targeted start location.
2. The master then issues a type 2 command, identifying the individual 32KB-aligned area within the targeted 16MB block that contains the targeted loca-

tion. The type 2 command also contains the transaction type: in this example, long read.

3. Finally, the first transaction request is enqueued when the master issues a type 1 command indicating (using A[14::3]) the quadword-aligned start address of the first 256 bytes to be transferred. In this example, since the start address is aligned on a 256KB address boundary, A[14::3] would all be zeros. The transfer length is set to 256 bytes.

4. To enqueue the next transaction request to read the next 256 bytes of texture information only requires the generation of a type 1 SBA command to change A[14::3] to point to the start address of the next 256-byte block to be transferred.

A total of 1024 requests must be enqueued to read the entire 256KB texture map. A type 2 SBA command would only need to be issued when crossing a 32KB address boundary. Because of the natural alignment of the texture map, only the initial type 3 command would be required.

SBA Idle Time

When the SBA port is idle, the master must actively drive the SBA[7::0] signals to FFh (i.e., all 1s). This is referred to as a NOP (short for "no operation"). A NOP indicates that the SBA is idle. In 1X mode, a NOP is one AGP clock in length (one byte). In 2X and 4X modes, a valid NOP requires 16-bits, or two bytes, of FFh to be sent over the SBA port.

The SBA port can be driven by the master at any time to enqueue a transaction request. There is no need for the master to assert REQ#, or to wait for the arbiter to assert GNT#, before driving an SBA command.

SBA Data Transfer Modes

The rate at which SBA commands are issued is the same as the rate selected for data transfers:

- If the selected data transfer rate is the 1X mode, then the SBA is operating in 1X mode.
- If the selected data transfer rate is the 2X mode, then the SBA is operating in 2X mode.
- If the selected data transfer rate is the 4X mode, then the SBA is operating in 4X mode.

The data transfer rate (and therefore the SBA transfer rate) is determined at configuration time and cannot be changed during runtime.

Sideband Addressing in 1X Mode

In 1X mode, the SBA signals are qualified on the rising edge of the AGP clock. Refer to Figure 7-3 for an example of Sideband addressing in 1X mode.

Figure 7-3: Sideband Addressing in 1X Mode

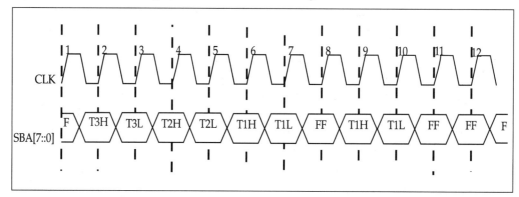

Clock 1. On the rising edge of the clock, the target latches a NOP command (SBA[7::0] is driven to FFh by the master).

Clock 2. On the rising edge of the clock, the target latches the high byte of the first SBA request command (T3H). "T3H" is an abbreviation for Type 3 command, High byte.

Clock 3. On the rising edge of the clock, the target latches the lower byte of the first SBA request command (T3L). "T3L" is an abbreviation for Type 3 command, Low byte. Clocks 2 and 3 complete the first SBA operation.

Clock 4. On the rising edge of the clock, the target latches the high byte of the second SBA request command (T2H). As an example, this could be the high byte of a type 2 SBA command.

Clock 5. On the rising edge of the clock, the target latches the low byte of the second SBA request command (T2L). This could be the low byte of a type 2 SBA command.

Clock 6. On the rising edge of the clock, the target latches the high byte of the third SBA request command (T1H). As an example, this could be the high byte of a type 1 SBA command.

Clock 7. On the rising edge of the clock, the target latches the low byte of the third SBA request command (T1L). This could be the low byte of a type 1 SBA command. With the receipt of the type 1 SBA command, the target enqueues a transaction request in its AGP request queue. The target has all of the information it needs to compose a request:

- The 32-bit start address supplied in the type 1, 2, and 3 commands.
- The transaction type supplied in the type 2 command.
- The transaction length supplied in the type 1 command.

Clock 8. On the rising edge of the clock, the target latches a NOP command.

Clock 9. On the rising edge of the clock, the target latches the high byte of the fourth SBA request command (T1H). As an example, this could be the high byte of another type 1 SBA command.

Clock 10. On the rising edge of the clock, the target latches the low byte of the fourth SBA request command (T1L). This could be the low byte of a second type 1 SBA command. Upon the receipt of another type 1 SBA command, the target enqueues another transaction request in its AGP request queue. The target uses this type 1 command, and the information supplied in the type 3 and 2 commands transferred on clocks 2-through-5, to compose the request. The type 3 and 2 commands are sticky. Those commands only need to be issued when changes need to be made to the information supplied in the earlier SBA commands.

Clocks 11 and 12. On the rising edge of these two clocks, the target latches a NOP command.

Sideband Addressing in 2X Mode

Refer to Figure 7-4 on page 126. When using sideband addressing in 2X mode, one new SBA operation can be issued to the target during each AGP clock. The high and low bytes of the SBA command are transferred within the same AGP clock period. The command information is latched by the target on the falling and rising edges of the master-sourced Sideband Strobe signal, SB_STB. The high byte of the SBA command is latched on the falling edge of SB_STB, and the low byte is latched on the rising edge of SB_STB.

Figure 7-4: Sideband Addressing in 2X Mode

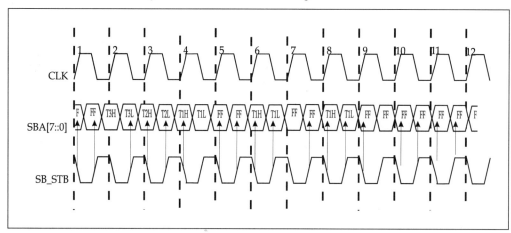

Clock 1. On the falling and rising edges of the SB_STB, the target latches a NOP (NOP's come in pairs in 2X mode: two bytes of FFh are required to signal a NOP).

Clock 2. The target latches T3H on the falling edge of SB_STB and T3L on the rising edge of SB_STB. These two bytes could comprise a type 3 command.

Clock 3. The target latches T2H on the falling edge of the SB_STB and T2L on the rising edge of SB_STB. These two bytes could comprise a type 2 command.

Clock 4. The target latches T1H on the falling edge of SB_STB and T1L on the rising edge of the SB_STB. This could comprise a type 1 command. Upon receipt of a type 1 SBA command, the target enqueues a transaction request in its AGP request queue. Using the information captured in the type 1, 2, and 3 commands, the target has a complete transaction request.

Clock 5. On the falling and rising edges of the SB_STB, the target latches a NOP.

Clock 6. The target latches T1H on the falling edge of SB_STB and T1L on the rising edge of SB_STB. These bytes could represent another type 1 command. Upon receipt of another type 1 SBA command, the target enqueues a second transaction request in its AGP request queue. It uses the previously received type 3 and type 2 command information latched during clocks 2 and 3, respectively, to compose this new request.

Clock 7. On the falling and rising edges of the SB_STB, the target latches a NOP.

Clock 8. The target latches T1H on the falling edge of SB_STB and T1L on the rising edge of SB_STB. These bytes could represent another type 1 command. Upon receipt of another type 1 SBA command, the target enqueues a third transaction request in its AGP request queue. It uses the previously received type 3 and type 2 command information latched during clocks 2 and 3, respectively, to compose this new request.

Clocks 9, 10, and 11. On the falling and rising edges of the SB_STB, the target latches NOPs.

Sideband Addressing in 4X Mode

Refer to Figure 7-5 on page 128. Two SBA operations can be issued during each AGP clock in 4X mode. In other words, the high and low bytes of two commands can be transferred within one AGP clock period. Only one of those commands, however, can be a type 1 command, not both.

The command information is latched by the target on the falling edges of the master-sourced Sideband Strobe (SB_STB) and Sideband Strobe Complement (SB_STB#) signals. The high byte of the pair of bytes that comprise the first SBA command is latched on the first falling edge of SB_STB and its corresponding low byte on the first falling edge of SB_STB#. The high byte of the pair of bytes that comprise the second SBA command is latched on the second falling edge of SB_STB, while the low byte is latched on the second falling edge of SB_STB#.

Figure 7-5: Sideband Addressing in 4X Mode

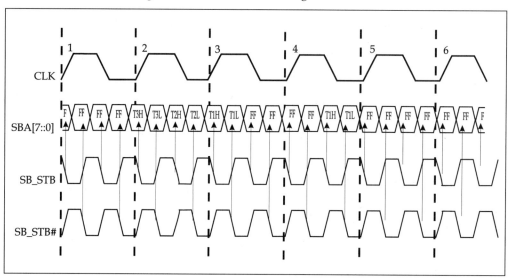

Clock 1. NOPs come in pairs in 4X mode and two bytes of FFh are required to signal a NOP. The target latches the two NOPs on the falling edges of SB_STB and SB_STB#.

Clock 2. The target latches T3H on the first falling edge of SB_STB, T3L on the first falling edge of SB_STB#, T2H on the second falling edge of SB_STB, and T2L on the second falling edge of SB_STB#. This could represent the two bytes that comprise a type 3 command and the two bytes that comprise a type 2 command. Either command could be a type 1 command, but not both.

Clock 3. The target latches T1H on the first falling edge of SB_STB, T1L on the first falling edge of SB_STB#, the first byte of a NOP on the second falling edge of SB_STB, and the second byte of the NOP, on the second falling edge of SB_STB#. The first two bytes could represent another type 1 command. Upon receipt of a type 1 SBA command, the target enqueues a transaction request in its AGP request queue. The target uses the previously received type 3 and type 2 command information, transferred during clock 2, to compose this new request.

Clock 4. The target latches the first byte of a NOP on the first falling edge of SB_STB, the second byte of the NOP on the first falling edge of SB_STB#, T1H on the second falling edge of SB_STB, and T1L on the second falling edge of SB_STB#. The second two bytes could represent another type 1 command. Upon receipt of another type 1 SBA command, the target enqueues another transaction request in its AGP request queue, and uses the previously-received type 3 and type 2 command information, transferred during clock 2, to compose this new request.

Clock 5. On the falling edges of the SB_STB and SB_STB# signals, the target latches NOPs.

Sideband Strobe Synchronization Protocol

The sideband strobe synchronization protocol is relevant whenever the SB_STB signal has been stopped, including after reset. The SB_STB may be stopped to reduce power consumption. SBA commands are considered undefined by the target until the master transmits the synchronization cycle. The synchronization cycle is used by the receiver within the target to determine the appropriate clock phase (T1 or T2) for inner loop timings.

The synchronization cycle consists of the data value of FEh presented on the SBA port for a single AGP clock. During this clock, FEh meets the 1X timing specifications. After the synchronization cycle, the contents of the SBA is no longer valid relative to the 1X clock, but valid relative to the first 2X or 4X strobe point. The first valid 2X or 4X strobe point occurs two 1X clocks after the synchronization cycle is sampled by the target. At this point, the first valid SBA command can be transmitted. The first valid command may be a NOP.

AGP 2X or 4X timing continues unless SB_STB is stopped. Before stopping SB_STB, NOPs must be transmitted for a minimum of four AGP clocks. When stopped, SB_STB must be driven high and either held high or tri-stated. Once stopped, SB_STB must remain stopped for a minimum of eight AGP clocks.

AGP Request Transaction Flow Control

The number of requests that can be enqueued by the master is determined during configuration. Although not architecturally limited, the target's request queue depth is specified at a maximum of 256 transactions. The maximum number of requests that can be enqueued is the smaller of the master's and the target's request queue depth. The master is responsible for not enqueuing more transaction requests than the target can handle.

The request queue depth of the target and the master are indicated in their respective AGP status configuration registers (see Table 7-1 on page 110). The

OS configuration software reads these registers and then programs the request queue depth in the master's command register (see Table 7-2 on page 111) accordingly. When the request queue of the target is larger than the request queue of the master, the master limits the number of transactions enqueued by design. The master simply stops enqueuing transaction requests when its own request queue is full. When the request queue of the master is larger than the request queue of the target, the master is configured with the request queue depth of the target.

Only read, long read, write, and flush commands occupy a slot in the request queue. The fence command does not. When the data begins to transfer, the slot occupied by the request corresponding to the data transfer is freed in the queue.

An interesting phenomena to note is that the request queue depth of the master is reported in its AGP status configuration register. The value reported may be misleading, however, because the master could simply stop issuing requests at any time. Therefore, the master may just stop issuing requests when its request queue is full, regardless of what is reported in its AGP status configuration register.

8 *AGP versus PCI Transactions*

The Previous Chapter

AGP transactions are broken into two distinct bus operations: the issuance of the transaction request by the AGP graphics accelerator (referred to as the AGP master), and the matching data transaction that is initiated later in time by the core logic (referred to as the AGP target). The previous chapter provided a detailed description of the issuance of transaction requests using the AD and C/BE busses, as well as the SBA port.

This Chapter

There are two categories of transactions that can be performed on the AGP bus: AGP transactions and PCI transactions. This chapter explores the differences between the two.

The Next Chapter

The next chapter provides a detailed description of AGP data transactions in 1X, 2X, and 4X data transfer modes.

Decoupled versus Coupled Data Transactions

The data transfers that occur within a PCI transaction (i.e., the data phases) are tightly coupled to the transaction's address phase.

Each PCI transaction begins with the address phase, during which the master drives out the start address and the transaction type (also referred to as the command) for a period of one PCI clock cycle. This can be thought of as the transaction request.

All devices on the PCI bus latch the request and decode it to determine which of them is the target of the request. Data is then transferred between the master and the target in a series of one or more data phases. In any data phase, either the master, the target, or both may need additional time before they are ready to transfer the current data item. Either or both of them can stretch out the data phase by adding wait states to it, thereby delaying its completion. The PCI bus is being wasted during this "dead" time and no other device can use it.

AGP transactions are intrinsically different than PCI transactions in that the request and data phases are treated as completely separate transactions. The transaction request is issued to the target by the master in a request transaction. The target latches the request and will deal with it off-line from the AGP bus. In the meantime, the master can issue additional transactions requests to the target. The target queues them up and deals with each of them off-line.

When the target is ready to transfer data to (in response to a memory read request) or from (in response to a memory write request) the master, it re-establishes the connection with the master and the data is transferred between the two.

The decoupled nature of AGP request transactions and data transactions allows the target latency on a read to be overlapped with the issuance of subsequent requests. This pipelining of requests allows more efficient data transfers on the AGP bus when compared to the PCI bus. The data transaction on AGP can be thought of as a stream of data, in either direction, transmitted from a high-speed buffer within the source to a high-speed buffer within the destination.

PCI Flow Control

In PCI transactions, a data item is transferred during each data phase. The size of a data item is a dword (in a 32-bit PCI bus environment), or a quadword (in a 64-bit PCI environment). A data phase ends when the data item is transferred between the master and the target. Both the master and the target must be ready to transfer the data item in order for the data phase to complete. The master indicates to the target that it is ready to transfer a data item by asserting IRDY#, and the target indicates to the master that it is ready to transfer it by asserting TRDY#.

Both IRDY# and TRDY# must both be sampled asserted on the same rising edge of the PCI clock in order to transfer data between the master and the target. Both the master and the target have the opportunity to add wait states into a data phase by deasserting their respective ready signals. In other words, the data transfer can be throttled, or slowed, by either the master, the target, or both.

AGP Data Flow Control

General

AGP flow control is handled very differently than PCI flow control. The specifics of throttling a data transfer from a signaling protocol perspective depends on the type of transaction. Regardless of transaction type, AGP flow control is based on individual blocks of data. A **block** of data is **defined as** the **amount of data** that can be **transferred during four AGP clock periods**. The amount of data transferred in a block, therefore, depends on the transfer mode, (1X, 2X, or 4X). In this discussion, the term "AGP clock" refers to the 66 MHz AGP bus clock. This clock synchronizes the data transfer in 1X mode and provides timing for control signals in all transfer modes.

- In AGP **1X mode**, four bytes of data can be transferred during each AGP clock period, therefore a **block** of data **consists of 16 bytes**.
- In AGP **2X mode**, eight bytes of data can be transferred during each AGP clock period, therefore a **block** of data **consists of 32 bytes**.
- In AGP **4X mode**, 16 bytes of data can be transferred during each AGP clock period, therefore a **block** of data **consists of 64 bytes**.

A block of data is always aligned on an address divisible by eight (in other words, on a quadword address boundary). A data transaction that can complete the overall data transfer in four AGP clocks or less only has only an initial block of data. Transactions that transfer more than one block of data have one initial block and one or more subsequent blocks.

The master and the target only have an opportunity to insert wait states prior to the transmission of a subsequent data block. They do not have the ability to insert wait states into the transmission of the individual dwords that make up a data block. They must be transferred at full speed. The point at which the master or target can indicate that one or more wait states must be inserted prior to the transmission of a data block is referred to as the block's **throttle point**.

The throttle point is abbreviated *TP* in the timing diagrams, and always occurs on the rising edge of the AGP clock two clocks prior to the point in time when the next data block would normally begin to transfer. The number of AGP clocks between the throttle points for adjacent data blocks is always four.

If wait states are added prior to the transfer of a data block, then the throttle point is extended (in other words, instead of it being a point in time, it is extended into a period of time one or more clocks in duration). The **throttle point** for the next data block ends when both the master and target indicate that they will be ready to start the transmission of the next data block two clocks later. The throttle point for the next data block is four AGP clocks after the rising edge of the clock in which the current throttle point ends.

Three Times Where Data Can Be Delayed

The transmission of requested read or write data can be delayed at three points in time:

- After the transaction request has been issued, but before the target indicates that it's ready to transfer the data. In other words, **before** the **data transaction begins**.
- During the data transaction, but **before** the transfer of the **initial data block**.
- **Before** the transfer of **each subsequent data block**.

At the throttle point for each subsequent data block, the master and the target may add a number of wait states to delay the transfer of the data block. If the master adds any wait states to read data transactions, the latency guarantee associated with all high-priority transactions in the queue may be adversely affected. The target incorporates any target-added wait states into the guaranteed latency that it reports for high-priority transactions. The target, however, cannot anticipate wait states that may be added by the master. When wait states are added by the master, the resulting behavior of the target with respect to the latency of pending high-priority transactions is implementation-specific.

AGP Master Flow Control

Flow control for the master is best represented in a table. Table 8-1 on page 135 describes the signals that the master can use to add wait states to a data transaction. There is also a corresponding table for the target (Table 8-2 on page 137) later in this chapter. An entry of "None" indicates that the master has no mechanism for adding wait states for that particular transaction type, at that particular time. The following terms are used in the table:

- LP Read is a low-priority read data transaction.
- HP Read is a high-priority read data transaction.
- AGP Write is a high- or low-priority write data transaction. The protocol is the same for both transaction types.
- Fast Write is an AGP fast write transaction.

A fast write transaction is a modified form of a PCI write transaction. The initiator of the fast write transaction is always the core logic. The target of the fast write is always the graphics accelerator. The core logic uses fast write transactions to perform writes to the AGP master on behalf of the processor or a PCI bus master.

Flow control for a fast write is similar to flow control for AGP transactions. Wait states are added based on data blocks. This is different than PCI write transactions. PCI write transactions can have data throttled on the dword-level. More information on fast writes can be found in Chapter 10, entitled "Fast Write Transactions," on page 187.

Table 8-1: AGP Master Flow Control

Transaction Type	LP Read	HP Read	AGP Write	Fast Write
Before Data Transaction	RBF#	None	None	WBF#
Before Initial Data Block	None	None	IRDY#	None
Before Subsequent Block	IRDY#	IRDY#	None	TRDY#/STOP#

Column 2, Row 2. The master can assert the RBF# signal to prevent the core logic from returning previously requested low-priority read data.

Columns 2 and 3, Row 4. The master can deassert the IRDY# signal at the throttle point to add wait states before the return of a subsequent block of low or high-priority read data.

Column 3, Rows 2 and 3. Once high-priority read data is requested, the master cannot delay the return of the initial block coming from the core logic. The master must be ready to accept it when the core logic is ready to source it. This is a reasonable assumption, considering the master requested it in the first place. The core logic could reorder high-priority read data being returned in front of a processor access to memory. If the master were allowed to delay its return, the processor could potentially be stalled.

Column 4, Row 3. After the arbiter has given permission to the master (by asserting GNT#) to supply write data to the target, the master may delay sourcing the first data block by one AGP clock by keeping IRDY# deasserted. However, the first data block transmission must begin within two clock periods after GNT# is sampled asserted.

Column 4, Row 4. The master has no mechanism for throttling the transfer of subsequent data blocks during write transactions. Once it asserts IRDY# to transfer the initial block of data, the master must be ready to source all of the data for the write transaction at full speed (in other words, the master must transfer the subsequent blocks without wait states). This is reasonable, considering that it is the master that chooses the transaction size when it first issues the memory write request.

Column 5, Row 2. If the write buffers within the master are full, the master cannot accept fast write data at this time. The master can prevent the core logic from initiating a fast write transaction by asserting the WBF# signal. In PCI protocol, if a target cannot accept write data due to a buffer full condition, the target signals a retry to the PCI initiator. In AGP, if the master were allowed to signal a retry in this scenario, bus bandwidth is wasted.

Column 5, Row 3. The AGP master has no mechanism to delay (i.e., throttle) the transmission of the initial data block in an AGP fast write transaction. The AGP master, acting as the target of the fast write, must be able to accept the first four AGP clocks of data (in other words, the first data block).

Column 5, Row 4. The master (i.e., the AGP graphics accelerator) can insert wait states to delay the transfer of a subsequent data block by deasserting TRDY# at the throttle point (remember that the master is acting as the target of the fast write transaction, so it uses TRDY# to insert wait states). The master can also terminate the transaction prematurely (before all of the data has been transferred) by using the PCI disconnect protocol (by asserting the STOP# signal).

AGP Target Flow Control

Flow control for the target is best represented in a table. Table 8-2 on page 137 describes the signals that can be used by the target to add wait states to a data transaction. There is also a corresponding table for the master earlier in this chapter (Table 8-1 on page 135). An entry of "None" indicates that the target has no mechanism for adding wait states for that particular transaction type, at that particular time.

Table 8-2: AGP Target Flow Control

Transaction Type	LP Read	HP Read	AGP Write	Fast Write
Before Data Transaction	GNT#/ST[2::0]	GNT#/ST[2::0]	GNT#/ST[2::0]	GNT#/ST[2::0]
Before Initial Data Block	TRDY#	TRDY#	None	IRDY#
Before Subsequent Block	TRDY#	TRDY#	TRDY#	IRDY#

Row 2, All Columns. Regardless of transaction type, the target (which contains the arbiter) can always delay the data transfer by not granting bus ownership to the master (using the arbitration signals GNT# and ST[2::0]).

Columns 2 and 3, Row 3. Relative to the assertion of the GNT# signal, the core logic can delay the transfer of the initial block of LP or HP read data by one clock by deasserting TRDY#.

Columns 2, 3, and 4, Row 4. By deasserting TRDY# at the throttle point, the core logic can insert one or more wait states before the transmission of a subsequent data block.

Column 4, Row 3. In write data transactions, once the arbiter (within the core logic) has granted bus ownership to the master to supply the write data, there is no mechanism that permits the target to throttle the transfer of the initial data block.

Column 5, Row 2. In fast write transactions, the core logic is the initiator. Since the arbiter is internal to the core logic, the GNT# and ST[2::0] signals are internal to the chip.

Column 5, Row 3. Once the fast write transaction has begun, the core logic can delay the transfer of the initial data block for one AGP clock by deasserting IRDY#. However, the initial data block must be delivered within two clocks of the transaction initiation.

Column 5, Row 4. By deasserting IRDY#, the core logic can insert one or more wait states prior to the transmission of a subsequent data block. During fast write transactions, the assertion of IRDY# qualifies the subsequent data block.

Use of the RBF# Signal

The AGP master asserts the Read Buffer Full (RBF#) signal to indicate that it's unable to accept previously requested low-priority read data. Upon sampling RBF# asserted, the arbiter will not allow the target to initiate the return of previously requested low-priority read data (while RBF# remains asserted). An AGP master can be designed to always be ready to accept the first data block of a low-priority read transaction. In this case, the graphics accelerator does not need to implement RBF# as an output to the core logic. The use of the RBF# signal depends on the length of the current transaction, the length of the next transaction, and the data transfer rate.

Regardless of the data transfer rate, once RBF# is deasserted the master is always required to accept all of the data in the initial data block of a low-priority read transaction without throttling. The master chooses the transfer size for each transaction. The length of each transaction depends on the available buffer space within the master. It is not the intention of the specification that the master assert RBF# as part of "normal" operation. The RBF# signal should only be used by the master under those unusual conditions where the master cannot consume the data it requested as fast as the target is able to source it.

Data Buffering Required to Deassert RBF# in 1X Mode

In 1X data transfer mode, four bytes of data can be transferred during each AGP clock period. The block size is equal to four clocks of data, or 16 bytes. The master is required to have adequate buffering to accept the initial block of data for the current transaction without wait states. This initial block can be up to 16 bytes in length. In transactions that have a length of greater than 16 bytes, the master can use flow control, by deasserting IRDY# at the throttle point, to delay the return of subsequent data blocks.

Regardless of the length of the current transaction, there is always sufficient time to assert RBF# to block additional low-priority read transactions in 1X mode. In order to keep RBF# deasserted, the master must have buffering sufficient to accept all of the data associated with the next data transaction (if the next transfer were 16 bytes or less). If the next transfer were greater than 16 bytes, the master must accept the first block (16 bytes).

Assume the worst-case scenario, where the length of the first transaction is 16 bytes, and the length of the second transaction is greater than or equal to 16 bytes. For RBF# to remain deasserted, the master must have 16 + 16 = 32 bytes of data buffering.

Data Buffering Required to Deassert RBF# in 2X Mode

In 2X data transfer mode, eight bytes of data can be transferred during each AGP clock period. The block size is equal to four clocks of data, or 32 bytes. If the current transaction has a length greater than eight bytes, then only the current transaction must be accepted. The master will have sufficient time to assert RBF# to block the initiation of additional low-priority read transactions.

If the current transaction has a length of eight bytes, then the master must be able to accept two transactions of data without adding wait states. The master must have sufficient buffering to accept the data from the first transaction, eight bytes, and the data from the initial block of the second transaction (which can be up to four clocks x eight bytes per clock = 32 bytes). There is not sufficient time in the first transaction to assert RBF# to prevent the second transaction. As an example, if the length of the first transaction is eight bytes, and the length of the second transaction is greater than or equal to 32 bytes, then the master must, at a minimum, have 8 + 32 = 40 bytes of buffering.

As another example, if the length of the first transaction is eight bytes, and the length of the second transaction is 16 bytes, then the master must, at a minimum, have 8 + 16 = 24 bytes of buffering.

In order to always keep the RBF# signal deasserted, the master must be able to buffer the data from the initial block of the first transaction, and the initial block of the second transaction. Assume the worst-case scenario, where the length of the first transaction is 32 bytes, and the length of the second transaction is greater than, or equal to, 32 bytes. For RBF# to remain deasserted, the master must have 32 + 32 = 64 bytes of data buffering.

Data Buffering Required to Deassert RBF# in 4X Mode

In 4X data transfer mode, 16 bytes of data can be transferred during each AGP clock period. The block size is equal to four clocks of data, or 64 bytes. If the current transaction has a transaction length greater than 16 bytes, then only the current transaction must be accepted. The master will have sufficient time to assert RBF# to block the issuance of additional low-priority read transactions.

If the current transaction has a length of 16 bytes or eight bytes, then the master must be able to accept two transactions of data without adding wait states. The master must have sufficient buffering to accept the data from the first transaction, eight or 16 bytes, and the data from the initial block of the second transaction (which can be up to 64 bytes). There is not sufficient time in the first transaction to assert RBF# to prevent the issuance of the second transaction. As an example, if the length of the first transaction is 16 bytes, and the length of the second transaction is greater than or equal to 64 bytes, then the master must, at a minimum, have 16 + 64 = 80 bytes of buffering.

As another example, if the length of the first transaction is 16 bytes, and the length of the second transaction is 16 bytes, then the master must, at a minimum, have 16 + 16 = 32 bytes of buffering.

In order to keep RBF# deasserted, the master must be able to buffer the data from the initial block of the first transaction, and the initial block of the second transaction. Assume the worst-case scenario, where the length of the first transaction is 64 bytes, and the length of the second transaction is greater than or equal to 64 bytes. For RBF# to always remain deasserted, the master must have 64 + 64 = 128 bytes of data buffering.

9 1X, 2X, and 4X Data Transactions

The Previous Chapter

There are two categories of transactions that can be performed on the AGP bus: AGP transactions and PCI transactions. The previous chapter explored the differences between the two.

This Chapter

This chapter provides a detailed description of AGP data transactions in 1X, 2X, and 4X data transfer modes.

The Next Chapter

The next chapter provides a detailed description of Fast Write transactions in 1X, 2X, and 4X data transfer modes.

Introduction

The following sections describe 1X, 2X, and 4X mode data transactions. The discussion is limited to AGP read and write data transactions. In AGP transactions, the core logic is always the target and the graphics accelerator is always the master.

1X Transfer Mode Data Transactions

The data rate for these examples is 1X, meaning that four bytes of data can be transferred during each AGP clock cycle. The data transfer rate is established at configuration time. In 1X mode, all signals are driven and sampled on the rising edge of the AGP clock.

AGP System Architecture

Multiple Data Block Read Transaction

Figure 9-1 illustrates the target device (the core logic) responding with previously-requested read data. The assumption is that the transaction request was for 32 bytes of data. With 32 bytes to transfer, this transaction has an initial block of 16 bytes, and one subsequent block, also of 16 bytes. The transaction length was encoded in the previously issued request. This example shows no wait states added by either the master (the graphics accelerator) or the target (the core logic).

Figure 9-1: Multiple Block Read, 1X Mode

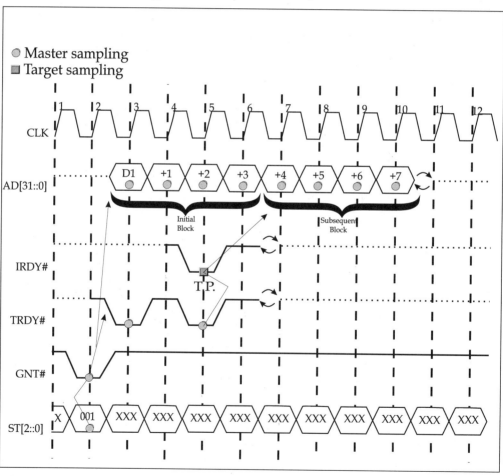

Chapter 9: 1X, 2X, and 4X Data Transactions

Clock 1. The target begins the data transaction by asserting the GNT# signal and placing a value of 001b on the Status bus (ST[2::0]). A status of 001b indicates that previously requested high-priority read data is being returned to the master. When GNT# is sampled asserted on the rising edge of Clock 2, the master begins (one clock later) latching data from the AD bus on the rising edge of each clock.

Clock 2. TRDY# is asserted (by the core logic) in response to the bus grant. The assertion of TRDY# indicates when the target will start supplying each data block. TRDY# is only asserted for one clock period. The assertion of TRDY# indicates that the target is ready to transfer the initial data block. In this example, 16 bytes make up the initial block. This example shows the minimum delay in asserting TRDY# in response to the grant. The maximum delay would be if TRDY# were not asserted until Clock 3. This would indicate that the target is adding one wait state prior to the transfer of the first data block (for this type of transaction, a maximum of one wait state is allowed to be inserted by the target).

GNT# is deasserted in this clock and the status bus goes to a "don't care" state. The target deasserted GNT# because it knows that the master detected the grant asserted on the rising edge of clock 2.

Clock 3. The first four bytes of data are latched by the master on the rising edge of the clock. The master sampled TRDY# asserted on the rising edge of the clock, indicating that the first block of data is being presented. The target sources the next four bytes of valid data in this clock. TRDY# is deasserted after a one clock assertion.

Clock 4. The next four bytes of data are latched by the master (for a total of eight bytes read so far) on the rising edge of the clock. The target sources the next four bytes of valid data in this clock. TRDY# is asserted by the core logic, indicating that the target is ready to source the next 16 byte block of data (the subsequent block) with no wait states, immediately after the transfer of the first block completes. IRDY# is asserted by the graphics accelerator, indicating that the master will be ready to accept the next 16 byte block, with no wait states, immediately after the transmission of the first data block.

Clock 5. The rising edge of Clock 5 is the throttle point (labeled T.P.) for the subsequent data block. This throttle point is two AGP clocks prior to the earliest point where the next block could begin transferring. On the throttle point clock edge is where both the master and the target have the opportunity to add wait states prior to the transfer of the subsequent data block. In this example, no wait states are being added by either agent, so the transmission of the next data block will start one clock later (on the rising edge of clock 6). The next four bytes of data are latched by the master (for a total of 12 bytes read so far) on the rising edge of the clock. The target sources the next four bytes of valid data in this clock. TRDY# is deasserted by the target after a one clock assertion. IRDY# is deasserted by the master after a one clock assertion.

Clock 6. The final four bytes of the initial data block are latched by the master (for a total of 16 bytes read so far) on the rising edge of the clock. The next four bytes are driven out by the target (these are the first four bytes of the subsequent data block). TRDY# is released by the target (in other words, it backs its output driver off of the TRDY# signal line), and IRDY# is released by the master. TRDY# and IRDY# are then in a high-impedance condition. These signals are kept high by a required pull-up resistor.

Clock 7. The first four bytes of the subsequent data block are latched by the master (for a total of 20 bytes read so far) on the rising edge of the clock. The target sources the next four bytes of data in this clock.

Clock 8. The second four bytes of the subsequent data block are latched by the master (for a total of 24 bytes read so far) on the rising edge of the clock. The target sources the next four bytes of data in this clock.

Clock 9. The third four bytes of the subsequent data block are latched by the master (for a total of 28 bytes read so far) on the rising edge of the clock. The target sources the final four bytes of data in this clock. Had there been another subsequent data block for this data transaction, the rising edge of this clock would be the next throttle point. TRDY# and IRDY# would have to be sampled asserted to continue the data transfer with zero wait states.

Clock 10. The final four bytes of the subsequent data block are latched by the master (for a total of 32 bytes read) on the rising edge of the clock. The target returns the AD and C/BE busses to a high-impedance state (represented by the turn-around symbol).

Multiple Block Read Data Transaction with Wait States

Figure 9-2 on page 145 illustrates the target device responding with read data corresponding to a previously enqueued transaction request. The assumption is that the transaction request is for 32 bytes of read data. With 32 bytes of data to be transferred, this transaction has an initial block of 16 bytes, and one subsequent block, also 16 bytes. Wait states are added at the subsequent data block's throttle point.

Figure 9-2: Read Data Transaction, 1X Mode, Wait States Added

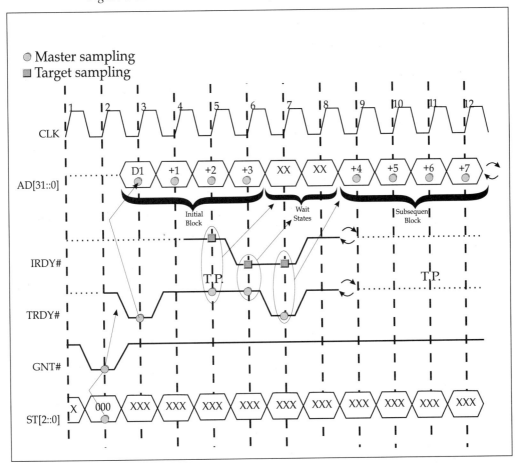

Clock 1. The target begins the data transaction by asserting the GNT# signal and placing a value of 000b on the Status bus (ST[2::0]). A status of 000b indicates that previously requested low-priority read data is being returned to the master. When GNT# is sampled asserted on the rising edge of Clock 2, the master begins (one clock later) latching data from the AD bus on the rising edge of each clock.

Clock 2. TRDY# is asserted (by the core logic) in response to the bus grant. The assertion of TRDY# indicates when the target will start supplying each data block. TRDY# is only asserted for one clock period. The assertion of TRDY# indicates that the target is ready to transfer the initial data block. In this example, 16 bytes make up the initial block. This example shows the minimum delay in asserting TRDY# in response to the grant. The maximum delay would be if TRDY# were not asserted until Clock 3. This would indicate that the target is adding one wait state prior to the transfer of the first data block (for this type of transaction, a maximum of one wait state is allowed to be inserted by the target).

GNT# is deasserted in this clock and the status bus goes to a "don't care" state. The target deasserted GNT# because it knows that the master detected the grant asserted on the rising edge of clock 2.

Clock 3. The first four bytes of data are latched by the master on the rising edge of the clock. The master samples TRDY# asserted on the rising edge of the clock, indicating that the first block of data is valid. The target sources the next four bytes of data in this clock. The TRDY# signal is deasserted after a one clock assertion.

Clock 4. The next four bytes of data are latched by the master (for a total of eight bytes read so far) on the rising edge of the clock. The target sources the next four bytes of data in this clock.

TRDY# is deasserted by the core logic, indicating that the target will not be ready to start sourcing the next 16 byte block of data (the subsequent block) one clock later. IRDY# is also deasserted (by the graphics accelerator), indicating that the master will not be ready to accept the next 16 byte block two clocks later. The specification requires that IRDY# and TRDY# be actively driven during throttle points.

Clock 5. The rising edge of Clock 5 is the throttle point (T.P.) for the subsequent data block. The throttle point is two AGP clocks prior to the earliest that the next block could begin transferring. The throttle point clock edge is where both the master and the target have the opportunity to add wait states prior to the transfer of the subsequent data block. When the master and the target will both be ready to start transferring the subsequent data block two clocks later, they assert their respective ready lines. This ends the throttle point. The throttle point for the next data block is always four AGP clocks after the previous throttle point ends. In this example, two wait states are being added by the target and one is being added by the master, prior to the transmission of the second data block.

Chapter 9: 1X, 2X, and 4X Data Transactions

The next four bytes of data are latched by the master on the rising edge of the clock (for a total of 12 bytes read so far). The target sources the next four bytes of data in this clock. TRDY# remains deasserted during this clock. Another wait state is being added by the target. IRDY# is asserted by the master, indicating that the master will be ready to begin receiving the subsequent block of data two clocks later.

Clock 6. The final four bytes of the initial data block are latched by the master (for a total of 16 bytes read so far) on the rising edge of the clock. The target had previously indicated to the master (TRDY# sampled deasserted on the rising edge of clock 5) that it is not ready to source the first data item of the second data block. This is referred to as adding a wait state. The state of the AD bus is undefined, and the data is shown as "XX" or "don't care." The data on the AD bus might actually be the data that was sourced by the target during the previous clock. The target samples IRDY# asserted on the rising edge of the clock, indicating that the master will be ready to receive the first dword of the second data block two clocks later. During this clock the target asserts TRDY#.

Clock 7. Because wait states were added prior to the transfer of the subsequent block, the data latched by the master on the rising edge of the clock is ignored. The target is not yet ready to source valid data in this clock. Thus, the transfer of the second block is delayed for a total of two clocks. When both IRDY# and TRDY# are sampled asserted on the rising edge of the clock, the throttle point for the subsequent data block ends. The subsequent block will begin to transfer two clocks later.

If this transaction had more data to transfer beyond the second data block, then the next throttle point would be four clocks later (on the rising edge of Clock 11). However, the next throttle point does not occur in this example due to the length of the transaction (only two data blocks). With the end of the second block's throttle point, the master deasserts IRDY# and the target deasserts TRDY#.

Clock 8. Due to the second wait state added by the target, the data on the AD bus on the rising edge of the clock is a "don't care" and the master ignores it. Both the master and the target have deasserted their respective ready signals. In this clock, the master and the target back off their output drivers from their respective ready signal lines, returning them to a high-impedance state (represented by the turn-around symbol). The target begins sourcing the first four bytes of the next data block during this clock.

Clock 9. The first four bytes of the subsequent data block are latched by the master (a total of 20 bytes read so far) on the rising edge of the clock. The target sources the next four bytes of valid data in this clock.

Clock 10. The second four bytes of the subsequent data block are latched by the master (24 bytes read so far) on the rising edge of the clock. The target sources the next four bytes of data in this clock.

Clock 11. The third four bytes of the subsequent data block are latched by the master (28 bytes read so far) on the rising edge of the clock. The target sources the final four bytes of data in this clock. Had there been another data block to transfer after the second one completes, the rising edge of this clock would be the throttle point for the next data block. This is indicated in the figure as "T.P.," and is where TRDY# and IRDY# would be sampled to determine whether or not the transmission of the third data block would be delayed.

Clock 12. The last four bytes of the subsequent data block are latched by the master (a total of 32 bytes read) on the rising edge of the clock. Since this is the final dword to be transferred for this transaction, the target terminates the transaction by returning the AD bus to an idle or float condition.

Read Data Transaction, Delay Prior to First Block

Figure 9-3 on page 149 illustrates the target (the core logic) delaying the transmission of the first data block of a read by one clock. This is the maximum delay permitted at this point in the transaction.

Since the arbiter and the target are the same device, the author is not sure why the core logic would delay the returning of the first data block after bus grant occurs. Regardless, this behavior is acceptable within the bus protocol. This example also illustrates a single block transfer in 1X mode. 16 bytes of data are transferred in four clocks.

By delaying the transfer of the initial block by one clock, the target has effectively pushed out the throttle point for the subsequent block by one clock. However, this transaction does not have a subsequent data block, therefore the throttle point does not actually occur.

Figure 9-3: Read Data Transaction with Delay Prior to Transmission of First Data Block, 1X Mode

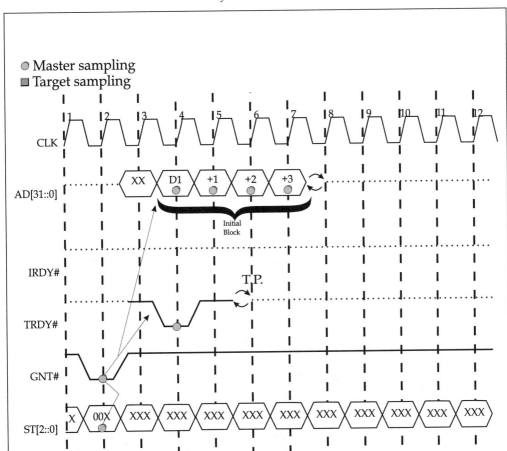

Clock 1. The arbiter begins the data transaction by asserting GNT# with a status of 00Xb, indicating that previously requested low- or high-priority read data is being returned to the master. If X = 1, then the data is high-priority. If X = 0, then the data is low-priority. Once the bus grant is detected on the rising edge of Clock 2, the master (the graphics accelerator) will begin latching data from the data bus beginning on the rising edge of Clock 3.

Clock 2. The target (the core logic) keeps TRDY# floating in this clock. The required pull-up resistor keeps TRDY# deasserted. The data on the AD bus during this clock is a "don't care." GNT# is deasserted in this clock and the status bus goes to a "don't care" state. The target deasserted GNT# because it knows that the master detected the grant on the rising edge of clock 2.

Clock 3. The master samples TRDY# deasserted on the rising edge of the clock, indicating to the master that the target is adding a wait state prior to the transmission of the first data block. The data latched by the master on the rising edge of the clock is ignored.

During this clock, the target asserts TRDY# for one clock, indicating that the target is ready to transfer all of the data for this transaction (in this example, 16 bytes will be transferred). When a data transaction can complete in four clocks or less, there is only one assertion of TRDY#.

The target is only allowed to add a single wait state prior to the transfer of the initial block of read data. The minimum delay for TRDY# assertion, relative to sampling a bus grant, would be if TRDY# were asserted in Clock 2 and were detected by the master on the rising edge of Clock 3.

Clock 4. The first four bytes of data are latched by the master (the graphics accelerator) on the rising edge of the clock. The master samples TRDY# asserted, indicating that the data block is valid. The target sources the next four bytes of data in this clock. TRDY# signal is deasserted after a one clock assertion.

Clock 5. The next four bytes of data are latched by the master (eight bytes have been read) on the rising edge of the clock. The target sources the next four bytes of data in this clock. TRDY# is in a turn-around clock; and the target is disengaging from driving this signal in this clock (the target is returning TRDY# to a high-impedance state). The pull-up resistor on TRDY# will then keep it deasserted.

Clock 6. The next four bytes of data are latched by the master (12 bytes have been read) on the rising edge of the clock. The target sources the final four bytes of data in this clock. The rising edge of this clock would be the throttle point for the second data block, if there were one. Notice that the T.P. was delayed due to the wait state before the transmission of the first data block.

Clock 7. The final four bytes of data are latched by the master (16 bytes have been read) on the rising edge of the clock. The AD bus is returned to a high-impedance state by the master during this clock.

Chapter 9: 1X, 2X, and 4X Data Transactions

Write Data Transaction, Minimum Delay

Figure 9-4 on page 152 illustrates the target responding to a previously issued write transaction request by granting bus ownership to the master so it can start delivering the write data.

The transaction length is 16 bytes, so this transaction will only transfer one data block. No wait states are added by the master or the target. In an AGP write transaction, the target cannot add wait states prior to the transfer of the initial data block.

The master is allowed to add one (and only one) wait state prior to the transfer of the first data block. This example illustrates zero wait state operation. Once IRDY# is asserted by the master to indicate its readiness to transfer the first block of write data, the master must source all of the write data for the entire transaction at full-speed. No wait states may be added by the master for a write transaction that has multiple blocks. Although the target cannot delay the transmission of the first data block, it can insert wait states prior to the transmission of any of the subsequent data blocks (if there are any). In this example, only one data block of 16 bytes is being transferred.

As each dword is driven by the master, it also drives the four bytes enable signals, C/BE[3::0]#, to indicate which of the four data paths contain valid bytes to be written within the current dword. As the target (the core logic) accepts each dword, it examines the byte enables to identify which of the four locations within the current dword are being written to.

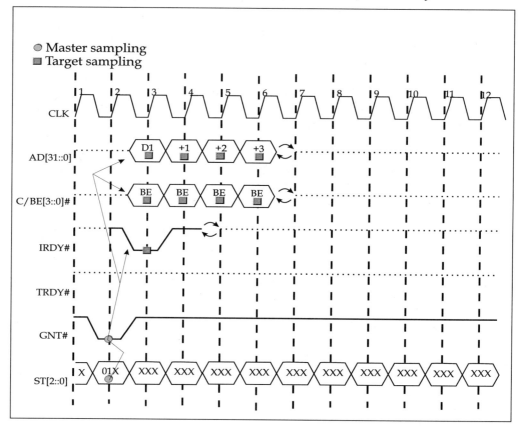

Figure 9-4: Write Data Transaction, 1X Mode, Minimum Delay

Clock 1. The arbiter begins the data transaction by asserting GNT# with a status of 01Xb, indicating that a previously requested low- or high-priority write data transfer can begin. If X = 1, then the data is high-priority. If X = 0, then the data is low-priority.

Clock 2. Once the grant is detected on the rising edge of the clock, the master (the graphics accelerator) begins sourcing the first dword of write data on the AD bus and the byte enables for the first dword. The master asserts IRDY# to indicate to the target that it has begun sourcing the first (and only) data block during this clock. This is the fastest that the master can start sourcing data after the grant (in other words, it's a minimum delay write).

GNT# is deasserted in this clock and the status bus goes to a "don't care" state. The target deasserted GNT# because it knows that the master detected the grant on the rising edge of clock 2.

Chapter 9: 1X, 2X, and 4X Data Transactions

Clock 3. The target (the core logic) starts latching data on the rising edge of the clock, and the asserted state of IRDY# indicates that the master has started sourcing the write data. The master will source valid write data during each clock. The target must consume four bytes of data and their respective byte enables (supplied on C/BE[3::0]#) on each rising edge of the AGP clock. There is no mechanism that permits the target to throttle the transfer of the data block once it has begun.

The master deasserts IRDY# in this clock after a one clock assertion and it will not be asserted again during this transaction. TRDY# is not used in this transaction because only one data block is being transferred and there is therefore no throttle point for a second data block. TRDY# remains deasserted, pulled high by the required pull-up resistor. During this clock, the master sources the next four bytes of the transaction and their respective byte enables on C/BE[3::0]#.

Clock 4. The target latches the second dword and second set of byte enables (eight bytes written so far) on the rising edge of the clock. The master sources the next dword and byte enables during this clock. Also during this clock, the master disengages from driving IRDY#. By turning off its IRDY# output driver, the master returns IRDY# to a high-impedance state (represented by the turn-around symbol).

Clock 5. The target latches the third dword and byte enables (a total of 12 bytes written) on the rising edge of the clock. The master sources the final dword and byte enables during this clock.

Clock 6. The target latches the final dword and byte enables (a total of 16 bytes written) on the rising edge of the clock. The master tri-states its AD and C/BE bus output drivers, returning those signals to the high-impedance state (represented by the turn-around symbol).

Back-to-Back Write Data Transactions, No Delays

Figure 9-5 on page 154 illustrates the master responding with a series of write data transactions in response to a series of previously enqueued write transaction requests. Each transaction in the example has a length of eight bytes. Because each of these transactions only transfers one data block, the TRDY# signal is not required (there are no subsequent data blocks and therefore no throttle points).

Figure 9-5: Back-to-Back Write Data Transactions, No Delays

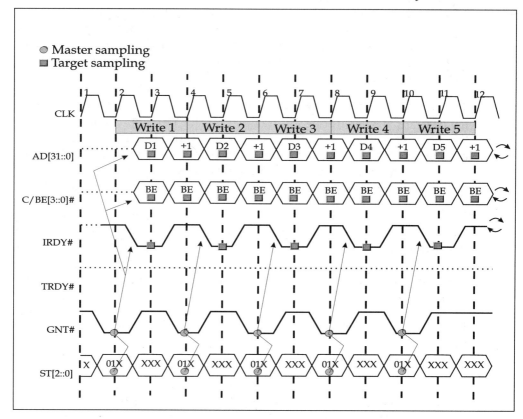

Clock 1. The arbiter grants the master ownership of the data bus to perform the first write data transaction by asserting GNT# and providing a status of 01Xb, where 01Xb indicates that a previously requested low- or high-priority write data transfer can begin.

Clock 2. The master samples the GNT# plus the status bus and recognizes that it has acquired ownership of the bus to perform the previously requested low- or high-priority write data transfer. In response, the master begins to source the first dword of data and its byte enables during this clock. The master asserts IRDY#, indicating that has started writing data in this clock. There is no delay between the grant and the sourcing of data and assertion of IRDY#. This is the fastest that the master could respond to the grant. The maximum permissible delay would be if IRDY# were asserted in clock 3. GNT# is deasserted in this clock to prepare for the pipelining of the GNT# signal in Clock 3 for the next transaction.

Chapter 9: 1X, 2X, and 4X Data Transactions

Clock 3. On the rising edge of the clock, the target latches the first four bytes of data and their byte enables. The target samples IRDY# asserted, qualifying the latched data and byte enables as valid.

During this clock, the master sources the final four bytes of data and their byte enables for the first transaction (only eight bytes are being written). The initiator deasserts IRDY# after a one clock assertion. GNT# is again asserted by the arbiter during this clock (for the next transaction). This allows the master to make the most efficient use of the AD bus bandwidth. By pipelining the GNT# signal, the arbiter is giving permission to the master to perform back-to-back write data transactions, without idle clocks in between the transactions.

Clock 4. On the rising edge of the clock, the target latches the final four bytes of data and their byte enables for the first transaction. The GNT# signal and Status of 01Xb is detected asserted by the master, giving the master permission to begin transferring the data and byte enables for the next transaction immediately. The master begins sourcing the first four bytes of data and their byte enables for the second transaction. The master asserts IRDY# in this clock, qualifying the data and byte enables as valid. The arbiter deasserts GNT# during this clock, preparing to pipeline GNT# for the next transaction.

Clock 5. On the rising edge of the clock, the target latches the first four bytes of data and their byte enables for the second transaction. The target samples IRDY# asserted, qualifying the latched data and byte enables as valid.

During this clock, the master sources the final four bytes of data and their byte enables for the second transaction. The master deasserts IRDY# after a one clock assertion. The GNT# signal is asserted by the arbiter for the next transaction.

Clock 6. On the rising edge of the clock, the target latches the final four bytes of data and their byte enables for the second transaction. The GNT# signal and a Status of 01Xb is detected by the master, giving the master permission to begin transferring the data and byte enables for the third transaction immediately.

The master begins sourcing the first four bytes of data and their byte enables for the third transaction. The master asserts IRDY# in this clock, qualifying the data and byte enables as valid. The arbiter deasserts GNT# during this clock, preparing to pipeline GNT# for the next transaction.

Clock 7. On the rising edge of the clock, the target latches the first four bytes of data and their byte enables for the third transaction. The target samples IRDY# asserted, qualifying the latched data and byte enables as valid.

The master sources the final four bytes of data and their byte enables for the third transaction. The master deasserts IRDY# after a one clock assertion. The GNT# signal is asserted by the arbiter during this clock for the next transaction.

Clock 8. On the rising edge of the clock, the target latches the final four bytes of data and their byte enables for the third transaction. The GNT# signal and a Status of 01Xb is detected by the master, giving the master permission to begin transferring the data and byte enables for the next transaction immediately.

The master begins sourcing the first four bytes of data and their byte enables for the fourth transaction. The master asserts IRDY# in this clock, qualifying the data and byte enables as valid. The arbiter deasserts GNT# during this clock, preparing to pipeline GNT# for the next transaction.

Clock 9. On the rising edge of the clock, the target latches the first four bytes of data and their byte enables for the fourth transaction. The target samples IRDY# asserted, qualifying the latched data and byte enables as valid.

During this clock, the master sources the final four bytes of data and their byte enables for the fourth transaction. The master deasserts IRDY# after a one clock assertion. The GNT# signal is asserted by the arbiter during this clock for the next transaction.

Clock 10. On the rising edge of the clock, the target latches the final four bytes of data and their byte enables for the fourth transaction. The GNT# signal and a Status of 01Xb is detected by the master, giving the master permission to begin transferring the data and byte enables for the next transaction immediately.

During this clock, in response to sampling GNT# asserted and the appropriate status code, the master begins sourcing the first four bytes of data and their byte enables for the fifth transaction. The master asserts IRDY# in this clock, qualifying the data and byte enables as valid. The arbiter deasserts GNT# during this clock.

Clock 11. On the rising edge of the clock, the target latches the first four bytes of data and their byte enables for the fifth and final transaction. The target samples IRDY# asserted, qualifying the latched data and byte enables as valid.

During this clock, the master sources the final four bytes of data and their byte enables for the fifth transaction. The master deasserts IRDY# after a one clock assertion.

Clock 12. On the rising edge of the clock, the target latches the final four bytes of data and their byte enables for the fifth transaction.

During this clock, in response to GNT# being detected deasserted, the master begins tri-stating its AD and C/BE bus drivers, and also floats the IRDY# signal in this clock.

2X Transfer Mode Data Transactions

2X transfer mode data transactions allow eight bytes to be transferred during each AGP clock period. When operating in 2X mode, the available bandwidth is 532 MB/s. To transfer eight bytes per clock period across a 32-bit AD bus, two four-byte transfers are performed in a single clock period. The protocol and control signals in 2X mode are identical to the protocol and control signals in 1X mode.

The data is latched by the recipient using data strobes, AD_STB0 and AD_STB1, that are supplied along with the data by the same device that sources the data. AD_STB0 is used to latch the data on AD[15::0], while AD_STB1 is used to latch the data on AD[31::16]. The transmitter of the data positions the strobes so that the edges are at approximately the middle of the data valid windows. These source-synchronized strobes present the consumer of the data with an optimized input data sampling window. Clock skew and flight time delay problems are minimized by using the strobes, as opposed to the clock, at the higher transfer rates.

The receiver of the data latches the first four bytes of data on the falling edge of the two strobes and the second four bytes of data on the next rising edge of the two strobes.

Back-to-Back Read Data Transactions, No Delays

Figure 9-6 on page 158 illustrates the target device (the core logic) responding to a series of previously enqueued transaction requests with a series of back-to-back read data transactions. The data rate for this example is 2X and each transaction request was for eight bytes of read data. The example illustrates either low-priority or high-priority read data being returned.

AGP System Architecture

Figure 9-6: Back-to-Back Read Data Transactions, 2X Mode

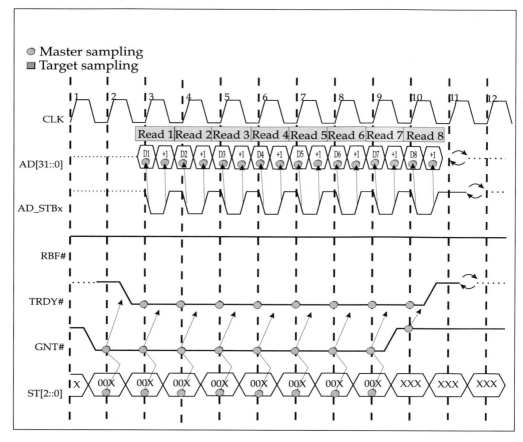

Clock 1. The target (the core logic) prepares to begin the first read data transaction by asserting GNT# and supplying Status of 00Xb, indicating that either low- or high-priority data is being returned to the master (the graphics accelerator).

Clock 2. Once the GNT# and a Status of 00Xb is detected on the rising edge of the clock, the master begins latching data on the first falling edges of the two AD_STBx strobe signals. The latched data is qualified as valid by sampling TRDY# asserted.

During this clock, the target asserts TRDY# to indicate that the read data being sourced on the AD bus is valid. This example shows the minimum delay in asserting TRDY# after the bus grant is detected. Near the end of Clock 2, the target begins sourcing read data on the AD bus, and positions the falling edge of the two strobes at the center point of the data valid window.

Normally, GNT# would be deasserted in this clock, but it is kept asserted for the next transaction of this back-to-back read data transaction series. The GNT# and Status for a new transaction can be driven in the final clock of the current transaction. Since the length of each of these transactions is eight bytes and eight bytes can be transferred in one clock in 2X mode, this clock is the first and final clock of the current transaction.

Clock 3. TRDY# is detected asserted by the master, indicating that the core logic is returning the requested read data on the strobe edges. The master latches the first four bytes of read data for the first transaction on the falling edges of the two AD_STBx strobes, and the second four bytes of read data on the rising edges of the two strobes. GNT# is detected asserted on the rising edge of the clock and the status indicates that the target will return requested read data in the next transaction. By pipelining the GNT# signal, the second transaction can begin in the next clock. This GNT# pipelining allows the most efficient use of the AD bus bandwidth. In this series of back-to-back eight-byte read data transactions, eight bytes of data is transferred during each AGP clock period, with no idle clocks between transactions.

TRDY# remains asserted, indicating that the data latched on the next falling and rising edges of the strobes is read data for the second transaction. Near the end of this clock, the target begins sourcing valid data for the second transaction.

Clock 4. TRDY# is detected asserted by the master, indicating that the core logic is returning the requested read data on the strobe edges. The master latches the first four bytes of read data for the second transaction on the falling edges of the two strobes, and the second four bytes of read data on the rising edges of the two strobes. GNT# is detected asserted on the rising edge of the clock and the status bus indicates that the target will return requested read data in the next transaction.

TRDY# remains asserted, indicating that the data latched on the next falling and rising edges of the strobes is valid data for the third transaction.

Clock 5. TRDY# is detected asserted by the master, indicating that the core logic is returning the requested read data on the strobe edges. The master latches the first four bytes of read data for the third transaction on the falling edges of the two strobes, and the second four bytes of read data on the rising edges of the two strobes. GNT# is detected asserted on the rising edge of the clock and the status bus indicates that the target will return requested read data in the next transaction. TRDY# remains asserted, indicating that the data latched on the next falling and rising edges of the strobes is valid read data for the fourth transaction.

Clock 6. The master latches the first four bytes of read data for the fourth transaction on the falling edges of the two strobes, and the second four bytes of read data on the rising edges of the two strobes.

Clocks 7 & 8. During each of these two clocks, the master latches the first four bytes of read data for the fifth and sixth transactions on the falling edges of the two strobes, and the second four bytes of read data on the rising edges of the two strobes.

Clock 9. The master latches the first four bytes of read data for the seventh transaction on the falling edges of the two strobes, and the second four bytes of read data on the rising edges of the two strobes.

During this clock, the target deasserts the GNT# signal and the contents of the status bus is no longer valid. This indicates that this series of transactions will complete in the next clock, upon the completion of the eighth read data transaction.

Clock 10. The master latches the first four bytes of read data for the eighth transaction on the falling edges of the two strobes, and the second four bytes of read data on the rising edges of the two strobes. The target deasserts TRDY#, indicating that valid data is no longer being sourced. After the transfer of the data for the eighth transaction, the target drives the two strobe signals high, before floating its strobe output drivers.

Clock 11. This clock is a turn-around clock for the signals used during the previous transaction. During this clock, the target disengages from the AD bus, returning it to the high-impedance state. The target also disconnects from the strobe lines and TRDY# during this clock. Pull-up resistors on these signals keep them deasserted when they are not being driven by any device.

Multiple Block Read, No Delays

Figure 9-7 on page 161 illustrates the target device responding with the read data for a previously enqueued transaction request. The transaction request was for 64 bytes of read data (the transaction length was encoded in the request). There are no wait states added by either the master (the graphics accelerator) or the target (the core logic). At the 2X data transfer rate, eight bytes can be trans-

Chapter 9: 1X, 2X, and 4X Data Transactions

ferred during each clock. With 64 bytes to transfer in the example, this transaction has an initial data block of 32 bytes, and one subsequent data block, also of 32 bytes. An assumption is that the data is low-priority read data. However, this example is representative of a high- or low-priority read data transaction.

Figure 9-7: Multiple Block Read, No Delays, 2X Mode

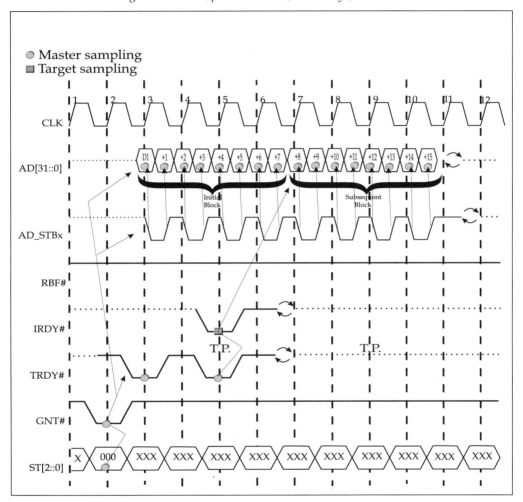

Clock 1. On the rising edge of the clock, the arbiter samples RBF# deasserted, indicating that the master can handle low-priority read data at the current time (it has buffer space available). In response, the arbiter begins the read data transaction by asserting GNT# during this clock and driving Status of 000b out. This grants ownership of the bus to the master to transfer previously requested low-priority read data.

Clock 2. On the rising edge of the clock, the master samples GNT# and the status bus. The status indicates that the target will be returning low-priority read data. The master will begin latching data on the falling and rising edges of the two strobes, AD_STB[1::0].

During this clock, the target asserts TRDY# to indicate to the master that the first block of data will begin transferring on the falling and rising edges of the strobes. Near the end of this clock, the target begins sourcing the first four bytes of read data for the initial data block. The GNT# signal is deasserted and the status bus goes to an invalid state.

Clock 3. The master samples TRDY# asserted on the rising edge on the clock, indicating that the target is sourcing the initial 32-byte data block starting on the first falling edges of the two strobes. The master latches the first four bytes of read data for the transaction on the falling edges of the strobes, and the second four bytes of read data on the rising edges of the strobes. During this clock, the target deasserts the TRDY# signal.

Clock 4. The master latches another four bytes of read data (12 bytes have been read) for the transaction on the falling edges of the strobes, and four bytes of read data on the rising edges of the strobes (16 bytes have been read). The state of the TRDY# signal at this point is a "don't care," because TRDY# was already sampled asserted on the rising edge of Clock 3 to indicate that the target is ready to transfer the initial block.

In preparation for the second data blocks throttle point, the target asserts TRDY# and the master asserts IRDY#, indicating that both agents will be ready to begin transferring the subsequent data block two clocks after the throttle point.

Clock 5. The rising edge of the clock marks the first and only throttle point (T.P.) of this transaction. This is the point in time where the master and the target have the opportunity to insert wait states prior to the transmission of the second data block. In this case, both IRDY# and TRDY# are sampled asserted, ending the throttle point for the second data block. Both agents have indicated that they will be ready to start the transmission of the second data block two clocks later. During Clock 5, IRDY# and TRDY# are actively driven deasserted.

Chapter 9: 1X, 2X, and 4X Data Transactions

The master latches another four bytes of read data (20 bytes have been read) on the falling edges of the strobes, and four bytes of read data are latched on the rising edges of the strobes (24 bytes have been read).

Clock 6. The master latches another four bytes of read data on the falling edges of the strobes (28 bytes have been read), and four bytes of read data on the rising edges of the strobes (32 bytes have been read). These are the final eight bytes of the initial block. The master and target tri-state their respective ready signal drivers in this clock. The target begins sourcing the second 32-byte data block near the end of this clock. This is two clocks after the completion of the second data block's throttle point.

Clock 7. The master latches the first four bytes of the second data block on the falling edges of the strobes (36 bytes have been read), and the second four bytes on the rising edges of the strobes (40 bytes have been read).

Clock 8. The master latches another four bytes of read data on the falling edges of the strobes (44 bytes have been read), and four bytes of read data on the rising edges of the strobes (48 bytes have been read).

Clock 9. The master latches another four bytes of read data on the falling edges of the strobes (52 bytes have been read), and four bytes of read data on the rising edges of the strobes (56 bytes have been read). The rising edge of clock 9 would have been the throttle point for the next data block if this transfer were longer than 64 bytes.

Clock 10. The master latches another four bytes of read data on the falling edges of the strobes (60 bytes have been read), and four bytes of read data on the rising edges of the strobes (64 bytes have been read). These are the final eight bytes of the second data block.

Clock 11. During this clock, the target tri-states its AD bus drivers and ceases to drive the strobe signals. The strobe signals have pull-up resistors to keep them in the deasserted state when they are not being driven by any device.

Multiple Block Write with Wait States

Figure 9-8 on page 164 illustrates the master responding with write data corresponding to a previously enqueued write transaction request. The transaction length is 64 bytes. Since the data block size in 2X transfer mode is 32 bytes, this transaction will have an initial block followed by one subsequent block. There is one wait state added by the target prior to the transmission of the second data block.

The master is allowed to delay, at a maximum, one wait state prior to the transmission of the first data block and must then be prepared to source all of the write data for the first and any subsequent blocks at full speed. The target must be prepared to accept the first block at full speed, but may insert wait states to delay the transmission of the subsequent data blocks.

This example shows the master immediately ready to transfer the first data block, and the target inserting one wait state prior to the transmission of the second data block.

Figure 9-8: Multiple Block Write, 2X Mode, Wait States Added

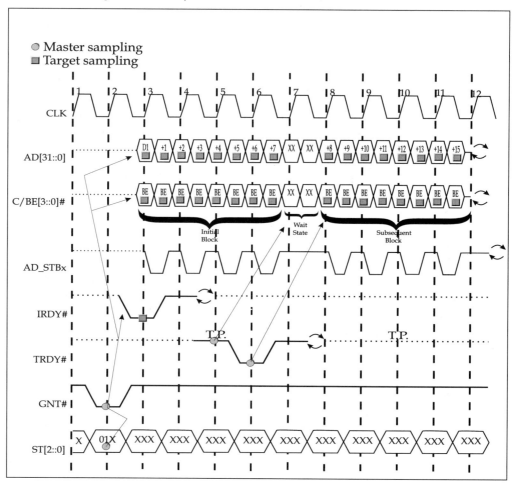

Chapter 9: 1X, 2X, and 4X Data Transactions

Clock 1. The arbiter begins the write data transaction by asserting GNT# and supplying a Status of 01Xb. This indicates that the master is being granted bus ownership to write data into memory. A status of 01Xb indicates that a previously-requested low- or high-priority write data transfer can begin. If X = 1, then the data is high-priority. If X = 0, then the data is low-priority.

Clock 2. Once the grant is detected on the rising edge of the clock, the master begins sourcing four bytes of write data on the AD bus, their byte enables on C/BE[3::0]#, and the two data strobes on AD_STB[1::0]. The master indicates that it is ready to transfer the first data block by asserting IRDY# during this clock. By asserting IRDY# during clock 2, the master is exhibiting zero wait state operation. This is the fastest that the master could begin sourcing data relative to the assertion of GNT#. The GNT# signal is deasserted by the arbiter, returning the status bus to a "don't care" state.

Clock 3. The target samples IRDY# asserted on the rising edge on the clock, indicating that the master is ready to source all of the write data for the transaction at full speed. The target latches the first four bytes of write data and their byte enables on the falling edges of the strobes, and the second four bytes of write data and byte enables on the rising edges of the strobes. During this clock, the master deasserts the IRDY# signal. The IRDY# signal is only asserted for one clock for write data transactions and indicates that the master is ready to source all of the write data at full speed.

Clock 4. The target latches another four bytes of write data and the byte enables on the falling edges of the strobes, and another four bytes of write data and the byte enables on the rising edges of the strobes. During this clock, the master tri-states its IRDY# output driver. TRDY# is deasserted by the target in preparation for the second data block's throttle point on the rising edge of the next clock.

Clock 5. The target latches another four bytes of write data and byte enables on the falling edges of the strobes, and another four bytes of write data and byte enables on the rising edges of the strobes. The master samples TRDY# deasserted, indicating that the target will not be ready to accept the subsequent data block two clocks later. By adding one wait state, the target delays the transfer of the subsequent data block by one clock period. During this clock, the target asserts TRDY# to indicate that it will be ready to transfer the second data block starting three clocks later (in clock 8).

Clock 6. The target latches the final eight bytes of write data (two dwords and their byte enables) for the initial data block on the falling and rising edges of the strobes. The master samples TRDY# asserted, indicating that the target will be ready to accept the subsequent data block starting two clocks later. Sampling TRDY# asserted ends the second data block's throttle point. TRDY# only needs to be asserted for one clock, so the target deasserts TRDY#.

Clock 7. During a wait state, the content of the AD bus is "don't care." During this clock, the master could drive the first four bytes of the second data block, the last four bytes of the first data block, or it could drive meaningless data. The data strobes remain driven high during the wait state. TRDY# is no longer needed for this transaction so it is released by the target during this clock and goes to the high-impedance state.

Clock 8. The target latches the first four bytes of write data and the byte enables of the second data block on the falling edges of the strobes, and the second four bytes of write data and the byte enables on the rising edges of the strobes.

Clock 9. The target latches another four bytes of write data and byte enables on the falling edges of the strobes, and another four bytes of write data and byte enables on the rising edges of the strobes.

Clock 10. The target latches another four bytes of write data and byte enables on the falling edges of the strobes, and another four bytes of write data and byte enables on the rising edges of the strobes. This would have been the throttle point for the third data block, had this transaction been longer than 64 bytes. Notice that the throttle point for the third data block was delayed due to the wait state that was injected prior to the transfer of the second data block. The throttle point for the next data block always falls four clocks after the throttle point for the previous data block ends.

Clock 11. The target latches the final eight bytes of valid data (two dwords and their respective byte enables) of the second data block on the falling and rising edges of the two strobes.

Clock 12. The transaction ends with the master tri-stating its AD and C/BE output drivers. The AD_STBx signals cease to be driven in this clock.

Back-to-Back Write Data Transactions, Minimum Delay

Figure 9-9 on page 167 illustrates the master transferring write data, corresponding to a series of previously-enqueued write transaction requests. The data is transferred using a series of back-to-back write data transactions. Each transaction has a length of eight bytes. It takes one clock to transfer eight bytes in 2X data transfer mode, so each of these transactions only requires an initial data block, without any subsequent blocks. TRDY# is therefore not required to be used for any of the transactions (because there are no throttle points for subsequent data blocks).

Figure 9-9: Back-to-Back 8-Byte Write Data Transactions, 2X Mode, No Delays

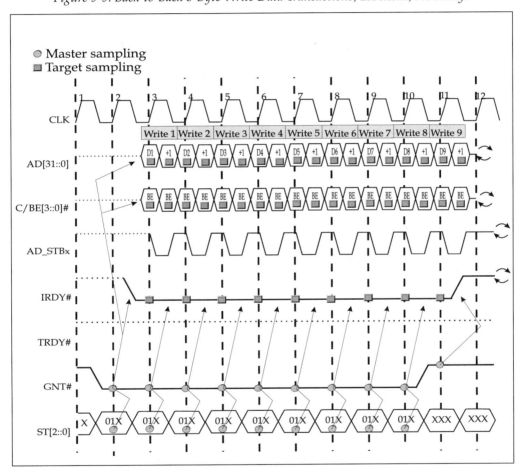

Clock 1. The arbiter begins the data transaction by asserting the GNT# signal. A status of 01Xb indicates that a previously requested low- or high-priority write data transfer can begin.

Clock 2. The master (the graphics accelerator) responds to the assertion of GNT# and the Status by sourcing the first dword of write data on the AD bus and the byte enables on C/BE[3::0]#. The master asserts IRDY# to indicate that it is ready to source the requested eight bytes at full speed. The first transfer is only eight bytes in length, so the arbiter can keep GNT# asserted in this clock for the second transaction. The arbiter is allowed to assert the GNT# signal for the next transaction in the final clock of the current transaction. Since the first transaction can complete in one clock, the arbiter can keep the GNT# signal asserted, thus pipelining the GNT# for the second transaction.

Clock 3. The target samples IRDY# asserted on the rising edge on the clock, indicating that the master is ready to source all of the data for the first transaction (eight bytes) at full speed. The target latches the first four bytes of write data and byte enables on the falling edges of the two strobes, and the second four bytes of write data and byte enables on the rising edges of the two strobes. In response to sampling GNT# asserted on the rising edge of the clock, the master keeps IRDY# asserted. IRDY# asserted indicates that the master is sourcing valid data for the second transaction immediately after this transaction.

Clock 4. The target samples IRDY# asserted on the rising edge on the clock, indicating that the master is ready to source all of the data for the second transaction (eight bytes) at full speed. The target latches the first four bytes of write data and byte enables on the falling edges of the two strobes, and the second four bytes of write data and byte enables on the rising edges of the two strobes. In response to sampling GNT# asserted on the rising edge of the clock, the master keeps IRDY# asserted. IRDY# asserted indicates that the master is sourcing valid data for the third transaction immediately after this transaction.

Clock 5. The target samples IRDY# asserted on the rising edge on the clock, indicating that the master is ready to source all of the data for the third transaction at full speed. The data is latched on the falling and rising edges of the two strobes. In response to sampling GNT# asserted on the rising edge of the clock, the master keeps IRDY# asserted. IRDY# asserted indicates that the master is sourcing valid data for the fourth transaction immediately after this transaction.

Clocks 6, 7, 8, and 9. The target samples IRDY# asserted on the rising edges of each of these clocks, indicating that the master is ready to source all of the data for each transaction at full speed. The target latches the first four bytes of write data and byte enables for the respective transaction on the falling edges of the two strobes, and the second four bytes of write data and byte enables on the rising edges of the two strobes. In response to sampling GNT# asserted on the rising edge of the clock, the master keeps IRDY# asserted. IRDY# asserted indicates that the master is sourcing valid data for the next transaction immediately after this transaction. This pipelining of the GNT# signal allows eight bytes of data to be transferred during each clock without idle clocks on the bus.

Clock 10. The target samples IRDY# asserted on the rising edge on the clock, indicating that the master is ready to transfer all of the requested data at full speed. The target latches the first four bytes of write data and byte enables for the transaction eight on the falling edges of the two strobes, and the second four bytes of write data and the byte enables on the rising edges of the two strobes. In response to sampling GNT# asserted on the rising edge of the clock, the master keeps IRDY# asserted. IRDY# asserted indicates that the master is sourcing valid data for the next transaction immediately after this transaction. Also during this clock, the arbiter deasserts GNT#, indicating that the next transaction is the last in this series.

Clock 11. The target samples IRDY# asserted on the rising edge on the clock, indicating that the master is ready to source all of the data for the final transaction at full speed. The target latches the first four bytes of write data and byte enables for the last transaction on the falling edges of the two strobes, and the second four bytes of write data and byte enables on the rising edges of the two strobes. During this clock, the master deasserts IRDY# in response to sampling GNT# deasserted on the rising edge of the clock. When GNT# is deasserted, the Status bus is now in a "don't care" state.

Clock 12. The master tri-states its AD and C/BE output drivers, as well as its strobe and IRDY# output drivers.

Maximum Shift between Generation of Ready and Arrival of Data Strobes at Receiver

The use of strobe signals to indicate data latch points in AGP 2X and 4X transfers is fairly straightforward, but can complicate the reading of AGP timing diagrams because other signal events, such as IRDY# and TRDY#, are clocked only by the rising edge of the AGP clock. For example, in the previous 2X timing diagrams, there might appear to be a correlation between the first data transferred, and the rising edge of AGP Clock 3. This illusion results from the following conditions:

- The AGP clock is running at its highest speed — 66 MHz. Each clock is 15ns in duration.
- The AGP 2.0 specification references the AGP clock at which either TRDY# or IRDY# is asserted to the beginning of valid data and strobe cycles. Because of how tight the timing is for 2X and 4X data transfers, the specification takes advantage of the fact that the sender provides both the data **and** the strobe, and allows the arrival of the first data and strobe at the

receiver to be delayed (measured from the rising edge of the sender's AGP clock on which xRDY# was clocked out) by as much as 12ns **plus** the maximum AGP propagation delay of 2.5ns. This 14.5ns total delay (12ns + 2.5ns) is very close to the 15ns period of a full speed, 66MHz AGP clock, and represents the maximum shift allowed in the specification. Once again, this is measured from the rising edge of the sender's AGP clock in which it asserted xRDY#, to the arrival of the first valid data strobe at the receiver.

Figure 9-10 on page 171 illustrates the timing components involved in the maximum shift described above.

- The subscripts t and r in this diagram (and the next) refer to 2X signals at the "transmitter" and "receiver," respectively.
- **TTSf** is the delay from clock to AD_STBx at the transmitter (**12ns max**)
- **TPROP** is the AGP propagation delay (**2.5ns max**)

Note that the apparent arrival of valid data on the rising edge of AGP Clock 2 is coincidental; the arrival of data at the receiver is strictly a function of how much delay the sender employed in asserting the strobe after Clock 1 **plus** whatever propagation delay exists in the AGP signal group. In AGP 2X (and 4X, too) a receiver latches data on valid strobe edges, not on the rising edges of the AGP clock.

Figure 9-10: Maximum Shift between xRDY# and AD_STBx, 2X Mode

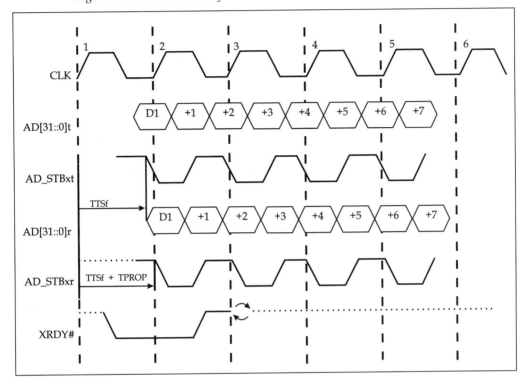

Minimum Shift between Generation of Ready and Arrival of Data Strobes at Receiver

In addition to the maximum delay of 12ns described above, the AGP specification also requires a minimum time from the rising edge of the AGP clock on which xRDY# is asserted to the falling edge of the first data strobe. Here TTSf is 2ns and, if a maximum propagation delay of 2.5ns is again used, the minimum shift at the receiver is 4.5ns.

As indicated in Figure 9-11 on page 172, the first data is transferred very quickly after the rising edge of Clock 1. In fact, two transfers have been latched before the arrival of the rising edge of Clock 2. Again, in AGP 2X and 4X the receiver is latching data based on accompanying strobes, not on the rising edges of the AGP clock.

Figure 9-11: Minimum Shift between xRDY# and AD_STBx

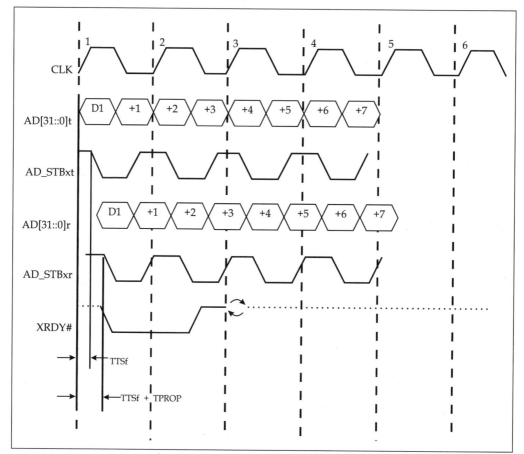

4X Transfer Mode Data Transactions

The data block size when using 4X transfer mode data transactions is 64 bytes. 16 bytes are transferred during each AGP clock period. When operating in 4X mode, the available bandwidth is 1064MB/s (1GB/s). To transfer 16 bytes per clock period across a 32-bit AD bus, four dword transfers are performed in a single clock period. The protocol and control signals in 4X mode are identical to the protocol and control signals in 1X and 2X modes.

Chapter 9: 1X, 2X, and 4X Data Transactions

The data is latched by the recipient using strobes supplied by the same device that transits the data. There are four data strobes: the two data strobes used in 2X mode, AD_STB[1::0], and the two complement strobes, AD_STB[1::0]#. The complement strobes are the inverted forms of the two data strobe signals. They are used as follows:

- The first falling edges of AD_STB[1::0] are used to latch four bytes from AD[31::0] and the bytes enables on C/BE[3::0]#.
- The first falling edges of complement strobe AD_STB[1::]# are used to latch four bytes from AD[31::0].
- The second falling edges of AD_STB[1::0] are used to latch four bytes from AD[31::0] and the bytes enables on C/BE[3::0]#.
- The second falling edges of complement strobe AD_STB[1::]# are used to latch four bytes from AD[31::0].

Just as in 2X mode, the transmitter of the data positions the strobes approximately at the center of the data valid window.

In 4X mode, the designer of the receiving device has two choices as to how to use the strobes to latch data. The first choice is to use them as documented in the bulleted list that immediately precedes this text.

The second choice provides better noise immunity. AD_STB0 and AD_STB0# are used as one differential signal pair, while AD_STB1 and AD_STB1# are used as another differential signal pair. At the receiving device, each signal pair is connected to a differential receiver. Any noise that may be induced in one signal of the pair is typically induced (in inverted form) on the sibling signal. When they arrive at the receiver, they tend to cancel each other out.

The differential receiver produces an output pulse whenever the falling edge of the active high strobe crosses over the rising edge of the complement strobe. This pulse is used as an internal latch signal. The receiver connected to AD_STB0 and AD_STB0# produces the internal AD_STB0 strobe (to latch the lower two data bytes) at the crossover point of the two signals, while the receiver connected to AD_STB1 and AD_STB1# produces the internal AD_STB1 strobe to latch the upper two bytes of data.

The receiver of the data latches the first four bytes of data on the first edge of the strobes, the second four bytes of data on the second edge of the strobes, the third four bytes of data on the third edge of the strobes, and the fourth four bytes of data on the fourth edge of the strobes.

Back-to-Back Read Data Transactions, No Delay

Figure 9-12 on page 175 illustrates the target (the core logic) responding to a series of previously-enqueued read transaction requests, by performing a series of back-to-back read data transactions. At a data rate of 4X, the amount of data that can be transferred in one clock cycle is 16 bytes, so the data block size is 64 bytes (4 clocks * 16 bytes per clock = 64). Note that the drawing of the clock has been scaled for 4X operation, relative to the 1X and 2X examples. The clock frequency, 66 MHz, is still the same as the previous examples. The assumption is that each transaction request was for 16 bytes of read data. The example illustrates either low-priority or high-priority read data being returned.

Note that, in the timing diagrams in this section:

*   AD_STBx represents both the AD_STB0 and AD_STB1 strobes.
*   AD_STBx# represents both the AD_STB0# and AD_STB1# strobes.

Also note that the byte enables are shown in the timing diagram and are always set to 0000b (all asserted). It is a rule that the target (the core logic) must always return all four bytes in each dword in a read data stream. The master ignores the bytes enables, however (because it "knows" that all four bytes are valid).

Chapter 9: 1X, 2X, and 4X Data Transactions

Figure 9-12: Back-to-Back Read Data Transactions, No Delays, 4X Mode

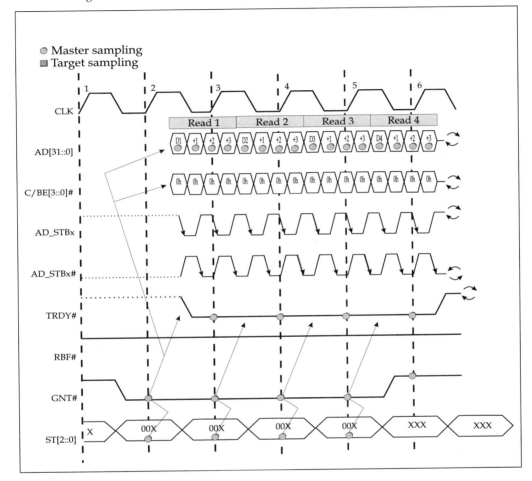

Clock 1. The arbiter begins the data transaction by asserting the GNT# signal. A status of 00Xb indicates that a previously requested low- or high-priority read data transfer can begin.

Clock 2. When GNT# is sampled asserted on the rising edge of the clock, the master (the graphics accelerator) decodes the status to determine the use of the AD bus in the next transaction. 00Xb indicates that the bus will be used to return read data, so the master begins latching data on the first falling edges of the AD_STB[1::0] and AD_STB[1::0]# strobes. The master will sample TRDY# to determine when the target has started delivery of the data.

During this clock, the target asserts TRDY# indicating that it has started delivery of the read data. This example shows the fastest assertion of TRDY# relative to recognition of the bus grant. The target begins sourcing valid data on the AD bus during Clock 2, positioning the falling edges of the strobes at the center point of the data valid window.

If the target only wanted to perform one transaction, it would deassert GNT# in this clock, thereby instructing the master to relinquish bus ownership. Because the core logic has another read data transaction to perform, it keeps GNT# asserted in this clock. GNT# can be asserted for the next transaction in the final clock of the current transaction. Since the length of each of the example transactions is 16 bytes and 16 bytes can be transferred in one clock cycle in 4X mode, this clock is the first and final clock of the current transaction.

Clock 3. TRDY# is sampled asserted by the master. The master latches the first four bytes of read data for the first transaction on the first falling edges of the AD_STBx strobes and the second four bytes of read data for the first transaction on the first falling edges of the AD_STBx# strobes. The master latches the third four bytes of read data for the first transaction on the second falling edges of the AD_STBx strobes and the fourth and final four bytes of read data for the first transaction on the second falling edges of the AD_STBx# strobes.

GNT# is still asserted on the rising edge of the clock and the status bus indicates that the target will again return read data in the next transaction. By pipelining the GNT# signal, the second transaction can begin in the next clock. GNT# pipelining allows the most efficient use of the AD bus bandwidth. In this series of 16 byte read data transactions, 16 bytes of read data is transferred in each AGP clock period, with no idle clocks between transactions.

TRDY# remains asserted, indicating that the target has started delivery of the read data for the second transaction.

Clock 4. TRDY# is detected asserted by the master. The master latches the first four bytes of read data for the second transaction on the first falling edges of the AD_STBx strobes and the second four bytes of read data for the second transaction on the first falling edges of the AD_STBx# strobes. Notice that these eight bytes are actually transferred during Clock 3. The master latches the third four bytes of read data for the second transaction on the second falling edges of the AD_STBx strobes and the fourth and final four bytes of read data for the second transaction on the second falling edges of AD_STBx#.

GNT# is still asserted on the rising edge of the clock and the status indicates that the target will again return read data in the next transaction. TRDY# remains asserted, indicating that the target has started delivery of the read data for the third transaction.

Clock 5. TRDY# is detected asserted by the master. The master latches the first four bytes of read data for the third transaction on the first falling edges of the AD_STBx strobes and the second four bytes of read data for the third transaction on the first falling edges of the AD_STBx# strobes. The master latches the third four bytes of read data for the third transaction on the second falling edges of the AD_STBx strobes and the fourth four bytes of read data on the second falling edges of the AD_STBx# strobes.

GNT# is deasserted during this clock because the target doesn't have any more data transactions to initiate. TRDY# remains asserted, however, indicating that the target has started delivery of the read data for the fourth and final transaction in this series.

Clock 6. TRDY# is detected asserted by the master. The master latches the first four bytes of read data for the fourth transaction on the first falling edges of the AD_STBx strobes and the second four bytes of read data for the fourth transaction on the first falling edges of the AD_STBx# strobes. The master latches the third four bytes of read data for the fourth transaction on the second falling edges of the AD_STBx strobes and the fourth and final four bytes of read data for the fourth transaction on the second falling edges of the AD_STBx# strobes.

GNT# is sampled deasserted on the rising edge of the clock, instructing the master to release the bus. TRDY# is deasserted by the target. This ends this series of back-to-back read data transactions. The target tri-states its AD and C/BE output drivers during this clock, and also turns off the output drivers for the AD_STBx strobes, the AD_STBx# strobes, and TRDY#. Required pull-down resistors keep the AD_STBx# strobes deasserted (low) when not being driven.

Multiple Block Read, No Delays

Figure 9-13 on page 178 illustrates the target device responding with read data, corresponding to a single previously-enqueued transaction request. The read transaction request was for more than 64 bytes of data (the transfer length was encoded in the read request). Since 16 bytes can be transferred in one clock cycle in 4X mode, the data block size is 64 bytes (16 bytes per clock cycle * 4 clock cycles = 64 bytes per data block). This means that this transfer will have an initial 64-byte data block and at least one additional data block.

There are no wait states added by either the master (the graphics accelerator) or the target (the core logic). There isn't room to show the entire transaction.

Figure 9-13: Multiple Block Read Transfer, No Delays, 4X Mode

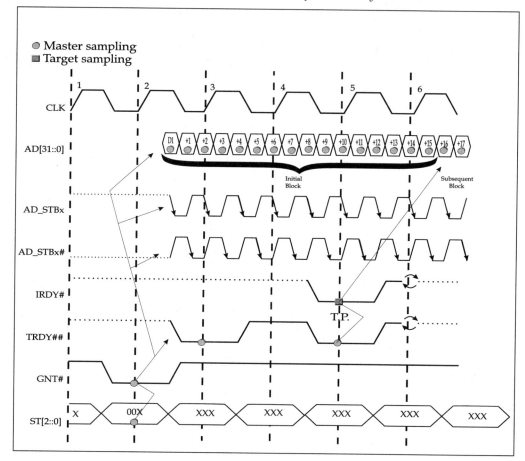

Clock 1. The arbiter begins the transaction by asserting GNT# and driving a Status of 00Xb, indicating that the bus will be used to return previously-requested low- or high-priority read data.

Clock 2. On the rising edge of the clock, the master recognizes the bus grant and begins latching data on the falling edges of the AD_STBx and AD_STBx# strobes.

During this clock, the target asserts TRDY# to indicate to the master that it has started delivery of the first data block. The target deasserts GNT# because it has no more transactions to perform and the status bus goes to an invalid state.

Chapter 9: 1X, 2X, and 4X Data Transactions

Clock 3. The master samples TRDY# asserted, indicating that the target has started delivery of the first 64-byte data block. The master latches the first four bytes of read data on the first falling edges of the AD_STBx strobes, and the second four bytes of read data on the first falling edges of the AD_STBx# strobes. Notice that this actually occurs during Clock 2. During this clock, the master latches the third four bytes on the second falling edges of the AD_STBx strobes, and the fourth four bytes on the second falling edges of the AD_STBx# strobes. 16 bytes have been read so far. During this clock, the target deasserts TRDY# because it has already indicated the start of the first data block transmission.

Clock 4. The master latches the fifth four bytes on the first falling edges of the AD_STBx strobes, and the sixth four bytes on the first falling edges of the AD_STBx# strobes. Notice that this actually occurs during Clock 3. During this clock, the master latches the seventh four bytes on the second falling edges of the AD_STBx strobes, and the eighth four bytes on the second falling edges of the AD_STBx# strobes. 32 bytes have been read so far. In preparation for the second data block's throttle point, the target asserts TRDY# and the master asserts IRDY#. The throttle point for the second data block occurs on the rising edge of Clock 5.

Clock 5. On the rising edge of the clock, the master samples TRDY# asserted and the target samples IRDY# asserted. This indicates that both the master and the target will be ready to start the transfer of the second data block two clocks later. It also ends the throttle period for the second data block.

The throttle point for the third data block (if there is one) would occur four clocks later on the rising edge of Clock 9 (not shown). Between the throttle points the two ready signals may be driven asserted, deasserted, or floated. In this example, TRDY# and IRDY# are driven high during this clock. The remaining dwords of the initial data block are transferred starting in this clock.

Clock 6. The master and the target float their respective ready signals during this clock. The first dword of the second data block is transferred on the falling edge of the AD_STBx strobes.

Multiple Block Read with Delayed Second Data Block

Figure 9-14 on page 180 illustrates the target device (the core logic) responding with read data corresponding to a single previously enqueued read transaction request. The transaction request is for more than 64 bytes of data, so the transaction will transfer multiple 64-byte data blocks. One wait state is added by the master prior to the transfer of the second data block.

Figure 9-14: Read Data Transaction, Wait States Added, 4X Mode

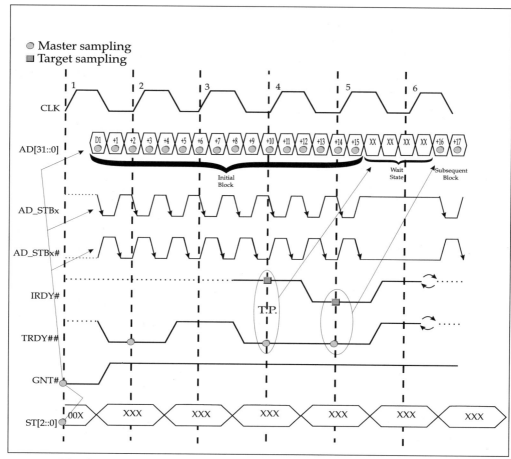

Clock 1. On the rising edge of the clock, the master detects GNT# asserted with a status of 00X, indicating that the target will be returning low- or high-priority read data. The master latches the first four bytes of read data on the first falling edges of the AD_STBx strobes, and the second four bytes of read data on the first falling edges of the AD_STBx# strobes. TRDY# is asserted by the target to indicate that it has started delivery of the first data block. The latest point at which the target can assert TRDY# and start delivery would be during clock 2.

During this clock, the arbiter deasserts GNT# and returns the status bus to an invalid state, because it doesn't have any other transactions to perform.

Clock 2. The master detects TRDY# asserted, indicating that the target started delivery of the first data block in clock 1. The master latches four more dwords during this clock on the falling edges of the AD_STBx and AD_STBx# strobes.

Clock 3. The master continues latching dwords of the initial data block on the falling edges of the strobes. The rising edge of clock 4 is the throttle point for the second data block. In preparation for the upcoming throttle point, the master deasserts IRDY# because the master will not be ready to start the transfer of the second data block two clocks later. This causes a wait state one clock cycle in duration to be inserted prior to the transmission of the second data block.

The specification states that the master and target ready signals must be driven during the throttle points. Had a wait state not been added, the subsequent block would begin to transfer two clocks later (in Clock 5).

The target will be ready to transfer the second data block two clocks later, as indicated by its assertion of TRDY# during this clock.

Clock 4. The master continues latching dwords of the initial data block on the falling edges of the strobes. When the target samples IRDY# deasserted at the throttle point, the target continues to assert TRDY# until the throttle point ends (on the rising edge on Clock 5) when both TRDY# and IRDY# are sampled asserted.

During this clock, the master asserts IRDY# to indicate that it will be ready to begin accepting the subsequent block two clocks later.

Clock 5. The master latches the final dwords of the initial data block on the falling edges of the strobes during this clock. The throttle point for the second data block ends when IRDY# and TRDY# are both sampled asserted.

Since the master indicated that it's not yet ready to start accepting the second data block, the target drives the contents of the AD bus to an undefined state after completing the transfer of the initial data block. The data shown as "XX" could be the last dword of the initial data block, the first dword of the second data block, or meaningless data. The strobe signals are driven to their respective idle states during the wait state. The idle state for the respective strobe signals is high for AD_STB[1::0] and low for AD_STB[1::0]#.

Since the throttle point has ended, the master and the target deassert their respective ready signals during this clock.

Clock 6. The transfer of the second data block can begin during this clock on the falling edges of the strobe signals. The master tri-states its IRDY# output driver and the target tri-states its TRDY# output driver.

Back-to-Back Write Data Transactions, No Delay

Figure 9-15 on page 183 illustrates the master providing write data corresponding to a series of previously enqueued write transaction requests. The data is transferred using a series of back-to-back write data transactions, each transaction with a length of 16 bytes. Because each of these transactions only requires an initial data block, the TRDY# signal is not required to be used in any of the transactions (because there are no throttle points for subsequent data blocks). TRDY# is not driven throughout the example. A required pull-up resistor keeps it deasserted.

Chapter 9: 1X, 2X, and 4X Data Transactions

Figure 9-15: Back-to-Back Write Data Transactions, No Delays, 4X Mode

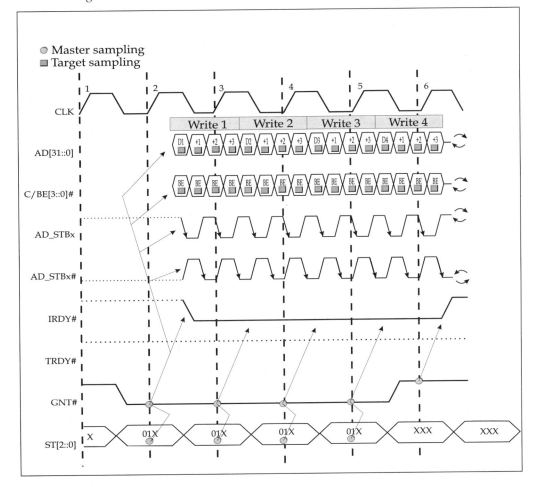

Clock 1. The arbiter asserts GNT# and provides a status of 01Xb, indicating that the target is ready for the master to begin delivery of either low- or high-priority write data.

Clock 2. The master detects the bus grant on the rising edge of clock 2 and asserts IRDY# immediately, indicating that it has started delivery of the first data block and is ready to source all of the write data at full speed. The target begins latching write data and byte enables on the falling edges of the AD_STBx strobes and the AD_STBx# strobes. The arbiter understands that the first transaction will complete in one clock (because there's less than one data block to deliver) and there is another transaction to perform. It therefore keeps GNT# asserted, pipelining it for the next transaction.

Clock 3. The target samples IRDY# asserted on the rising edge of clock 3, validating the eight bytes of data (and their byte enables) latched from the AD bus during clock 2 (and the remaining write data for the first transaction as well) as valid. The target latches the final two dwords and their byte enables, completing the 16 byte write data transfer for the first transaction in clock 3.

GNT# is detected asserted on the rising edge of clock 3, giving the master permission to begin sourcing data for the second transaction. As a result, IRDY# remains asserted, indicating to the target that the master has begun sourcing valid data for the second transaction. GNT# remains asserted during this clock, pipelining it for the third transaction.

Clock 4. The target samples IRDY# asserted on the rising edge of clock 4, validating the eight bytes of data (and their byte enables) latched from the AD bus during clock 3 (and the remaining write data for the second transaction as well) as valid. The target latches the final two dwords and their byte enables, completing the 16 byte write data transfer for the second transaction in clock 4.

GNT# is detected asserted on the rising edge of clock 4, giving the master permission to begin sourcing data for the third transaction. As a result, IRDY# remains asserted, indicating to the target that the master has begun sourcing valid data for the third transaction. GNT# remains asserted during this clock, pipelining it for the fourth transaction.

Clock 5. The target samples IRDY# asserted on the rising edge of clock 5, validating the eight bytes of data (and their byte enables) latched from the AD bus during clock 4 (and the remaining write data for the third transaction as well) as valid. The target latches the final two dwords and their byte enables, completing the 16 byte write data transfer for the third transaction in clock 5.

GNT# is detected asserted on the rising edge of clock 5, giving the master permission to begin sourcing data for the fourth transaction. As a result, IRDY# remains asserted, indicating to the target that the master has begun sourcing valid data for the fourth transaction. GNT# is deasserted, returning the status bus to a "don't care" state. The removal of the bus grant indicates that the current transaction is the final transaction in this series.

Clock 6. The target samples IRDY# asserted on the rising edge of clock 6, validating the eight bytes of data (and their byte enables) latched from the AD bus during clock 5 (and the remaining write data for the third transaction as well) as valid. The target latches the final two dwords and their byte enables, completing the 16 byte write data transfer for the fourth transaction in clock 6.

During this clock, the master ceases to drive the AD and C/BE busses, as well as the AD_STBx and AD_STBx# strobes. The master deasserts IRDY# and then tri-states its IRDY# output driver in the next clock.

10 *Fast Write Transactions*

The Previous Chapter

The previous chapter provided a detailed description of AGP data transactions in the 1X, 2X, and 4X data transfer modes.

This Chapter

This chapter provides a detailed description of Fast Write transactions in the 1X, 2X, and 4X data transfer modes.

The Next Chapter

The next chapter describes issues related to add-in cards, connectors, and the motherboard.

Introduction to the Fast Write Transaction

Whenever the processor or a PCI bus master needs to write data to the graphics accelerator, the core logic can act as the master of the transaction on the AGP bus. The core logic acts as the surrogate for the processor or the PCI bus master. The processor could be writing vertex data from a 3-D application. The PCI master could be a video capture device writing real-time video data. Because the core logic is always the target of AGP transactions, it cannot initiate an AGP write transaction to source the write data. Instead, the core logic initiates a PCI write transaction on the AGP bus to write the data to the graphics accelerator. In this PCI write transaction, the core logic (normally the target of AGP transactions) is the master, and the graphics accelerator (normally the master of AGP transactions) is the target.

At most, PCI write transactions performed on the AGP bus can transfer four bytes during an AGP clock period. At 66MHz, this yields a maximum data transfer rate of 264MB/s. Optionally, the core logic can implement the ability to perform what are called fast write transactions on the AGP bus. Fast writes allow PCI writes performed on the AGP bus by the core logic to be more efficient than standard PCI write transactions.

Essentially, a fast write transaction follows a hybrid protocol that includes aspects of both the PCI and AGP protocols. The signals involved in a fast write transaction are the same as those used in a PCI write transaction. However, flow control is implemented on a data block basis, rather than on a dword basis (as in PCI). Throttle points are used to determine when each data block will begin transmission. Fast writes can be used in 2X and 4X transfer modes, but not in 1X transfer mode. The commands issued during a fast write transaction are:

- the PCI Memory Write command, or
- the PCI Memory Write and Invalidate command.

Refer to Table 10-1. As in a PCI transaction, the command is presented on C/BE[3::0]# during the clock in which the FRAME# signal is initially asserted.

Table 10-1: PCI Command Encodings Supported for AGP Fast Write Transactions

PCI Command Type	C/BE[3::0]#
Memory Write	0111
Memory Write and Invalidate	1111

Write Transactions in 1X Mode

Refer to Figure 10-1 on page 190. To begin the discussion of fast write transactions, a standard PCI write transaction is examined. This provides a good foundation for a discussion of the fast write transaction and acts as an example for comparisons between the two.

It should also be noted that master/target combinations that do not both support fast write transaction capability, or when the core logic is performing writes to the graphics accelerator in 1X transfer mode, use standard PCI write transactions as pictured in the figure.

Chapter 10: Fast Write Transactions

The key points of difference between a standard PCI write transaction and a fast write transaction are:

- In PCI, the control signals, data, and byte enables are driven and are sampled on the rising edge of the clock. This limits the data transfer rate to a maximum of four bytes per clock period. In fast write transactions, the data is sampled using master-supplied data strobes.
- In PCI, there is a fundamental relationship between the FRAME# and IRDY# signals. The protocol for these signals must be followed for proper operation of the PCI bus. This relationship doesn't exist in fast write transactions.
- In PCI, data flow control is on a data phase basis. The initiator or the target, or both, may add wait states to any data phase to delay the transfer of the current dword. In fast write transactions, data flow control is on a data block basis, rather than a dword basis.

Figure 10-1: PCI Write Transaction

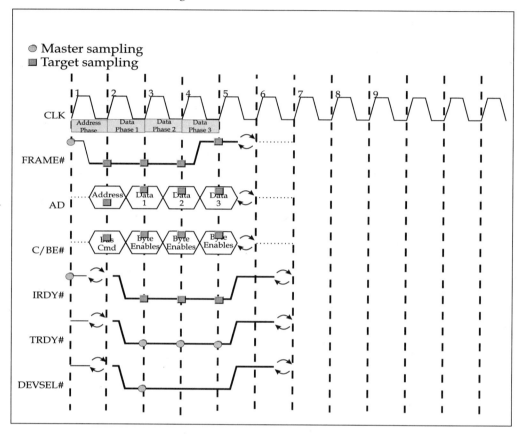

Clock 1. The bus master (the core logic) detects GNT# asserted on the rising edge of clock 1. Note that the GNT# is provided internally by the arbiter which also resides within the core logic. In addition, the bus master detects a PCI bus idle (FRAME# and IRDY# both deasserted) on the rising edge of the clock the bus master can initiate the transaction immediately in Clock 1.

The transaction starts on the rising edge of the clock when the core logic asserts FRAME# and drives out the start memory address on the AD bus and the command (memory write, or memory write and invalidate) on C/BE[3::]#.

A turn-around cycle is required on the IRDY#, TRDY#, and DEVSEL# signals to allow the previous owners of these signals to disengage their output drivers, before these signals are used in the current transaction. This eliminates any contention on these bussed signals.

Clock 2. On the rising edge of the clock, the target latches FRAME#, the address, and the command. Clock 1 is referred to as the address phase of the PCI transaction. The address phase has a duration of one clock period. The rising edge of clock 2 is the beginning of the transaction's first data phase.

During the clock, the master may begin (it can take as long as eight clocks to supply the data in any data phase) driving the first dword of write data onto the AD bus, and it must drive valid byte enables onto C/BE[3::0]# immediately upon entry into the first data phase. The master indicates the presence of the data on the AD bus by asserting IRDY# during this clock. The master keeps FRAME# asserted when it asserts IRDY#, thereby indicating to the target that the master would like to continue this transaction beyond the current data phase.

The target latched the address and command on the rising edge of the clock and, using a fast decoder, asserts DEVSEL# to claim the transaction. In this example, it also asserts TRDY# immediately (it actually has up to 16 clocks to assert TRDY# in the first data phase, and eight in any other data phase) to indicate its readiness to accept the first dword on the rising edge of clock 3.

Clock 3. On the rising edge of the clock, the target latches the data and byte enables. The data is qualified as valid by the asserted state of IRDY# on the rising edge of the clock. The master samples DEVSEL# and TRDY# asserted, indicating that the target has claimed the transaction and has accepted the first dword. The first data phase completes when the first dword has transferred, and the transaction advances to the second data phase.

During any data phase, either the master, the target, or both can throttle the transfer of a dword (in other words, delay the completion of a data phase) by keeping its respective ready signal deasserted until it is ready to transfer the dword.

During this clock, the master sources the next dword and byte enables and asserts IRDY# (actually, keeps it asserted) to indicate the presence of the data on the bus. The master indicates that this data phase is not the last by keeping FRAME# asserted when it asserts IRDY#. The target indicates its readiness to accept the data in the second data phase by keeping TRDY# asserted. DEVSEL# remains asserted throughout the transaction.

Clock 4. The second data phase completes on the rising edge of the clock when both IRDY# and TRDY# are sampled asserted. The target latches four more bytes of valid data and byte enables. The initiator keeps IRDY# asserted to indicate that it's immediately driving out the next dword, and also deasserts FRAME# to indicate that this is the final data phase.

The target indicates that it is ready to accept the next dword by keeping TRDY# asserted.

Clock 5. The final data phase completes on the rising edge of the clock. The target samples FRAME# deasserted and IRDY# asserted, indicating that the current data phase is the last. The target accepts the final four bytes of data and byte enables. In response to sampling FRAME# deasserted and IRDY# asserted, the target deasserts TRDY# and DEVSEL# during this clock.

During this clock, the master tri-states its FRAME#, AD bus, and C/BE bus output drivers. The master also deasserts IRDY#.

Clock 6. The bus returns to the idle state (FRAME# and IRDY# both deasserted). During this clock, the master tri-states its IRDY# output driver, and the target tri-states its TRDY# and DEVSEL# output drivers.

Fast Write Transactions in 2X Mode

Fast Write in 2X Mode, No Delays

Refer to Figure 10-2 on page 193. In 2X mode, eight bytes of data can be transferred during each AGP clock period. Fast write transactions in 2X mode can therefore approach a data transfer rate of 532 MB/s. In Figure 10-2 and Figure 10-3 AD_STBx represents both AD_STB0 and AD_STB1.

The key points of a fast write transaction are:

1. There is no FRAME#/IRDY# relationship as there is in PCI transactions.
2. In 2X mode, a fast write transaction can write eight bytes of data per clock period and the master supplies data strobes along with the data. The target uses the falling edge of the strobes, not the AGP clock, to latch the data.
3. Data flow control during a fast write is on the data block level rather than the dword level.
4. Only the PCI Memory Write and PCI Memory Write and Invalidate commands are supported for fast write transactions.
5. Just as in an AGP write transaction, the byte enable signals indicate which data lanes of the AD bus are used during the current dword transfer.
6. The generation and checking of PCI parity is not supported during fast write transactions.

Figure 10-2: Fast Write Transaction, No Delays, 2X Mode

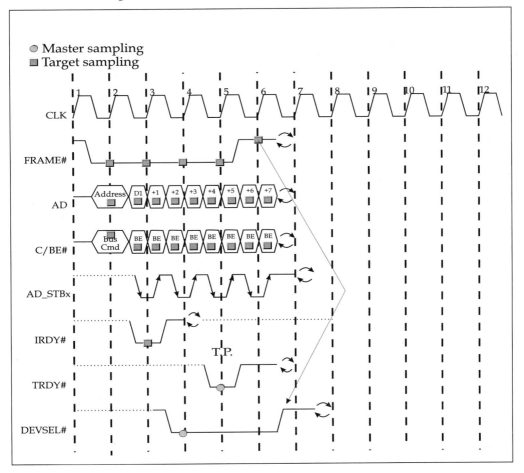

Clock 1. Just as in a PCI write transaction, a fast write begins with the master (the core logic) asserting FRAME#, driving the start address onto the AD bus, and the bus command onto the C/BE bus. The address phase of a fast write is identical to the address phase of a PCI write transaction and is one clock tick in duration.

Clock 2. On the rising edge of the clock, the target (the graphics accelerator) samples FRAME# asserted, indicating the beginning of the fast write transaction. The target latches the address and command and begins the decode.

The master begins driving the first dword of write data onto the AD bus and the byte enables onto the C/BE bus. They are latched by the target on the falling edges of the AD_STBx strobes. Once the transaction has begun, the target cannot throttle the data transfer of the initial block (in other words, it must be capable of accepting it at full speed). As a reminder, the block size in 2X mode is 32 bytes (eight bytes per clock * four clocks = 32 bytes per data block). During this clock, the master asserts IRDY# indicating that it has begun delivery of the initial block of data.

The assertion of IRDY# in clock 2 is the fastest that the master can begin sourcing the data. At the latest, the master could asserts IRDY# in clock 3. FRAME# remains asserted until the clock prior to the last transfer.

Clock 3. FRAME# remains asserted. The target latches valid write data and byte enables on the rising and falling edges of the AD_STBx strobes during this clock. IRDY# is only asserted for one clock to indicate that the master has started sourcing the data, so the master deasserts IRDY# during this clock. The target claims the transaction by asserting DEVSEL#. DEVSEL# could have been asserted during Clock 2 if the target had a fast decoder.

Clock 4. The master samples DEVSEL# asserted on the rising edge of the clock, indicating that the target has claimed the transaction. The throttle point for the second data block (if there is one) is the rising edge of clock 5. Unlike AGP transactions, which have the transfer length encoded in the transaction request, PCI and AGP fast write transactions do not provide transfer length information. The duration of the transaction, assuming the target does not terminate the transaction prematurely, is indicated by how long the master keeps FRAME# asserted.

FRAME# is still asserted, indicating that the transaction will not complete in the next clock. The target asserts TRDY#, indicating that it will be ready to start the transfer of the second data block (if there is one) two clocks later. Unknown to the target, this transaction has only one data block (32 bytes of data). The target prepares to accept the subsequent block. However, the throttle point on the rising edge of clock 5 is meaningless due to the length of the transaction.

The initiator stops driving IRDY# during this clock (because IRDY# is no longer required for this transaction). If the transaction had a second data block, then the IRDY# signal would be used by the initiator to indicate its readiness to transfer the subsequent block.

The target continues to latch data and byte enables on the rising and falling edges of the AD_STBx strobes during this clock.

Clock 5. During this clock, the master deasserts FRAME# to indicate that the next clock is the last clock of the transaction. The target continues latching four bytes of valid data and valid byte enables on the rising and falling edges of the AD_STBx strobes. IRDY# is not asserted during this clock because there isn't a second data block, and the throttle point for the second data block is therefore not used. When TRDY# is asserted by the target of a fast write transaction, it is only asserted for one clock per throttle point, so the target deasserts TRDY# during this clock.

Clock 6. The target samples FRAME# deasserted on the rising edge of the clock, indicating that is the final clock of the transaction. During this clock, the master stops driving FRAME#, returning it to the high-impedance state. The target latches the final four bytes of data and byte enables on the rising edges of the AD_STBx signals. A total of 32 bytes have been written to the graphics accelerator in this transaction. After the final dword is driven, the master stops driving the AD and C/BE busses during this clock. The master also stops driving the AD_STBx strobes.

The target stops driving TRDY# in this clock. DEVSEL# is deasserted by the target in response to sampling FRAME# deasserted on the rising edge of the clock. The target stops driving DEVSEL# in Clock 7.

Fast Write in 2X Mode, Wait States Added

The rules for adding wait states to a fast write transaction are as follows:

- The master may add one wait state between the address phase and start of the first data block transfer. The initiator keeps IRDY# deasserted for one extra clock to add this wait state.
- The target cannot delay the transfer of the first data block.
- Both the initiator and the target can add one or more wait states to the transfer of a subsequent block of data. The target adds wait states to a subsequent block by driving the TRDY# signal deasserted at the throttle point. The initiator adds wait states to a subsequent block by driving IRDY# deasserted unitil ready to begin transferring the subsequent block. The IRDY# signal is not relevant at the throttle point.

Figure 10-3 on page 196 illustrates a fast write transaction performed in 2X transfer mode. The amount of data to be transferred is 64 bytes. With 64 bytes to transfer, this transaction has an initial data block of 32 bytes, and a second data block, also of 32 bytes. At the throttle point for the second data block, the target delays the transfer of that block by one AGP clock.

Figure 10-3: Fast Write Transaction, Wait States Added, 2X Mode

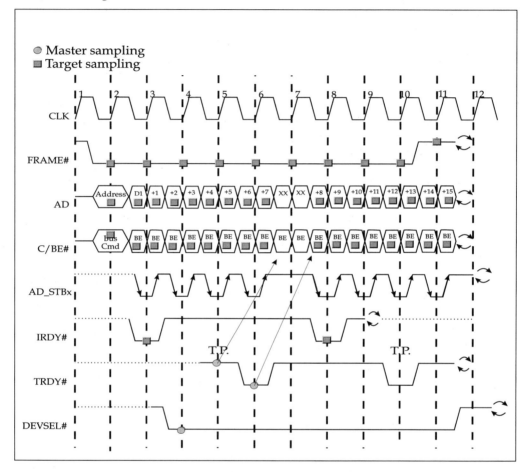

Clock 1. The transaction begins with the master asserting FRAME#, driving the start address onto the AD bus, and the bus command onto the C/BE bus.

Clock 2. The target samples FRAME#, the address, and the command on the rising edge of the clock.

The master begins driving the first dword of write data onto the AD bus and the byte enables onto the C/BE bus. They are latched by the target on the falling edges of the AD_STBx signals. During this clock, the master asserts IRDY# to indicate that it has begun sourcing the first data block.

Clock 3. The target latches valid write data and byte enables on the rising and falling edges of the AD_STBx signals during this clock. IRDY# is sampled asserted. The initiator then deasserts IRDY# after a one clock assertion. The target completes the decode and asserts DEVSEL# to claim the transaction. The master kept FRAME# asserted, indicating that the next clock is not the final clock of the transaction.

Clock 4. DEVSEL# is detected asserted on the rising edge of the clock, indicating that the target has claimed the transaction. The target continues to latch data and byte enables on the rising and falling edges of the AD_STBx strobes. FRAME# remains asserted, indicating that the next clock is not the final clock of the transaction.

Clock 5. The rising edge of clock 5 is the throttle point for the second data block of this transaction. The throttle point occurs two clocks before the earliest point at which the second data block could begin transferring. In fast write transactions, the target (the graphics accelerator) can deassert TRDY# at the throttle point to delay the transfer of the next data block. On the rising edge of clock 5, the master samples TRDY# deasserted, indicating that the second data block cannot begin to transfer two clocks later. The transfer of the second data block will be delayed by the number of clocks that TRDY# remains deasserted. In this example, TRDY# is only deasserted for one clock, so the start of the transfer of the subsequent block is only delayed by one clock.

During Clock 5, the target continues latching data for the first data block on the falling and rising edges of the strobe signals. FRAME# remains asserted, indicating that the next clock is not the final clock of the transaction.

Clock 6. On the rising edge of the clock, the initiator samples TRDY# asserted, indicating that the target will be ready to accept the entire subsequent block starting two clocks from this point. The final dword of the initial data block is latched by the target during this clock. The state of the AD bus and byte enables during the wait state is a "don't care." The data on the AD bus could be the last dword of the first data block, the first dword of the second data block, or meaningless data. The data and byte enables are not latched by the target during the wait state (because there are no data strobes generated by the master).

The AD_STBx signals are driven high during the wait state. IRDY# remains deasserted until the wait state is over (because the master only asserts IRDY# when it starts sourcing the next data block). TRDY# is only asserted for one clock at the throttle point and is then deasserted.

Clock 7. The wait state ends during this clock. The master asserts IRDY# and begins sourcing the first valid dword and byte enables of the second data block during this clock. The data is latched by the target on the falling and rising edges of the AD_STBx signals.

Clock 8. The target samples IRDY# asserted on the rising edge of the clock, indicating that the master has started sourcing all of the write data for the second data block. IRDY# is only asserted for one clock. The target latches data and byte enables on the rising and falling edges of the strobes during this clock.

Clock 9. The master stops driving IRDY# during this clock because there are no data blocks beyond the second one. The target latches data and byte enables on the rising and falling edges of the strobes during this clock. TRDY# is asserted by the target in anticipation of a third data block (there isn't one in this transaction).

Clock 10. This clock would be the throttle point for the third data block if there were one. Since this block is not required, the throttle point is also not required and the assertion of TRDY# has no meaning on this clock. The target only needs to assert TRDY# for one clock, so target deasserts TRDY# during this clock.

During this clock, the target continues latching dwords and byte enables of the second data block on the rising and falling edges of the strobes. The master deasserts FRAME#, indicating that the next clock is the final clock of the transaction.

Clock 11. On the rising edge of the clock, the target samples FRAME# deasserted, indicating that this is the final clock of this transaction. The target latches the final dword and byte enables on the rising edges of the AD_STBx signals. In response to sampling FRAME# deasserted, the target deasserts DEVSEL# during this clock and stops driving TRDY#.

After the final dword is transferred, the master stops driving the strobes, the AD bus, and the C/BE# bus. The master stops driving FRAME# in this clock.

Clock 12. The target stops driving DEVSEL# in this clock.

Fast Write Transactions in 4X Mode

Refer to Figure 10-4 on page 199. In 4X mode, 16 bytes of data can be transferred during each AGP clock period. Therefore, fast write transactions in 4X mode can approach a data transfer rate of 1GB/s. The block size in 4X mode is 64 bytes. The example that follows shows a fast write transaction with a single block of 64 bytes. The protocol for fast writes in 4X mode is identical to fast writes in 2X mode. The data rate is doubled, however, due to the addition of the complement strobes, AD_STB[1::0]#. As described earlier in "4X Transfer Mode Data Transactions" on page 172, the target could use the AD_STBx and AD_STBx# strobes as two differential signal pairs, or could just use the falling edges of both strobes to latch the data and byte enables (as pictured in Figure 10-4). In Figure 10-4:

- AD_STBx represents both AD_STB0 and AD_STB1.
- AD_STBx# represents both AD_STB0# and AD_STB1#.

Figure 10-4: Fast Write Transaction, 4X Mode

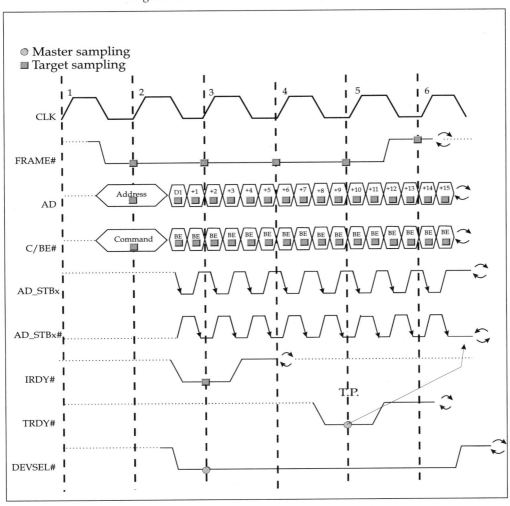

Clock 1. The transaction begins with the master (the core logic) asserting FRAME#, driving the start address onto the AD bus, and the command onto the C/BE bus. The address phase is always one AGP clock period in duration, regardless of the data transfer rate.

Clock 2. The target samples FRAME# asserted and latches the address and command on the rising edge of the clock. These signals are decoded and the target (the graphics accelerator) asserts DEVSEL# to claim the transaction.

The master sources the first two dwords of write data onto the AD bus and the byte enables onto the C/BE bus during this clock and they are latched by the target on the falling edges of the AD_STBx and AD_STBx# signals. During this clock, the initiator asserts IRDY#, indicating that it has started delivery of the first data block.

Clock 3. Four more dwords and four sets of byte enables are latched by the target on the falling edges of the strobes during this clock. IRDY# is detected asserted by the target, indicating that the core logic has started the delivery of the first data block and qualifying the data already latched as good. IRDY# need only be asserted for one clock for the entire initial block, so the master deasserts IRDY# during this clock.

Clock 4. Four additional dwords and their byte enables are transferred during this clock. The master stops driving IRDY# (it doesn't need it anymore because there are no additional data blocks beyond the first). The target asserts TRDY# during this clock in anticipation of another data block (but there won't be one). Since the transfer can be completed in a single data block, the throttle point and assertion of TRDY# are meaningless.

Clock 5. The master deasserts FRAME# during this clock, indicating that the transaction will end in the next clock. TRDY# is deasserted after a one clock assertion. The target latches an additional 16 bytes of data and their byte enables during this clock.

Clock 6. The target samples FRAME# deasserted on the rising edge of the clock, indicating that this is the final clock of the transaction. The master stops driving FRAME# during this clock and completes the transfer of the last two dwords. The master stops driving the AD and C/BE busses, as well as the AD_STBx and AD_STBx# strobes. In response to FRAME# being sampled deasserted, the target stops driving TRDY#. DEVSEL# is deasserted in this clock and the target stops driving it in the next clock.

Chapter 10: Fast Write Transactions

Target-Initiated Premature Transaction Termination

In the PCI protocol, the target can terminate a transaction prematurely before the master has transferred all of the data. To do this, the target asserts STOP#. Using a combination of the STOP#, TRDY#, and DEVSEL# signals, a PCI target can signal a retry, a disconnect, or a target abort. When acting as the target of a fast write transaction, the graphics accelerator can use STOP# to terminate a fast write transaction prematurely. Each of the termination types are discussed in the sections that follow.

Retry

The PCI **Retry** termination is **not supported** in fast write transactions. Retry is a premature termination of a PCI transaction that occurs in the first data phase before any data is transferred. The master of a transaction that results in a retry is required to terminate the current transaction with no data transferred and must periodically retry it until the data is transferred. The target (the graphics accelerator) of a fast write transaction must accept at least the initial data block of data, once the transaction has begun.

If a target (the graphics accelerator) cannot accept fast write transactions at this time, it must assert WBF# (Write Buffer Full) to the core logic. The core logic is prohibited from initiating fast write transactions while WBF# is asserted. Using WBF# eliminates the need to support PCI Retries. WBF# is described in more detail later in this chapter.

Disconnect

The PCI disconnect termination is supported in fast write transactions. There are two possible scenarios when a target issues a disconnect to the master:

- Disconnect after the subsequent data block has been transferred.
- Disconnect before the subsequent data block is transferred.

In both scenarios, the target claims the transaction by asserting DEVSEL#, receives at least the first data block from the master, and then asserts STOP# to indicate to the master that the transaction must be terminated. Both forms of disconnect are examined using examples.

Disconnect with Subsequent Data Block Transferred

A disconnect with subsequent data block transferred is signaled by asserting STOP# at a throttle point with TRDY# also asserted. This indicates to the master that the target is ready to accept the subsequent block of the transaction (TRDY#), but then it wants the master to stop the transaction (STOP#). Figure 10-5 illustrates this scenario in 2X transfer mode.

Figure 10-5: Fast Write Transaction, Disconnect with Subsequent Data Transferred

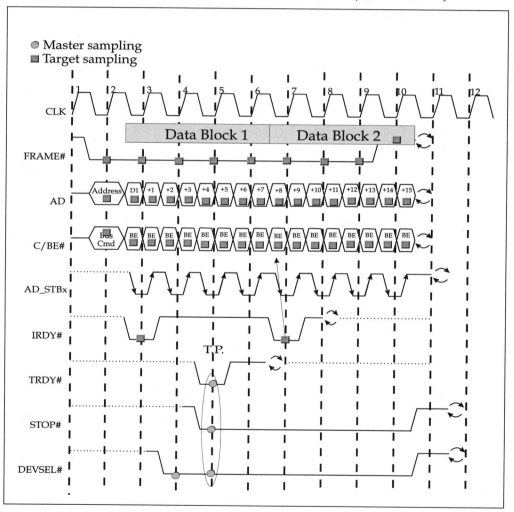

Clock 1. The transaction begins with the master asserting FRAME#, driving the start address onto the AD bus, and the command onto the C/BE bus.

Clock 2. On the rising edge of the clock, the target samples FRAME# asserted latches the address and command, and begins the decode of these signals.

The master begins driving the first dword of write data onto the AD bus and the byte enables onto the C/BE bus. These signals are latched by the target on the falling edges of the AD_STBx signals. During this clock, the master asserts IRDY#, indicating that has begun sourcing the first data block.

Clock 3. The target latches valid write data and byte enables on the rising and falling edges of the AD_STBx signals during this clock. The target samples IRDY# asserted, validating the data it has already latched as good. IRDY# is then deasserted.

The target claims the transaction by asserting the DEVSEL# signal during this clock.

Clock 4. The master samples DEVSEL# asserted on the rising edge of the clock. The rising edge of the next clock is the throttle point for the second data block. TRDY# is asserted during this clock, indicating that the target will be ready to accept the second data block starting two clocks after the throttle point. However, the target has also asserted STOP#, indicating to the master that the second data block is the last that the target is willing to accept in this transaction.

As was the case during the previous clock, the target continues to latch data and byte enables on the rising and falling edges of the AD_STBx strobes during this clock.

Clock 5. On the rising edge of the clock, the master samples TRDY# and STOP# asserted. This indicates that the target will be ready to accept the second data block starting two clocks later, but cannot accept any additional data blocks beyond that one at the current time. The target continues to latch data and byte enables on the rising and falling edges of the AD_STBx strobes during this clock. The target deasserts TRDY# during this clock.

Clock 6. Once the target asserts STOP#, it must remain asserted until the transaction is over. The target latches the final dword of the first data block on the rising edges of the AD_STBx signals. The target latches the first dword of the second data block on the falling edges of the AD_STBx signals. The master asserts IRDY# to indicate that it has started driving the second data block. The target stops driving TRDY# during this clock.

Clock 7. IRDY# is sampled asserted by the target, validating the second data block's data that it started latching on the falling edge of the strobes in the previous clock. The initiator now deasserts IRDY#. The second and third dwords of the second data block transfer during this clock.

Clock 8. The master stops driving IRDY#. The fourth and fifth dwords of the second data block transfer during this clock.

Clock 9. FRAME# is deasserted during this clock, indicating that the next clock is the final clock of the transaction. The sixth and seventh dwords of the second data block transfer during this clock.

Clock 10. FRAME# is sampled deasserted by the target on the rising edge of the clock. In response to this, the target deasserts DEVSEL# and STOP# during this clock. The master stops driving FRAME# during this clock. The final dword is transferred on the rising edges of the AD_STBx strobes, after which the master stops driving the AD and C/BE busses.

Clock 11. The target stops driving DEVSEL# and STOP# during this clock. Required pull-up resistors keep these signals deasserted when they are not being driven.

Disconnect without Subsequent Data Block Transferred

Refer to Figure 10-6 on page 205. A disconnect without transferring the subsequent data block is signaled when the target asserts STOP# at a throttle point with TRDY# deasserted. This indicates to the master that the target is not ready to accept the subsequent data block of the transaction (TRDY# high), and the data block just finishing its transfer is the final data block for this transaction (STOP#). The example is in 2X transfer mode.

Figure 10-6: Fast Write Transaction, Disconnect without Subsequent Data Transferred

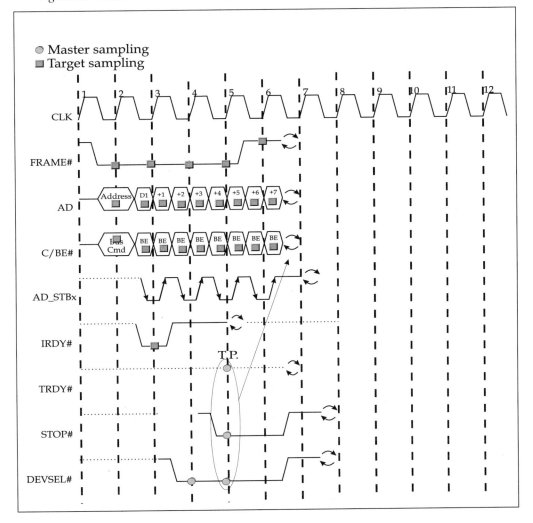

Clock 1. The transaction begins with the master asserting FRAME#, driving the start address onto the AD bus, and the command onto the C/BE bus.

Clock 2. On the rising edge of the clock, the target samples FRAME# asserted, indicating the beginning of the fast write transaction and latches the address and command. It begins the decode of these signals. The master begins driving the first dword of write data onto the AD bus and the byte enables onto the C/BE bus. These signals are latched by the target on the falling edges of the

AD_STBx signals. During this clock, the master asserts IRDY# indicating that it has started delivering the first data block.

Clock 3. The target samples IRDY# asserted on the rising edge of the clock, indicating that the master has started delivering the first data block. During this clock:

- The target latches four valid bytes and their byte enables on the rising and again on the falling edges of the AD bus strobes.
- IRDY# is deasserted by the master.
- DEVSEL# is asserted by the target to claim the transaction.

Clock 4. The master samples DEVSEL# asserted on the rising edge of the clock, indicating that the target has claimed the transaction. During this clock:

- The target latches four valid bytes and their byte enables on the rising and again on the falling edges of the AD bus strobes.
- The target asserts the STOP# signal.

Clock 5. The rising edge of the clock is the throttle point for the second data block. The master detects STOP# asserted and TRDY# deasserted. This indicates that the target is terminating the transaction after the completion of the transfer of the initial block, without any data from the second data block being transferred. A throttle point ends when either TRDY# or STOP# is detected asserted. During this clock:

- The target latches four valid bytes and their byte enables on the rising and again on the falling edges of the AD bus strobes.
- The master deasserts FRAME# in response to the target asserting STOP#. The next clock is the final clock of the initial data block transfer. Because of STOP#, it is also the final clock of the transaction. The subsequent data block, if it exists, will not be transferred during this transaction.
- In response to sampling STOP# asserted, the master also stops driving IRDY#.

Clock 6. The target samples FRAME# deasserted on the rising edge of the clock, indicating that this is the final clock of the transaction. The target deasserts DEVSEL# and STOP# in this clock. After the transfer of the final dword of the initial data block on the rising edges of the AD_STBx signals, the master stop driving the AD and C/BE busses, as well as the AD_STBx signals. It also stops driving FRAME# in this clock.

Clock 7. The target stops driving DEVSEL# and STOP# during this clock.

The arbiter within the core logic cannot grant the bus to another bus master until the current transaction is over. This is applicable when the current transaction is a fast write. The arbiter must ensure that granting the bus to another bus master will cause no contention on any signal. As an example, if the next transaction were a PCI transaction initiated by the graphics accelerator (acting as a PCI bus master), it could not start until clock 7, at the earliest. Therefore, to avoid contention the earliest that the core logic could grant the bus to the PCI bus master would be during Clock 6.

Target Abort

Refer to Figure 10-7 on page 208. The PCI target abort termination is supported in fast write transactions. In a fast write transaction, target abort is signaled at the throttle point. DEVSEL# is initially asserted by the target to claim the transaction. Subsequently, STOP# is asserted, while DEVSEL# and TRDY# are deasserted, at the throttle point. Essentially, the target abort indicates to the master that the transaction is terminated (STOP# asserted), with no subsequent data block transferred (TRDY# deasserted), and the target is no longer claiming this transaction (DEVSEL# deasserted). For reasons that are specific to the implementation of the target, the target can no longer participate in this transaction. The target also does not want this transaction repeated. Signaling a target abort is always abnormal behavior and implies an error condition.

Figure 10-7: Fast Write Transaction, Target Abort

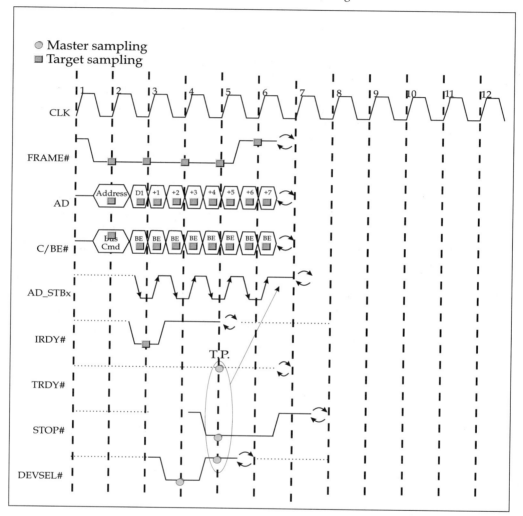

Clock 1. The transaction begins with the master asserting FRAME#, driving the start address onto the AD bus, and the command onto the C/BE bus.

Clock 2. On the rising edge of the clock, the target samples FRAME# asserted, indicating the beginning of the fast write transaction, latches the address and command, and begins the decode of these signals.

The master begins driving the first dword of write data onto the AD bus and the byte enables onto the C/BE bus and they are latched by the target on the falling edges of the AD_STBx signals. During this clock, the master asserts IRDY#, indicating that it has started delivery of the first data block.

Clock 3. The target samples IRDY# asserted on the rising edge of the clock, indicating that the master has started delivery of the first data block. During this clock, DEVSEL# is asserted by the target to claim the transaction. To signal a target abort, the target must first claim the transaction, by asserting DEVSEL#. The specification also states that the target must accept the first block of data. Keep in mind, that if the target is signaling a target abort, the successful receipt of the first data block is questionable.

Clock 4. The master detects DEVSEL# asserted on the rising edge of the clock. The master also continues sourcing valid data and byte enables during this clock on the rising and falling edges of the AD_STBx signals. During this clock, the target signals the target abort:

- it deasserts DEVSEL#,
- asserts STOP#, and
- keeps TRDY# deasserted.

The next rising edge of the clock is the throttle point for the subsequent block of the transaction.

Clock 5. On the rising edge of the clock, the master samples STOP#, TRDY#, and DEVSEL# and recognizes the target abort. The master interprets a target abort as a termination due to a target error condition. In response to the target abort, the master:

- Deasserts FRAME#, indicating that the next clock cycle is the final clock cycle of the transaction.
- Stops driving IRDY#, since it is no longer required for this transaction.
- The target stops driving DEVSEL# during this clock.

Clock 6. On the rising edge of the clock, the target samples FRAME# deasserted, indicating that this is the final clock of the transaction. In response, the target deasserts STOP# during this clock. After the completion of the transfer of the initial block, the master stops driving the AD and C/BE busses, as well as the AD_STBx strobes.

Clock 7. The target stops driving STOP# during this clock.

Master-Initiated Premature Transaction Termination

Refer to Figure 10-8 on page 211. The PCI master abort mechanism is supported in fast write transactions on the AGP bus. In PCI, a master is required to abort a transaction when no target claims the transaction (by asserting the DEVSEL#) within a predetermined amount of time. Likewise, the core logic is also required to master abort a fast write transaction after four clocks during which the graphics accelerator has not asserted DEVSEL#.

There is one difference between a PCI transaction that is terminated with a master abort and an AGP fast write transaction that is terminated with a master abort. In a PCI transaction, there is no transfer of data during an aborted transaction. In a fast write transaction, assuming that the WBF# signal has not been asserted by the graphics controller, the graphics controller is required to accept the first data block, *even if the transaction is terminated with a master abort*. However, the integrity of the data transfer is questionable.

Master abort of a fast write transaction is typically considered to be an error condition. The error reporting and handling of this error condition is core logic, implementation-specific.

Figure 10-8: Fast Write Transaction, Master Abort

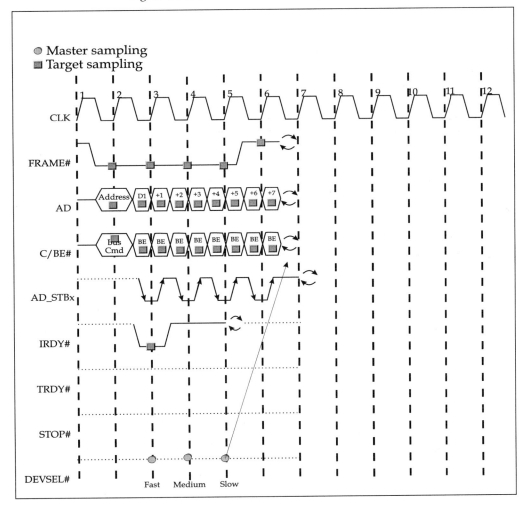

Clock 1. The transaction begins with the master asserting FRAME#, driving the start address onto the AD bus, and the command onto the C/BE bus.

Clock 2. On the rising edge of the clock, the address and command are valid, as indicated by the assertion of FRAME#. During this clock, the master drives the first dword and byte enables and asserts IRDY# to indicate that it has started delivery of the first data block. The target (the graphics controller) latches the dword and byte enables on the falling edge of the AD_STBx strobes.

Clock 3. On the rising edge of the clock, the master samples DEVSEL# for the first time and it has not yet been asserted. The assertion of DEVSEL# during Clock 2 is known as a fast decode.

IRDY# is sampled asserted, indicating that the master has started delivery of the first data block. IRDY# is then deasserted by the master. The master sources eight bytes of valid write data and byte enables on the rising and falling edges of the AD_STBx signals during this clock.

Clock 4. On the rising edge of the clock, the master again samples DEVSEL# and it's still not asserted. The assertion of DEVSEL# during Clock 3 is known as a medium speed decode.

The initiator sources eight bytes of valid write data and byte enables on the rising and falling edges of the AD_STBx signals during this clock.

Clock 5. On the rising edge of the clock, the master samples DEVSEL# for the final time and it's still not asserted. The assertion of DEVSEL# during Clock 4 is known as a slow decode. The master's DEVSEL# sampling logic times out and considers this to be a master abort (in other words, no target has responded).

In order to abort this transaction, the master:

- deasserts FRAME#, indicating that the next clock is the final clock of the transaction.
- stops driving IRDY# during this clock.
- must finish the transfer of the initial block of data.

The master sources eight bytes of valid write data and byte enables on the rising and falling edges of the AD_STBx signals during this clock.

Clock 6. During this clock, the master sources the final dword and byte enables of the initial data block. After doing so, the master stops driving the AD bus, the C/BE bus, the AD_STBx signals, and FRAME#.

Back-to-Back Fast Write Transactions

PCI transactions, AGP transactions, and Fast Write transactions can all be performed on the AGP bus. The AGP specification describes the relationship between two back-to-back transactions, when one of the transactions is a fast write. There is a table in the specification (not duplicated here) that describes for each possible combination whether a turn-around cycle is required between the first transaction and the second transaction.

To summarize the table:

- If a fast write transaction follows another fast write transaction, a turn-around clock may not be required between the two.
- If a fast write transaction precedes a PCI read transaction initiated by the core logic, a turn-around clock between the two may not be required.
- For every other type of transaction that could precede or follow a fast write, a turn around clock is required between the first and second transaction.

If two transactions occur without a turn-around clock between the transactions, then the transactions are referred to as fast back-to-back transactions.

Please note that the arbiter must consider the transaction type of the current transaction in deciding when to grant the bus for the next transaction. The arbiter cannot grant the bus to the next master in such a way that results in contention on any signals. IRDY# and TRDY# in particular, are signals that need to be taken into special consideration in this regard when designing an arbiter.

As the designer of a device that can initiate fast write transactions, there is no requirement to implement the ability to generate fast back-to-back transactions. An example of two back-to-back transactions that are not fast back-to-back is shown in Figure 10-9 on page 214. The example is in 2X transfer mode.

Figure 10-9: Back-to-Back, Fast Write Transactions

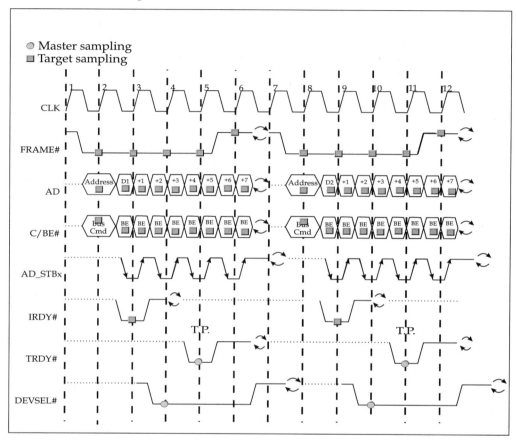

Clock 1. The first transaction begins with the master asserting FRAME#, driving the start address onto the AD bus, and the command onto the C/BE bus.

Clock 2. On the rising edge of the clock, the target samples FRAME# asserted, indicating the beginning of the fast write transaction, latches the address and command, and begins the decode of these signals. The master begins driving the first dword of write data onto the AD bus and the byte enables onto the C/BE bus, and they are latched by the target on the falling edges of the AD_STBx signals. During this clock, the master asserts IRDY#, indicating that it has started delivery of the first data block.

Clock 3. The target latches valid write data and byte enables on the rising and falling edges of the AD_STBx signals during this clock. The master deasserts IRDY#. The target claims the transaction by asserting DEVSEL#.

Clock 4. The master detects DEVSEL# asserted by the target on the rising edge of the clock. The target asserts TRDY#, indicating that it will be ready to accept the subsequent data block (if there were one, which there isn't) two clocks later. Due to the length of the transaction, this assertion of TRDY# and the throttle point on the rising edge of Clock 5 are meaningless.

The master stops driving IRDY# during this clock (it's no longer required for this transaction because there aren't any more data blocks). As in the previous clock, the target continues to latch data and byte enables on the rising and falling edges of the AD_STBx strobes during this clock.

Clock 5. During this clock, the master deasserts FRAME#, indicating that the next clock is the last clock of the transaction. The target continues latching four bytes of valid data and valid byte enables on the rising and falling edges of the AD_STBx strobes. TRDY# is deasserted because the next data block's throttle point is over.

Clock 6. The target samples FRAME# deasserted on the rising edge of the clock, indicating that this is the final clock of the transaction. During this clock, the master stops driving FRAME#, returning it to the high-impedance state. The target latches the final four bytes of data and byte enables on the rising edges of the AD_STBx signals. After the final dword is driven, the master stops driving the AD and C/BE busses during this clock.

Clock 7. The master stops driving the AD_STBx signals during this clock. The same master, the core logic, initiates another fast write transaction during this clock, by asserting FRAME#, and driving out the start address and command. Since the previous transaction was also a fast write, the same agent that's driving the AD and C/BE busses and FRAME# during clock 5 is driving those signals during this clock. Potentially, clock 6 could have been eliminated, reducing the latency for performing the next transaction by one clock period.

If, in clock 6 of the first transaction, the master used the maximum delay after the rising edge of the clock to drive AD_STBx low, then clock 6, the turn around clock, cannot be eliminated. This is because the data transfer in clock 6 would consume most of the clock period. By doing so, there would be insufficient time in clock 6 to drive the address and command for the next transaction before the rising edge of Clock 7. The minimum setup time specification, relative to the rising edge of Clock 7, cannot be violated when performing these "fast" back-to-back transactions.

Clock 8. From this point forward, the second transaction proceeds identically to the first transaction.

AGP System Architecture

Fast Back-to-Back, Fast Write Transactions

Figure 10-10 shows the idle clock removed between the two transactions. This can be done when performing back-to-back fast write transactions if the core logic is able to assert the AD_STBx signals fast enough in the final clock of the first transaction, such that there is sufficient time left in that clock to drive the address and command information for the next transaction. This is referred to as a *fast* back-to-back pair of transactions. The example uses 2X transfer mode.

Figure 10-10: Fast Back-to-Back, Fast Write Transactions

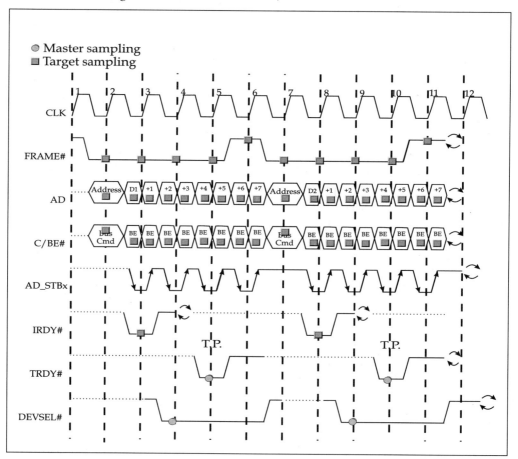

Clock 1. In this clock, the master asserts FRAME#, drives the start address onto the AD bus, and the command onto the C/BE bus.

Clock 2. On the rising edge of the clock, the target samples FRAME# asserted, indicating the beginning of the fast write transaction, latches the address and command, and begins the decode of these signals. The master begins driving the first dword of write data onto the AD bus and the byte enables onto the C/BE bus, and they are latched by the target on the falling edges of the AD_STBx signals. During this clock, the master asserts IRDY#, indicating that it has begun delivery of the first data block.

The master is driving the AD_STBx strobes low as quickly as the spec permits, relative to the rising edge of clock 2. This minimum delay strobe occurs in each clock of the transaction, allowing the first transaction to finish early in Clock 6. There will be enough time for the next transaction to then begin in the latter part of clock 6.

Clock 3. The target latches valid write data and byte enables on the rising and falling edges of the AD_STBx signals during this clock. Notice that the second and third dwords transfer within clock 3. This is possible because the minimum delay for the AD_STBx strobes is being used by the master of this transaction.

The initiator deasserts IRDY#. The target claims the transaction by asserting DEVSEL# during this clock.

Clock 4. The master samples DEVSEL# asserted on the rising edge of the clock. The master stops driving IRDY# during this clock (because IRDY# is no longer required for this transaction). The target continues to latch data and byte enables on the rising and falling edges of the AD_STBx strobes, during this clock.

Clock 5. During this clock, the master deasserts FRAME#, indicating that the next clock is the last clock of the transaction. The target continues latching four bytes of valid data and valid byte enables on the rising and falling edges of the AD_STBx strobes. The target deasserts TRDY# during this clock.

Clock 6. The target samples FRAME# deasserted on the rising edge of the clock, indicating that this is the final clock of the transaction. During this clock, rather than turn off its FRAME# output driver, the master reasserts FRAME# to indicate the start of the next transaction. It also drives out the start address and command for the next transaction.

The target latches the final four bytes of data and byte enables on the rising edges of the AD_STBx signals. This occurs early in clock 6. After the final dword is latched, rather than turning off its output drivers, the master sources the address and command for the next transaction in the latter part of clock 6.

During this clock and throughout the first transaction, the master used the minimum delay after the rising edge of the clock to drive the strobes low. This permitted the first transaction's final data transfer to complete soon enough in clock 6 to allow the next transaction to start in the latter part of clock 6. Since the ownership of the bussed signals used in the two transactions does not change, the elimination of the turn around clock between the transactions is permitted. The graphics accelerator, acting as the target of fast write transactions, is required to handle this optimization. It is optional whether or not the core logic is capable of performing fast back-to-back fast write transaction pairs.

Clock 7. On the rising edge of the clock, the target samples FRAME# asserted, indicating the beginning of a new transaction. New address and command information is provided by the master of the transaction. The first dword also transfers during this clock on the falling edges of the AD_STBx signals. By eliminating the idle clock in between the transactions, this dword transfers one clock earlier than in the previous example (Figure 10-9 on page 214).

Clock 8. The second transaction proceeds identically to the first transaction, from this point forward.

Use of the WBF# Signal

When the core logic is designed to initiate fast write transactions, the WBF# signal (Write Buffer Full) must be implemented as an input to the arbiter. It is an optional output from the graphics accelerator. As the name implies, when WBF# is asserted, the target cannot tolerate the initiation of new fast write transactions due to a write buffer full condition. The core logic is not allowed to initiate fast write transactions while WBF# is asserted.

This signal is optional from the target's perspective, because, due to speed and/ or buffer depth, it may always be ready to accept the first data block of a fast write transaction. When WBF# is deasserted, the target must be able to accept a minimum of five clocks of data without terminating the transaction prematurely or adding wait states. Five clocks of data buffering are required (and not four) because there may be a scenario where the first transaction of a fast back-to-back transaction pair only transfers a single dword. In this case, there is not enough time to assert WBF# during the first transaction to prevent the initiation of the second transaction.

Five clocks of data in 2X mode would be 40 bytes. Five clocks of data in 4X mode would be 80 bytes.

Chapter 10: Fast Write Transactions

In order to prevent the next transaction from being initiated, WBF# is required to be asserted two clocks prior to when the next fast write transaction will begin. This is illustrated in Figure10-11.

Figure 10-11: Write Buffer Full Prevents Next Transaction

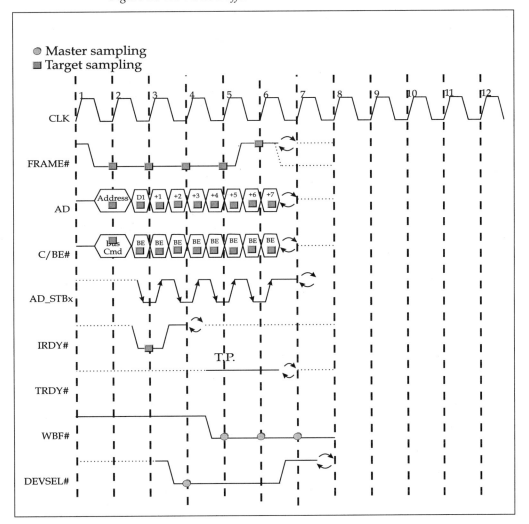

Clock 1. In this clock, the master asserts FRAME#, drives the start address onto the AD bus, and the command onto the C/BE bus.

Clock 2. On the rising edge of the clock, the target samples FRAME# asserted, indicating the beginning of the transaction, latches the address and command, and begins the decode of these signals. The master begins driving the first dword of write data onto the AD bus and the byte enables onto the C/BE bus, and they are latched by the target on the falling edges of the AD_STBx signals. During this clock, the master asserts IRDY#, indicating that it has started delivery of the first data block.

Clock 3. The target latches valid write data and byte enables on the rising and falling edges of the AD_STBx signals during this clock. The master deasserts IRDY#. The target claims the transaction by asserting DEVSEL#.

Clock 4. The master detects DEVSEL# asserted on the rising edge of the clock. The target continues to latch data and byte enables on the rising and falling edges of the AD_STBx strobes during this clock.

This transaction is filling the target's write buffers and, in this example, the target cannot deal with another write transaction immediately after this one. The target asserts WBF# during this clock, to prohibit the master from initiating another fast back-to-back fast write transaction in clock 6.

Also note that the target doesn't assert TRDY# in this clock. Due to the write buffer full condition, the target may opt to use TRDY# to delay the transfer of the next data block in this transaction. As another option, the target may signal a disconnect in this clock (by asserting STOP#).

Clock 5. On the rising edge of the clock, WBF# is detected asserted by the core logic. The master is prohibited from initiating a fast write transaction until WBF# is detected deasserted. If the next transaction were not a fast back-to-back fast write transaction, then WBF# could have been asserted in this clock to prevent the next transaction from beginning in clock 7. The target has no way of knowing in advance if the next transaction will be fast back-to-back.

In this clock, the master deasserts FRAME#, indicating that the next clock is the final clock of the transaction. Assuming that a disconnect was not signaled by the target (i.e., STOP# was not asserted), the deassertion of FRAME# in this clock is the beginning of a "normal" termination for this transaction. The assumption here is that the transaction was just one block (32 bytes) in length.

Clock 6. The transfer of the final dword occurs during this clock on the rising edges of the AD_STBx signals. The target sampled FRAME# deasserted on the rising edge of the clock. In response, the target deasserts DEVSEL# and stops driving TRDY# during this clock. Since the master cannot initiate another fast write transaction during this clock, the master stops driving the FRAME# signal. The master also stops driving the AD and C/BE busses, and the AD_STBx signals, after the transfer of the final dword completes.

Clock 7. During this clock, the target stops driving DEVSEL#. Since WBF# was sampled asserted on the rising edge of Clock 6, the master cannot start a fast write transaction during this clock. WBF# is detected asserted on the rising edge of this clock, preventing the master from starting a transaction in clock 8.

Short, Fast Write Transactions and DEVSEL#

Refer to Figure 10-12 on page 222. When the amount of data to be transferred during a fast write transaction is small, some interesting conditions exist. These conditions warrant discussion.

Figure 10-12: Short, Fast Write Transaction and DEVSEL#

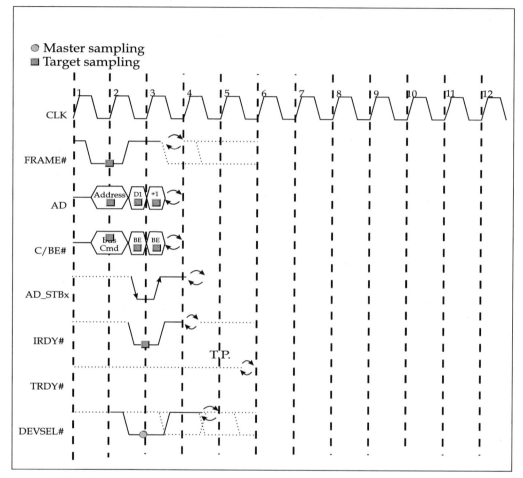

Clock 1. The transaction begins with the master asserting FRAME#, driving the start address onto the AD bus, and the command onto the C/BE bus.

Clock 2. On the rising edge of the clock, the target samples FRAME# asserted, indicating the beginning of the transaction, latches the address and command, and begins the decode of these signals. If the target does a fast decode, then it asserts DEVSEL# during this clock.

The master begins driving the first dword of write data onto the AD bus and the byte enables onto the C/BE bus, and they are latched by the target on the falling edges of the AD_STBx signals. During this clock, the master asserts IRDY#, indicating that it has started delivery of the first data block.

During this clock, the master deasserts FRAME#, indicating that the next clock is the final clock of the transaction.

Clock 3. The target latches the final dword and the byte enables on the rising edges of the AD_STBx signals during this clock. If the target does a medium decode, it asserts DEVSEL# during this clock. Because the data transfer completes before the target has finished the decode, the assertion of DEVSEL# is optional in this transaction. In fast write transactions, DEVSEL# is required to be asserted before or with the assertion of STOP# or TRDY#. If DEVSEL# is asserted in the current transaction, it must be deasserted during the clock in which FRAME# is detected deasserted.

Regardless of completing the decode, the target must accept the data for this transaction. If the target that accepted the data discovered that, after completing the address and command decode, it was not the target of the transaction, it must discard the latched data.

The master deasserts IRDY#, during this clock. After completing the transfer of data, the initiator could:

* Initiate a new fast back-to-back fast write transaction by asserting FRAME# during this clock.
* Stop driving FRAME#, the AD bus, the AD_STBx strobes, and the C/BE bus during this clock.

If the target had asserted DEVSEL# in clock 2, the target would be required to deassert DEVSEL# during this clock, after detecting FRAME# deasserted on the rising edge.

Clock 4. During this clock, the master may initiate a new transaction by asserting FRAME#. If not, then the master stops driving IRDY#.

If the target was a medium decode device and asserted DEVSEL# during clock 3, then DEVSEL# must be deasserted during this clock. If the master did not initiate a new transaction in clock 3, then a fast decode target would stop driving DEVSEL# during this clock. If the master did initiate a new transaction in clock 3, then a fast decode target would assert DEVSEL# during this clock.

Clock 5. Because of the short duration of this transaction, a throttle point is not needed. If the target was a medium decode device and asserted DEVSEL# during clock 3, then the target would stop driving DEVSEL# during this clock (assuming that the master has not initiated a new transaction). If the master did initiate a new transaction in clock 3, then a medium decode target would assert DEVSEL# during this clock. If the master initiated a new transaction in clock 4, then a fast decode target would assert DEVSEL# during this clock.

11 *The Physical Environment*

The Previous Chapter

The previous chapter provided a detailed description of Fast Write transactions in the 1X, 2X, and 4X data transfer modes.

This Chapter

This chapter describes issues related to add-in cards, connectors, and the motherboard.

The Next Chapter

The next chapter describes the responsibilities of the software required for initializing and configuring AGP devices. The AGP-specific configuration registers used in the configuration process are described.

Point-to-Point Topology

The AGP bus was architected as an interface between one active master and one active target. The target is integrated on the motherboard, while the master may be implemented on an add-in card through a connector, or integrated onto the motherboard. The specification strongly recommends that, due to the high speed nature of the bus, the routing of the traces be chosen based on simulation, in order to optimize signal quality and minimize signal skew due to trace mismatch, cross talk, and data dependencies. This is consistent with high-speed digital design techniques.

If three loads are implemented on the motherboard (the core logic, an on-board graphics accelerator, and an add-in connector), thorough simulation is required to ensure adequate signal quality and adherence to timing specifications.

Signal Routing and Layout

Routing and layout of AGP signals is critical to meet the timing and signal quality requirements of the specification. Simulation of the board routing should be done to verify that the specifications are met with regard to flight times, signal quality, and skews due to trace mismatch, cross talk, and data pattern dependency. **Total flight time** for the AGP trace is a maximum of **2.5ns**. The trace lengths of a group of signals must be selected to match the length of that group's strobe within a maximum of 0.5ns. Stated another way, the length of each signal trace must be either equal to that of the strobe trace, or up to 0.5 inches shorter for 2X operation, or 0.1 inches shorter for 4X operation. The strobe should always be the longest trace in the group. Serpentines may be used to match the trace lengths.

In 4X transfer mode, it is important to route the source synchronous data and strobe traces with a spacing of greater than or equal to three times the maximum dielectric thickness between the layer that the traces are routed on and the nearest plane. It is highly recommended that the strobe pairs be routed next to each other and that the spacing between be three to four times the maximum dielectric thickness. The strobes should be spaced from other traces by a minimum of five times the maximum dielectric thickness. It is recommended that the length of the strobe pairs be matched to within 0.1 inches.

Trace Impedance and Line Termination

Motherboard impedances should be controlled to minimize the impact of any mismatch between motherboard and add-in card. An impedance of 65 +/-15 Ohms is strongly recommended for 2X operation. An impedance of 60 Ohms +/- 10% is strongly recommended for 4X operation. Otherwise, signal integrity requirements may be violated.

Internal or external line termination may be used to meet signal integrity requirements as long as other specifications are not violated. Active clamping devices and slew rate controlled output buffers may be used to control signal reflection, overshoot, undershoot, and ringback. Termination may be more critical at the lower 1.5V level (due to tighter signal integrity requirements). Any clamp diodes on any AGP signal must only connect to Vddq and not to another supply.

Chapter 11: The Physical Environment

Add-In Card Clock Skew Specifications

The clock trace on the add-in card shall be routed to achieve an interconnect delay of 0.6ns +/- 0.1ns. Motherboard designers will assume that delay when accounting for clock skew.

Vref Generation

The motherboard generates the reference voltage Vref locally for all components that require it.

For 3.3V AGP in 2X Data Transfer Mode

For 3.3V operation, Vref must be generated from the AGP I/O voltage, Vddq, not from the 3.3V power supply voltage or from any other source. Vref must be generated at the receiver for 3.3V operation. This is why Vref is not defined on the AGP 3.3V connector. If the 3.3V AGP add-in card were to require Vref for the differential receivers, that reference would not be common with the reference for the core logic on the motherboard. Instead, Vref for the add-in card would be generated on the card itself.

Vref also needs proper decoupling to ground in order to manage switching currents. As with any decoupling scheme, the capacitors should be in close proximity to the receiver for best results. The actual value of the decoupling is not specified. The decoupling could vary depending on the implementation of the platform.

For 1.5V AGP in 2X and 4X Data Transfer Modes

Unlike Vref for 3.3V operation, Vref for 1.5V operation must be generated at the driving agent. This will help preserve the common mode relationship between the data and reference voltage at the receiver. The Vref is generated with a simple resistor voltage divider from the Vddq and Vss at the source. There are two unidirectional Vref signals on the motherboard and on the connector (for add-in cards). The master sources one of the Vref signals (A66 on the connector). The target sources the other (B66 on the connector). The circuits are shown in the specification and are not duplicated here. The circuits should be physically as close as possible to the AGP interface, to leverage the common mode power supply benefits.

Use of the Vref is not required, but is strongly recommended at this voltage level and in the high-speed data transfer modes.

AGP System Architecture

Component Pinout Recommendations

The component pinout of the master should follow the pinouts recommended in the specification. This will allow components mounted on add-in cards to match the specified connector pinout. By aligning the pins as indicated in the spec, signal trace crossing will be minimized, reducing the complexity of the layout of the add-in card. These pinouts will also minimize add-in card trace lengths and aid in matching the trace lengths within the associated data groups.

The strobe signals must be grouped with their associated data groups:

- AD_STB0 with AD[15::0] and C/BE[1::0]#
- AD_STB1 with AD[31:16] and C/BE[3::2]#
- SB_STB with SBA[7::0]

In 4X transfer mode operation, in addition to the above groupings:

- AD_STB0# with AD[15::0] and C/BE[1::0]#
- AD_STB1# with AD[31::16] and C/BE[3::2]#
- SB_STB# with SBA[7::0]

Motherboard/Add-In Card Interoperability

The most critical issue associated with motherboard and add-in card interoperability is the interface voltage. Although one might think that the data transfer rate is also important, remember that all AGP agents must be able to support all data transfer rates slower than the maximum that it supports. For example, if the add-in card only supports 1X mode, but the core logic supports 4X mode, the system will work and the resulting transfer rate will be 1X mode. The core logic device at a minimum must support 1X and 2X data transfer modes. If the add-in card supports 4X mode, it must also support 2X mode, in order to be interoperable with core logic devices that do not support 4X mode, but support 2X mode. The transfer rate will be the fastest common rate of the AGP master and target.

The Vddq I/O buffer voltage interoperability is enforced by the physical design of the AGP connector. A 1.5V card will not fit into a 3.3V connector, and vice-versa. A key prevents add-in cards from being plugged into incompatible motherboards. The 1.5V and 3.3V connectors are mounted on the motherboard, but are rotated 180 degrees, relative to one another. The universal connector will have no key and is therefore able to accept 1.5V or 3.3V add-in cards. The TYP-DET# pin on the add-in card communicates the card's voltage requirements to the motherboard. The symmetrical universal connector provides for the transition from 3.3V to 1.5V signaling.

Table 11-1: Motherboard/Add-In Card Interoperability

Motherboard	1.5 V Add-in Card 1X Capable	1.5 V Add-in Card 2X Capable	1.5 V Add-in Card 4X Capable	3.3 V Add-in Card 1X Capable	3.3 V Add-in Card 2X Capable
1.5 V - 2X Mode Capable	Yes	Yes	Yes*	No	No
1.5 V - 4X Mode Capable	Yes	Yes	Yes	No	No
3.3 V - 2X Mode Capable	No	No	No	Yes	Yes
Universal-2X Mode Capable	Yes	Yes	Yes*	Yes	Yes
Universal-4X Mode Capable	Yes	Yes	Yes	Yes	Yes

- **No** indicates a combination precluded by the key position on the connector.
- **Yes** indicates an acceptable combination.
- **Yes*** indicates an acceptable combination, but the resulting data transfer rate will be 2X.

Pull-Up/Pull-Down Resistors

S/T/S and O/D signal types require pull-up resistors on the motherboard, or integrated into the core logic. The signals that require pull-ups include: FRAME#, TRDY#, IRDY#, DEVSEL#, STOP#, SERR#, PERR#, RBF#, INTA#, INTB#, PIPE#, AD_STB[1::0], and SB_STB. The core logic may also require a specific value of pull-up on the REQ# and SBA[7::0] signals, so that those signals do not float when the card slot is unoccupied.

Pull-ups are allowed on any AGP signal with the exception of AD_STB[1::0]# and SB_STB#, which require pull-downs to ground. When attaching pull-ups to the AD, C/BE, or SBA busses and their corresponding strobes, care should be taken to keep the trace stub length to the resistor to less than 0.1 inch. This will minimize the signal reflections from the stub.

Table 11-2: Pull-Up/Pull-Down Resistor Values

	Rmin	Rtypical	Rmax
Pull-up/Pull-down	4 K Ohm	8.2 K Ohm @ 10%	16 K Ohm

Maximum AC Ratings and Device Protection

All AGP input, bi-directional, and tri-state output buffers should, by design, be able to withstand continuous exposure to the maximum AC signaling waveform shown in the specification. The voltage swing of the waveform depends on the Vddq value. For 3.3V signaling, the minimum peak-to-peak voltage is 7.1V. For 1.5V signaling, the minimum peak-to-peak voltage is 3.1V.

Power Supply

The power supply to the add-in card for the component core (Vcc) and Vddq must be separated on the die, package, and card. Vddq must never be more than 0.5V above Vcc3.3. Add-in cards must use all of the ground pins on the connector. Any unused power pins must be bypassed to ground on the card with low-inductance 0.01uF (or larger) capacitors.

Mechanicals

The AGP expansion card for ATX systems is based on the PCI expansion card design with the same maximum dimensions. The NLX version of the AGP card has reduced dimensions. The connector shall hold the add-in card at right angles to the motherboard. The connector is not hot-pluggable or hot-unpluggable. System power must be off when inserting or removing an add-in card.

AGP Pro

The AGP Pro specification is a connector definition for high-end servers and workstations. It is specifically designed for 4X mode operation, although it will support 1X and 2X mode operation with either 1.5V or 3.3V signalling. AGP Pro will electrically, mechanically, and thermally support up to 110 Watts through the connector. Since the specification had just been released at the time of this writing, more details are not included.

Connector Pinout

Table 11-3: AGP Motherboard Connector Pinout

Pin#	3.3 Volt B	3.3 Volt A	Universal B	Universal A	1.5 Volt B	1.5 Volt A
1	OVRCNT#	12V	OVRCNT#	12V	OVRCNT#	12V
2	5.0V	TYPEDET#	5.0V	TYPEDET#	5.0V	TYPEDET#
3	5.0V	Reserved	5.0V	Reserved	5.0V	Reserved
4	USB+	USB-	USB+	USB-	USB+	USB-
5	GND	GND	GND	GND	GND	GND
6	INTB#	INTA#	INTB#	INTA#	INTB#	INTA#
7	CLK	RST#	CLK	RST#	CLK	RST#
8	REQ#	GNT#	REQ#	GNT#	REQ#	GNT#
9	VCC3.3	VCC3.3	VCC3.3	VCC3.3	VCC3.3	VCC3.3
10	ST0	ST1	ST0	ST1	ST0	ST1
11	ST2	Reserved	ST2	Reserved	ST2	Reserved
12	RBF#	PIPE#	RBF#	PIPE#	RBF#	PIPE#
13	GND	GND	GND	GND	GND	GND
14	Reserved	Reserved	Reserved	WBF#	Reserved	WBF#
15	SBA0	SBA1	SBA0	SBA1	SBA0	SBA1
16	VCC3.3	VCC3.3	VCC3.3	VCC3.3	VCC3.3	VCC3.3
17	SBA2	SBA3	SBA2	SBA3	SBA2	SBA3
18	SB_STB	Reserved	SB_STB	SB_STB#	SB_STB	SB_STB#
19	GND	GND	GND	GND	GND	GND
20	SBA4	SBA5	SBA4	SBA5	SBA4	SBA5
21	SBA6	SBA7	SBA6	SBA7	SBA6	SBA7

Table 11-3: AGP Motherboard Connector Pinout (Continued)

Pin#	3.3 Volt B	3.3 Volt A	Universal B	Universal A	1.5 Volt B	1.5 Volt A
22	KEY	KEY	Reserved	Reserved	Reserved	Reserved
23	KEY	KEY	GND	GND	GND	GND
24	KEY	KEY	3.3Vaux	Reserved	3.3Vaux	Reserved
25	KEY	KEY	VCC3.3	VCC3.3	VCC3.3	VCC3.3
26	AD31	AD30	AD31	AD30	AD31	AD30
27	AD29	AD28	AD29	AD28	AD29	AD28
28	VCC3.3	VCC3.3	VCC3.3	VCC3.3	VCC3.3	VCC3.3
29	AD27	AD28	AD27	AD28	AD27	AD28
30	AD25	AD24	AD25	AD24	AD25	AD24
31	GND	GND	GND	GND	GND	GND
32	AD_STB1	Reserved	AD_STB1	AD_STB1#	AD_STB1	AD_STB1#
33	AD23	C/BE3#	AD23	C/BE3#	AD23	C/BE3#
34	Vddq3.3	Vddq3.3	Vddq	Vddq	Vddq1.5	Vddq1.5
35	AD21	AD22	AD21	AD22	AD21	AD22
36	AD19	AD20	AD19	AD20	AD19	AD20
37	GND	GND	GND	GND	GND	GND
38	AD17	AD18	AD17	AD18	AD17	AD18
39	C/BE2#	AD16	C/BE2#	AD16	C/BE2#	AD16
40	Vddq3.3	Vddq3.3	Vddq	Vddq	Vddq1.5	Vddq1.5
41	IRDY#	FRAME#	IRDY#	FRAME#	IRDY#	FRAME#
42	3.3Vaux	Reserved	3.3Vaux	Reserved	KEY	KEY
43	GND	GND	GND	GND	KEY	KEY
44	Reserved	Reserved	Reserved	Reserved	KEY	KEY

Table 11-3: AGP Motherboard Connector Pinout (Continued)

Pin#	3.3 Volt B	3.3 Volt A	Universal B	Universal A	1.5 Volt B	1.5 Volt A
45	VCC3.3	VCC3.3	VCC3.3	VCC3.3	KEY	KEY
46	DEVSEL#	TRDY#	DEVSEL#	TRDY#	DEVSEL#	TRDY#
47	Vddq3.3	STOP#	Vddq	STOP#	Vddq1.5	STOP#
48	PERR#	PME#	PERR#	PME#	PERR#	PME#
49	GND	GND	GND	GND	GND	GND
50	SERR#	PAR	SERR#	PAR	SERR#	PAR
51	C/BE1#	AD15	C/BE1#	AD15	C/BE1#	AD15
52	Vddq3.3	Vddq3.3	Vddq	Vddq	Vddq1.5	Vddq1.5
53	AD14	AD13	AD14	AD13	AD14	AD13
54	AD12	AD11	AD12	AD11	AD12	AD11
55	GND	GND	GND	GND	GND	GND
56	AD10	AD9	AD10	AD9	AD10	AD9
57	AD8	C/BE0#	AD8	C/BE0#	AD8	C/BE0#
58	Vddq3.3	Vddq3.3	Vddq	Vddq	Vddq1.5	Vddq1.5
59	AD_STB0	Reserved	AD_STB0	AD_STB0#	AD_STB0	AD_STB0#
60	AD7	AD6	AD7	AD6	AD7	AD6
61	GND	GND	GND	GND	GND	GND
62	AD5	AD4	AD5	AD4	AD5	AD4
63	AD3	AD2	AD3	AD2	AD3	AD2
64	Vddq3.3	Vddq3.3	Vddq	Vddq	Vddq1.5	Vddq1.5
65	AD1	AD0	AD1	AD0	AD1	AD0
66	Reserved	Reserved	Vrefcg	Vrefgc	Vrefcg	Vrefgc

12 *AGP Configuration*

The Previous Chapter

The previous chapter described issues related to add-in cards, connectors, and the motherboard.

This Chapter

This chapter describes the responsibilities of the software required for initializing and configuring AGP devices. The AGP-specific configuration registers used in the configuration process are described.

System Configuration and AGP Device Initialization

Three software elements are involved in configuring the AGP master and AGP target:

- The system BIOS (platform-specific).
- The operating system (Windows 9X, or NT 5.0 and higher).
- Microsoft DirectDraw.

Each of these software entities is discussed in this chapter.

BIOS Initialization Requirements

The system BIOS is responsible for the enumeration of the system busses. During bus enumeration, the BIOS determines what components exist, queries each device to determine its resource requirements, and allocates resources to each device. In order to perform the enumeration and configuration for PCI and AGP devices, the BIOS examines and programs the device's PCI configuration registers. AGP masters and targets are required to support the PCI configuration header registers as described in the PCI Bus Specification. For more information on PCI configuration, refer to the MindShare book entitled *PCI System Architecture, Fourth Edition* (published by Addison-Wesley).

AGP masters and targets are accessed using the PCI configuration mechanism. For Intel-based platforms, the PCI Configuration mechanism is defined in the PCI specification. This mechanism converts special IO accesses that appear on the host processor bus into PCI configuration read or write accesses on the PCI or AGP bus. The AGP bus is assigned a PCI bus number that is used to access the master, through a virtual PCI-to-PCI bridge within the core logic.

One possible implementation of the core logic treats the **host/PCI bridge** within the core logic as **physical device zero on PCI bus zero**. The **virtual PCI-to-PCI bridge** is **physical device one on PCI bus zero**. Using a depth-first search algorithm, the virtual PCI-to-PCI bridge is programmed with a primary bus number of zero, a secondary bus number of one, and a subordinate bus number of one. Therefore, the PCI configuration space assigned to the AGP master is physical device zero on PCI bus one. The core logic converts accesses that target PCI bus one into Type zero PCI configuration transactions on the AGP interface. The core logic is required to assert AD16 for IDSEL generation, during these configuration transactions.

One of the critical responsibilities of the BIOS is to assign memory space to the operational control and communication registers of the AGP master (in other words, its control register set is mapped into memory-mapped IO space), and to assign a prefetchable physical memory address range to the linear frame buffer on the master. This is done by programming the master's PCI configuration base address registers. As of this writing, the system BIOS is unaware of the AGP interface or transfer mechanisms. Therefore, the system BIOS does not do any AGP-specific configuration.

One of the responsibilities of the BIOS is find the VGA-compatible display device. The search for this device typically includes searching the ISA bus (if one exists), the PCI bus, the AGP connector, if one exists, and then the motherboard AGP graphics accelerator.

The core logic will implement a PCI base address register to request memory address space for the Graphics Aperture.

Operating System Initialization Requirements

The OS initializes the AGP-specific features within the master and the target. As part of this configuration, the OS allocates memory for the GART (Graphics Address Remapping Table). The OS also uses a miniport driver (designed for the specific chipset), to initialize the GART hardware within the target (i.e., the core logic). The driver will be accessible through the API appropriate for that OS.

The OS is responsible for setting the memory type for the Graphics Aperture. If the platform is based on a P6-family processor, this is accomplished by programming the MTRR (Memory Type and Range Registers) within the host processor. A maximum size of the graphics aperture is established to limit the amount of main memory that can be allocated as AGP memory. This typically depends on the amount of memory in the system.

The OS is responsible for setting up the AGP transfer parameters. This is accomplished by reading and programming the linked list of PCI configuration registers (described in the next section).

Capabilities List

The 2.2 PCI specification has added a new bit to the PCI status register and a new, read-only configuration register. Figure 12-1 on page 238 illustrates the Capabilities List status bit, while Figure 12-2 on page 239 illustrates the position of the new, read-only configuration register (the New Capabilities List Pointer Register).

A device indicates whether or not it implements the pointer register using the Capabilities List bit in the status register. A hard-wired value of 0 indicates that the register is not implemented, while a value of one indicates that it is present. The AGP's status register bit must equal one, indicating that the pointer register is present.

The pointer register contains a one-byte dword-aligned pointer to a location within the function's configuration space (to a location within the lower-48 dwords of configuration space reserved for the implementation of device-specific configuration registers). The location pointed to is the first entry in a linked series of configuration register sets that support various new features. Each entry has the general format illustrated in Figure 12-3 on page 240. The first byte identifies the feature supported by this register set (e.g., 2 = AGP), while the second byte either points to the next feature's register set, or indicates that there are no additional features (with a pointer value of 0) for this function. The feature's register set immediately follows the first two bytes of the entry, and its length and format are defined by what type of feature it is. The AGP feature registers have the format illustrated in Figure 12-4 on page 240, and the sections that follow describe each register.

Figure 12-1: PCI Status Register

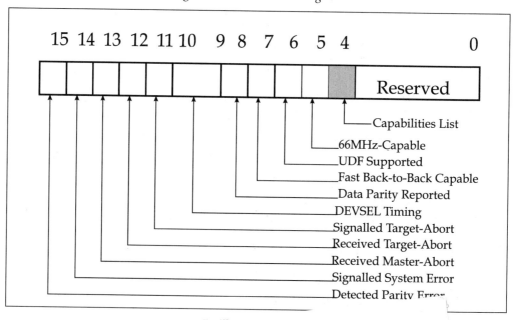

Figure 12-2: New Capabilities Pointer Register

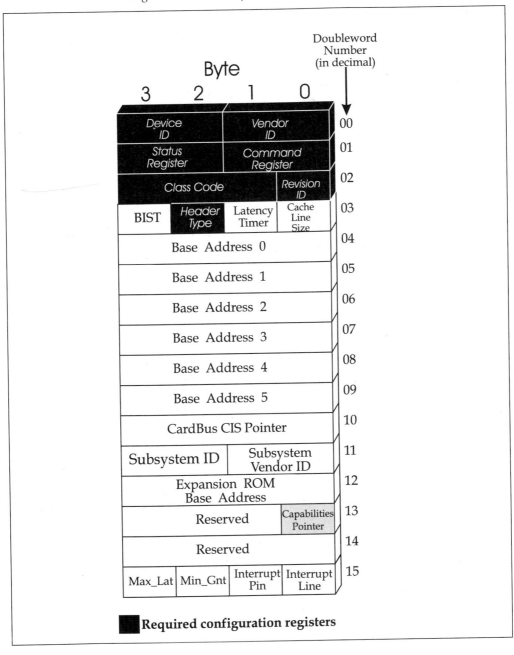

Required configuration registers

Figure 12-3: General Format of a New Capabilities List Entry

Feature-specific Configuration Registers	Pointer to Next Capability	Capability ID

Figure 12-4: Format of the AGP Capability Register Set

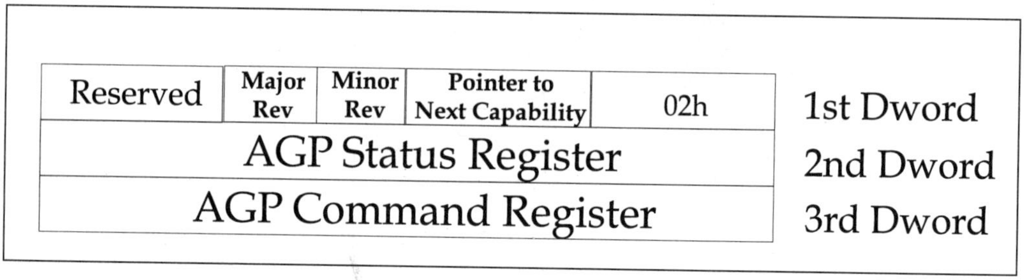

Reserved	Major Rev	Minor Rev	Pointer to Next Capability	02h	1st Dword
AGP Status Register					2nd Dword
AGP Command Register					3rd Dword

AGP Status Register

The AGP Status register is defined in Table 12-1. This is a read-only register. Writes have no effect. Reserved or unimplemented fields or bits always return zeros when read.

Table 12-1: AGP Status Register (Offset CAP_PTR + 4)

Bits	Field	Description
31:24	RQ	The RQ field contains the maximum depth of the AGP request queue. Therefore, this number is the maximum number of command requests this device can manage. A "0" is interpreted as a depth of one, while FFh is interpreted as a depth of 256.
23:10	Reserved	Writes have no effect. Reads return zeros.
9	SBA	If set, this device supports sideband addressing.

Table 12-1: AGP Status Register (Offset CAP_PTR + 4) (Continued)

Bits	Field	Description
8:6	Reserved	Writes have no effect. Reads return zeros.
5	4G	If set, this device supports addresses greater than 4 GB.
4	FW	If set, this device supports Fast Write transactions.
3	Reserved	Writes have no effect. Reads return a zero
2:0	RATE	The RATE field is a bit map that indicates the data transfer rates supported by this device. AGP devices must report all that apply. The RATE field applies to AD, C/BE#, and SBA busses. **Bit Set** **Transfer Rate** 0 1X 1 2X 2 4X

AGP Command Register

The AGP Command register is defined in Table 12-2 on page 242. This is a read/ writable register, with reserved fields hard-wired to zeros. All bits in the AGP command register are cleared to zero after reset. This register is programmed during configuration. With one exception, the behavior of a device if this register is modified during runtime is not specified. If the AGP_ENABLE bit is cleared, the AGP master is not allowed to initiate a new request.

Table 12-2: AGP Command Register (Offset CAP_PTR + 8)

Bits	Field	Description
31:24	RQ_DEPTH	**Master**: The RQ_DEPTH field must be programmed with the maximum number of requests the master is allowed to enqueue into the target. The value programmed into this field must be equal to or less than the value reported by the target in the RQ field of its AGP Status Register. A "0" value indicates a request queue depth of one entry, while a value of FFh indicates a request queue depth of 256. **Target**: The RQ_DEPTH field is reserved.
23:10	Reserved	Writes have no effect. Reads return zeros.
9	SBA_ENABLE	When set, the sideband address mechanism is enabled in this device.
8	AGP_ENABLE	**Master**: Setting the AGP_ENABLE bit allows the master to initiate AGP operations. When cleared, the master cannot initiate AGP operations. Also when cleared, the master is allowed to stop driving the SBA port. If bits 1 or 2 are set, the master must perform a re-synch cycle, before initiating a new request. **Target**: Setting the AGP_ENABLE bit allows the target to accept AGP operations. When cleared, the target ignores incoming AGP operations. The target must be completely configured and enabled before the master is enabled. The AGP_ENABLE bit is the last to be set. Reset clears this bit.
7:6	Reserved	Writes have no effect. Reads return zeros.

Table 12-2: AGP Command Register (Offset CAP_PTR + 8) (Continued)

Bits	Field	Description
5	4G	**Master**: Setting the 4G bit allows the master to initiate AGP requests to addresses at or above the 4GB address boundary. When cleared, the master is only allowed to access addresses in the lower 4 GB of addressable space. **Target**: Setting the 4G bit enables the target to accept AGP DAC commands, when bit 9 is cleared. When bits 5 and 9 are set, the target can accept a Type 4 SBA command and utilize A[35::32] of the Type 3 SBA command.
4	FW_ENABLE	When this bit is set, memory write transactions initiated by the core logic will follow the fast write protocol. When this bit is cleared, memory write transactions initiated by the core logic will follow the PCI protocol.
3	Reserved	Writes have no effect. Reads return zeros.
2:0	DATA_RATE	Only one bit in the DATA_RATE field must be set to indicate the maximum data transfer rate supported. The same bit must be set in both the master and the target. **Bit Set** **Transfer Rate** 0 1X 1 2X 2 4X

Microsoft DirectDraw

A future edition of this book will describe this software interface as it relates to the AGP memory management activity during runtime. This is integral to the dynamic memory allocation capability of the AGP interface.

Multifunction AGP Devices

An AGP master could be implemented as a PCI multifunction device. As an example, consider a graphics accelerator that also supports a video capture function. In this example, the graphics accelerator function could be implemented as PCI function zero, for configuration purposes, while the video capture function could be implemented as PCI function one (or any function number within the range 1 through 7). Again, these function numbers are used when accessing a function's PCI configuration registers. Although not required, each function within a multifunction PCI device typically has its own dedicated device driver.

As with a PCI multifunction device, the functions within an AGP multifunction device share a single physical interface to the AGP bus. The AGP master can only request a single data transfer rate that all functions within the multifunction device will use. There is absolutely no switching from 1X to 2X to 4X during runtime. Each function uses either the SBA or the AD bus to enqueue transaction requests, but not both. The Request Queue Depth value (RQ_DEPTH) must be shared among the multiple functions. The exact implementation of this sharing scheme is outside the scope of the specification.

Index

Index

Index

Addison-Wesley Computer and Engineering Publishing Group

How to Interact with Us

1. Visit our Web site

http://www.awl.com/cseng

When you think you've read enough, there's always more content for you at Addison-Wesley's web site. Our web site contains a directory of complete product information including:

- Chapters
- Exclusive author interviews
- Links to authors' pages
- Tables of contents
- Source code

You can also discover what tradeshows and conferences Addison-Wesley will be attending, read what others are saying about our titles, and find out where and when you can meet our authors and have them sign your book.

2. Subscribe to Our Email Mailing Lists

Subscribe to our electronic mailing lists and be the first to know when new books are publishing. Here's how it works: Sign up for our electronic mailing at **http://www.awl.com/cseng/mailinglists.html**. Just select the subject areas that interest you and you will receive notification via email when we publish a book in that area.

3. Contact Us via Email

cepubprof@awl.com

Ask general questions about our books.
Sign up for our electronic mailing lists.
Submit corrections for our web site.

bexpress@awl.com

Request an Addison-Wesley catalog.
Get answers to questions regarding your order or our products.

innovations@awl.com

Request a current Innovations Newsletter.

webmaster@awl.com

Send comments about our web site.

cepubeditors@awl.com

Submit a book proposal.
Send errata for an Addison-Wesley book.

cepubpublicity@awl.com

Request a review copy for a member of the media interested in reviewing new Addison-Wesley titles.

We encourage you to patronize the many fine retailers who stock Addison-Wesley titles. Visit our online directory to find stores near you or visit our online store: **http://store.awl.com/** or call **800-824-7799**.

Addison Wesley Longman
Computer and Engineering Publishing Group
One Jacob Way, Reading, Massachusetts 01867 USA
TEL 781-944-3700 • FAX 781-942-3076